# LET LOVE BE THE VICTOR

by

## Jack R. McClellan

authorHOUSE®

*AuthorHouse*™
*1663 Liberty Drive*
*Bloomington, IN 47403*
*www.authorhouse.com*
*Phone: 1-800-839-8640*

*First published by AuthorHouse      12/05/2011*

*ISBN: 978-1-4567-3672-9 (sc)*
*ISBN: 978-1-4567-5452-5 (hc)*
*ISBN: 978-1-4567-3673-6 (ebk)*

*Library of Congress Control Number: 2011908014*

*Printed in the United States of America*

To Gilbert whose long friendship
and constant source of encouragement has made authorship possible.

# Chapter One

A scraping noise spiked the silence. Patience gasped as fear tensed her body. At her feet lay the dress she had just unfastened and dropped to the floor. "There it is again," she warned herself, "the same noise I heard last night when I undressed for bed. It began three nights ago, always as I undress."

The noise stopped abruptly the moment she tilted her head to listen. She looked intently at the south wall trying once more to identify the source of aggravation, then she allowed her eyes to dart about the room looking for some promising clues. A flickering of candle flame interrupted her concentration and she stared at the commode next to her bed. "A draft," she recognized and glanced at the window. One shutter had blown open. She moved across the room to close it but hesitated as she reached the window to watch the turmoil of angry clouds flying landward over the English Channel.

Pushed by a freshening wind, a bubbling mass of grey and black clouds floated swiftly toward her, momentarily blurring the stars, then slashing them from view. Moonlight faded and the earth blackened. "Should I consider this darkening sky a bad omen for me?" she wondered. "Nonsense. You are too superstitious. It is only nature preparing to create sustenance for the earth of Castelamer."

The temperature dropped suddenly. What had been a warm summer day became within an hour a cool fall night. Patience shivered, closed the shutter, then returned to the foot of her bed where her nightgown lay. She was about to loosen her shift when she heard the scratching noise again.

"That noise!" she mumbled. "It sounds as if it is in this room, but I can't find what is causing it. I've looked everywhere. What is it?" The question was asked in desperation. Her right hand went to her neck in a gesture of frustration. She directed her eyes to the south wall once again. "There is nothing. I've searched every inch of those panels." Her conclusion evidenced despair and fear began to close in once more. Quickly letting her shift fall, she slipped into her nightgown and returned to the window. She adjusted the open shutter, leaving it slightly ajar. A brisk breeze that flowed through the opening carried with it a damp odor of rain. She breathed deeply, blew out the candle and crawled into bed.

Sleep was long in coming. Uneasiness nagged at her as she let speculative questions dart in and out of the recesses of her mind. She tossed and turned, buried her face in her pillow, stared at the ceiling, tried to think of her school lessons, but she could not prevent the jabs of concern from surfacing. "What is it that scrapes? Where is it? Is someone making the noise? Why always at bedtime when I am undressing?" It was the notion that someone might be disturbing her deliberately that created the most alarm. "But why? Who would want to do that?"

A roar of thunder disturbed the sleep that had finally replaced her anxieties. She became aware of a gentle rhythmic patter of rain, and it occurred to her that rain drops would be coming through her window. Reluctantly she arose, quickly closed the shutter and returned to bed. She was dozing when something startled her. Becoming alert she sat up, threw the covers from her and prepared to leap from bed. Shaking a trembling fear, she glanced at the window. The shutters remained closed. Rapidly she made a visual exploration of the room. All was in order. "You are not only silly but a bit daft to think anyone in this house would want to disturb your sleep," she told herself. "You know the sounds of storms. Go to sleep."

The admonition failed. She lay awake, conscious of every disturbing sound. A scraping noise, louder than the others alerted her. "It's the door!" She bounded out of bed, grabbed her robe, swirled it about her shoulders and hastened to the entry leading into the hall. Perspiration dampened her forehead. "Is someone there?" she called out. Her right hand went to her throat as she awaited a reply. No response. "It would be impossible for anyone to enter," she reassured herself. "The door is bolted." She checked to prove her statement but was startled to see that the bolt was not secure. "I'm positive I put that bolt in place!" Her fingers enclosed the door knob. It turned within her hand even though she had not gripped it! She shuddered, petrified. She fought an impulse to scream.

"It is your imagination," Patience cautioned herself. She let eternity pass as she tried to shed her terror. She directed her fingers to close about the knob. Slowly she turned it. Her hand, functioning automatically, pulled the door open slightly. She moved a step and peered out. The hallway was dark. She could detect no one.

Cautiously, silently, she stepped back into her bedroom, closed the door, slid the bolt into its holder and leaned against the wall. Her heart beat audibly in cadenced pumps. She felt faint. She got herself to the window and threw open the shutters. A light, moist breeze immediately bathed her face and she took a deep breath. Rain had stopped falling, clouds were clearing and the landscape lay in silence. It was the moment between night and day.

From the open window on the second floor of Castelamer, Patience watched dawn break, letting herself be calmed by the wonder of the scene as first light touched tops of hills, slowly filled vales, then illumined familiar objects in the garden below. In the clear atmosphere she could see the undulating landscape of Cornwall stretching inland from the English Channel toward Bodmin Moors. The serrated coast that wound a dizzy line toward Plymouth was fringed with white fuzz made by waves breaking rhythmically along the shore. In the foreground beyond the garden was Hythe Haven, a small natural harbor set within a spit of land extending from Bodacombe Bluff, the rising crest on which Castelamer had been built.

Feeling refreshed she returned to the foot of her bed, intent on discovering the source of her distress. As she turned to study each part of her room, her eyes embraced old keepsakes, a collection of knickknacks, a doll, books, the treasures a child collects. Each object contributed to a feeling of calm which was being restored gradually. The doll particularly gave comfort for it had been a gift from her mother the day before the boat accident, and it was still her dearest possession.

"How could anyone want to disturb this joyful room?" she questioned. Lovely linen fold paneling covered the walls from floor to ceiling. Patience enjoyed letting her fingers roam about deep carvings just to feel the wood some hand many years ago had turned from flat surface to splendor with the wielding of a knife.

"This room I shared with my sister," she mused. "Here we grew up together. We played house, discussed secrets and told each other wondrous dreams. She moved to her own room. 'At fifteen you should be by yourself,' she admonished. 'And you, Patience, need to be more on your own.'

Her reverie was broken by a renewal of the scraping noise. "No!" Patience's heart beat increased to a frightening thump, thump, thump as fear took hold once more. She wanted to yell but her throat constricted. It could not produce a whisper. She wanted to move but alarm chained her to the floor. With the force of overwhelming determination, she took a step and then another until she reached the wall. Mustering what strength she had, she raised her arms and drove tight fists against the panel in front of her. They struck furiously again and again until she had no more strength to pound. She stepped backward exhausted and reached for her bed, falling onto it. Smothering her face in the covers, she wept.

She must have fallen asleep for bright sunshine flooding her bed awakened her. Rising quickly she washed her hands, bathed her face, then dressed for morning activities.

A knock sounded on the door. It opened before Patience could speak. It was Nancy, the upstairs maid who warned immediately, "Hurry, Miss Patty. You have breakfast awaitin' and Mr. Chivers will be here shortly for instruction. Penny is already at table. What a beautiful morning after that thunder storm last night. I wonder any one got any sleep. And the winds made all kinds of noises in the house. They liked to scared me out of my skin. Made me think someone was after me. Even Mrs. Battey said the same thing. That's all we talked about this morning. Hurry along."

"Good morning, Nancy. Let me get this locket on and I am out the door." Patience hastened along the hall thinking of Nancy's comments about the wind and feeling foolish for imagining the sound of scratching on the panels or the noises in the hallway. Down the back stairs she went and approached the breakfast room. She stopped abruptly, her hand clasping her throat. "The bolt! Nancy opened the door! That door was bolted." Before she could give it further thought, Mrs. Battey, the housekeeper, greeted her rather dolefully and added, "Penelope is not feeling well at all. Be gentle with her."

Although cautioned, Patience was not prepared for Penny's woeful appearance. Sitting down at table, she noted her twin sister had no color in her face and that she spoke without displaying any spirit whatsoever. That was not like Penny. Patience offered to do anything to help, but Penelope rose from the table saying she was not hungry and thought it best to return to bed.

Patience helped her stand up and noticed her sister's extended abdomen. "It is just bloated," came the explanation, but before questions could be asked, Mrs. Battey appeared. She motioned Patience away from Penny and then assisted the sick girl to her room.

Patience wanted to inquire about getting a doctor, but at that moment cook arrived with a tray. As the meal was finished, Nancy announced that Mr. Chivers had arrived.

Patience hurried to the school room where she was greeted by the tutor who, having been told Penny was ill, suggested a review rather than an introduction of new material.

Both had a jolly time testing one another.

Class over, Patience ran to Penelope's room but was told the sick girl was sleeping. She grabbed a shawl and hurried to the garden where the sun was bright and warm after the storm. A breeze off the Channel was brisk and stimulating. She found her favorite place on Bodacombe Bluff, a jagged cliff rising some one hundred feet above Hythe Haven, a small harbor snuggled within the curve of a cove protected by a spit of land jutting from Signal Bluff, a rising land opposite to Bodacombe Bluff.

Patience could identify the exact place in the sea beyond the spit where her father's boat was found. "Father was known as a fine sailor," she reminded herself. "People always said that Mr. Tatham was a master at sailing and gave his boat the utmost care. It happened on a Sunday. Seeing a gentle sea and feeling a sailor's breeze on his face, he talked mother into a sail. Off they went, gaily, arm in arm. They never returned or were their bodies ever found. The boat was located, a hole in the hull."

That hole continued to be a mystery and a source of considerable speculation. No one could reason how it got there. Even with the boat sinking so close to the harbor, nobody could understand why the Tathams did not swim to the spit since both were fine swimmers, but as some were want to say, accidents do happen and many are unexplainable.

Little was left by the Tathams in the way of material goods. What they had was sold to pay debts. A family in the north took their son who was seven while Patience and Penelope, then six, were taken by Mr. Tatham's cousin and his wife, Cecil and Anne Framsden, who inherited Castelamer shortly after the Tatham's deaths. They provided a tutor for classroom instruction, a seamstress to teach Patience needle work and sewing at which she became quite proficient, clothed the children and kept them in health.

Patience turned to face the great house which was the love of her life. The builder was a Norman who fought for William at Hastings and was awarded a land grant for loyalty. He had granite boulders pulled from the earth, shaped and sized, and then placed together to form the original part of the house, a massive entry two stories high, buttressed and topped with battlements. On either side of the entry were granite walls pierced with windows. He called his demi-fortress Castelamer, a corruption of "castle" for his adopted England and "la mer" in memory of his French sea. His descendants became one of the premier families of the west country, associates of the Gilberts and Raleighs, the Grenvilles and Drakes. Its members fought on Boswell Field for the Tudors, challenged the Spanish Armada for Queen Elizabeth and supported Charles II in his struggle to regain his throne.

During the sixteenth century, alterations were made in the original medieval house to modernize it. Two story Tudor wings were added. Each wing, identical to the other, was extended forward of the original granite building thus recessing the old entry which had been left intact. At the extremity of either wing a three story tower topped by a cupola and lantern was constructed.

Superb herringbone brickwork dominated the Tudor wing facades, a lasting tribute to the brilliant workmanship of bricklayers. At intervals, silhouetted against the sky, molded chimneys were stacked in twists and turns.

Patience liked to step gingerly to the edge of Bodacomb Bluff where it fell in a sheer tumble some one hundred feet to the beach below. She would get on her hands and knees then crawl to the very edge where she would stretch out on her stomach and gaze at waves crashing into a massive build up of boulders on the beach. The noise was loud and raucous as the sea rammed into the rocky barrier which protected a narrow strip of sand between the rocks and the base of the cliff. There was one opening among the rocks where waves could roll onto the beach unchallenged.

As she lay in solitude, she thought of stories she had heard of wicked men who, on stormy nights, posted lights on this bluff to guide an unsuspecting captain away from Hythe Haven and onto the boulders. When the ship floundered, these ruthless men would confiscate the cargo.

She was lost in musing when she thought she heard footsteps. Patience raised her head to listen but the noise stopped. She rolled over on her back to gaze at the heavens when all of sudden she found her eyes looking directly at the figure of Mr. Wyatt.

"Do not move, sweet child," he whispered, his eyes bright and eager. "Gently now. Stay as you are. You are a picture of heaven. Let me enjoy your loveliness."

Dudley Wyatt was a close personal friend of Mr. Framsden. He frequently was a visitor at Castelamer. He had the freedom to come and go and was entertained at house socials. Most often when he came calling, however, he was in private discussion with Mr. Framsden.

Prone as she was, Mr. Wyatt appeared to Patience as a giant. Actually he was of little more than average height and weight, but broad in the shoulders. There was the first suggestion of grey hair at his temples giving maturity to a handsome young face. His eyes had a green cast, and on this day they sparkled brightly in the sunlight. His mouth was in full smile, the kind a person uses to reflect appreciation. Fine white teeth added to the charm of his smile. Light brown hair was worn long. Usually he dressed in the latest fashion, but today he was garbed casually, wearing riding boots and a white shirt which was partially open at the chest.

He put out his hand to stay any move on Patience's part and began dropping to one knee. Without thinking she rolled quickly in the opposite direction and bounded to her feet while he was off balance.

"There, Patty, stay," he directed. "I want to spend a moment of this beautiful day with you. Tell me, what have you been thinking as you lay in the sunshine? Has it been of a young lover who chanced on Bodacombe Bluff, won your heart, and then carried you away in his arms? Tell me. Honest."

He extended his arm. She stepped backward to avoid his touch as he spoke amorously. "I could be that lover, Patty. No more longing for you. It could be real. Have you talked to Penny?"

Patience responded with a questioning tilt of her head when he spoke her sister's name and he immediately added, "Of course not. Innocent Patty. But not Penny. You think your sister was given her own room because you were old enough to be separated. A ha! Not so. She asked for her own room so I could visit her when it pleased her and that was often. I played with her. She was like a kitten wanting to be played with. We played often. Too often. That swelling which she wanted you to believe was a stomach bloating is my brat she is about to have!"

Patience was stunned. Penny! Before she could recover her senses, Mr. Wyatt had his hands on her shoulders holding her as a vice and staring down at her. "Those hazel eyes of yours! They always do me in! Some day I am going to hold you, look down onto those captivating eyes, and let their magic weave a complete spell over me. No. Not some day. Now! Yes, you have the face of an angel, but you will not be an angel after I have taken you!"

Fearfully Patience watched as his face developed a strong determined look, then quickly it relaxed to a quiet gentleness as he whispered, "Oh, Patty, you are no longer a child. You are a woman. Come, taste the kiss of love." He drew her to him, gently.

Patience was entranced. His eyes seemed to gather her in, mystifying her. He dominated every nerve, every part of her physical being. As her body swayed slowly, she could feel herself being drawn to him mentally and physically. She wanted him to touch her. She lost control of her senses as if transfixed by his overwhelming charm. There was a strange urge to collapse in his arms and to let him smother her. She wanted him to crush her. She was perplexed, her body trembled, not knowing what to do. She was frightened. What was this sensation she was enjoying? Never had she felt this way before.

"There. You are mine." His voice had softened. "You are about to know the greatest joy, a joy beyond your wildest imagination. I am the prince you dream of, ready to take you away to a strange world. Come, Patty. You are lovelier than Penny."

Penny. Penny! The mention of her sister's name broke his spell. Patience thought of her dear sister. Her suffering. This man. Her head cleared as she felt his breath on her face.

"I know you have looked at me with those fascinating eyes of yours, wanting me. I could feel your lust for me when I visited Castelamer. I have watched you in your room. No. You could not see me. This morning you heard me. Careless of me to be so noisy. It was I who turned the door handle, but the wind made me think someone was in the hall and I had to flee detection. I wanted to enter your room, to spend the rest of the night with you making our own storm. I must have you!"

"No!" Patience screamed and struggled free from his grasp. "Ah, my pretty Penny," he responded. "We have not finished the lesson. You have not learned what is is to be a woman."

Quickly she was in his clutches again. She fought his hold but his arms were binding hers and she could not strike. She tried to kick but her skirt would not allow for a forceful swing. Her shawl had fallen to the ground and his feet became entangled in it. Patience gave a lunge at him with all her might and he fell backward, landing on the ground, pulling her with him. She found herself on top of him, her face directly over his. A smile broke the angry surface. Again he was gentle. "Sweet Penny. You do want to learn. One roll and we shall be in perfect harmony for the lesson."

For a fleeting moment, Patience felt his hypnotism again, but this time she was prepared. "Here is your lesson," she cried out, and with her free hand she slapped him across his face, whipping out his lusting smile. A touch of red appeared.

"You dirty little vixen!" he sneered. "I shall give you more than a lesson." His hand grabbed the shoulder of Patience's dress and ripped it. She flailed her arms, aiming fists in every direction as fast as she could. As he tried to roll her over, she grabbed her shawl, now full of dirt, and rammed it into his face, rubbing hard on it to force grime into his mouth and eyes.

Wyatt relaxed his hold to pull at the shawl. As he did so, she struggled to get up. His one hand removed the shawl from his face and the other grabbed her leg. Patience's effort to run to the house was shattered.

Standing now and towering over him, she became aware that their grappling had carried them close to the edge of the bluff. Not wanting to fall, she stepped backward with her free leg. Then a thought struck! She swung her free leg with all her strength to drive her foot into his head.

Dropping his hold on Patience's leg, he raised both hands to his face. As he did so, he rolled to the brink of the bluff. Unaware of his closeness to the rim, he raised himself and moved his legs so they protruded over the edge. A particle of earth gave way. Then instantly a large piece fell. Before Patience could reach him, the earth on which he was sitting broke free and he fell from view. A scream, full of terror, pierced the silent day. It was like the cry of a seagull fleeing in fear.

Patience was stunned, too frightened to look over the brink to learn what had happened to Mr. Wyatt. She pictured his body spread on a pile of boulders, broken and bloody. Terror gripped her. "I am a murderess!" she yelled. She imagined the finger of accusation pointing at her. She envisioned a life in prison or death on the gallows. Panic brought her to her knees and she wept copiously.

When tears were no more, she stood, vigorously brushed her soiled, torn dress, shook her shawl and tossed it around her shoulders. She then walked slowly through the garden wondering what to do.

Once inside the house, she went immediately to her room. Quietly she removed her torn and soiled clothing, rolled every item into a bundle and placed it in a portmanteau she had taken from the bottom of the armoire. After ablutions she donned a fresh dress.

Seeing the portmanteau brought a rush of happy memories, for in the past its use meant adventure, visits to Plymouth for joyous shopping sprees, dining in inns, traveling in coaches, sleeping in strange rooms. Now there was no joy.

Noon was approaching. Patience thought of the Falmouth - Plymouth coach. It passed on the main road about three in the afternoon. She placed some personal things in the bag then unlocked a chest. In it she kept some money, some coins she had saved, and some jewelry. "There should be enough money for fare," she figured. She looked at a gold watch that had belonged to her father and a gold locket her mother had worn. These she considered she might need. Both went into a side pocket of the portmanteau, and the coins were dropped into a small purse and placed at the bottom of the bag.

Mrs. Battey greeted Patience very solemnly when the confused girl sat down for the noon meal. "After you have eaten, I need to speak to you," the housekeeper requested as she went to the kitchen.

Nancy brought a tray. Patience ate a second bowl of soup knowing this might be her last good meal for awhile. After Nancy cleared the tray, Mrs. Battey came in and sat down. "How is Penny getting along," Patience inquired, trying not to indicate in any way her knowledge of the problem. "I would like to see her now."

"My dear, I do not know how to tell you. It is all tragic. And Mr. and Mrs. Framsden not being here, not knowing. Your little sister gave birth to a still born baby during the morning. It was such a surprise. We did not suspect her feeling poorly was due to a pregnancy. We were not prepared. Mrs. Tully in the village helps with such things, but Nancy could not find her. Now we cannot find Dr. Peers. Penny is very sick. Maybe she wont be with us long."

With that Patience flew up to Penny's room, quietly opened the door and tiptoed to the bed. There was no life in the face that was an image of her own. Her eyes were closed and her mouth was drawn. Her skin looked grey. Slowly Patience reached out and gently brushed Penny's forehead. It was cold. Mrs. Battey entered the room, touched Penny's forehead, too, and commented almost inaudibly, "I am afraid the poor child is dead."

"Dead! My sister!" Tears spilled from her eyes, falling in streams over her cheeks. She knelt at the side of the bed and buried her face in the covers.

After the sobbing faded to silence, Mrs. Battey gently placed a hand on Patience's shoulder and urged, "Come, love. There is nothing we can do now. Let her rest in peace. We shall never know the man responsible for this tragedy. You go to the garden and walk. It will do you good."

Patience accepted the suggestion. The fresh salt air helped clear her head and walking calmed her nerves. She considered her plans to run away. "Mr. Wyatt!" she yelled out in a loud voice for her sorrow was turning to hate. Quickly she realized she had no proof of his relations with her sister. "He would deny all if I confronted him, and I would look silly." Then she remembered his body on the rocks. "I would be accused of his murder if any one saw me in the garden talking to him, or even if the disturbed area where our scuffle took place is discovered."

Thoughts of running again came to mind. "If I stay I will be questioned about Penny's death. In anger I will accuse Mr. Wyatt. Then they will say I killed him in revenge."

She returned to her room, put on her coat, picked up the portmanteau and opened the door. Mrs. Battey stood in front of her. They looked at each other questioningly. The housekeeper spoke first. "Now, love. What are you up to?"

Patience hesitated while thoughts caromed around her mind trying to find an answer. It had not occurred to her that anyone would question her actions. After what seemed ages, she spoke weakly. "The walk in the garden did not help, Mrs. Battey. I want to stay with someone. I want to spend the night with Claire in the village."

Mrs. Battey considered the proposal a moment then responded sympathetically. "Of course, child. You need to be with someone who will understand. The vicarage is a goodly spot. I shall call for you tomorrow to bring you home."

Patience's knees felt like willow sticks, barely strong enough to take her down stairs. "Fancy thinking of Claire." Patience had joined Claire with other children to receive religious instruction from the girl's father, the vicar, and Claire visited Castelamer to participate in some of Mr. Chiver's classes. The lie freed Patience from further questioning, for if Mrs. Battey approved of her actions, she had a blessing from the temporary head of household.

Patience left by the side door, hurried around the service area, then took a short cut through the copse to the main road. She needed time for the afternoon was fleeting and the coach schedule was rarely on time, being early or late.

On reaching the road, Patience waited, concealed behind a cluster of trees. "Better not be sighted here when I should be in Brixton Village." The sound of hoof beats brought her out of concealment. She ran to the road to see dust billowing in the distance. As the coach approached, she waved heartily but made every effort to hide her face as the coach slowed to a stop and then the driver got down to place her portmanteau with other luggage within the rack on top. Inside she was lodged with other passengers from Falmouth.

# Chapter Two

A late afternoon sun cast shadows on the landscape. Patience watched passing scenes through windows as a team of four pulled the coach up wooded hills, across streams and through open countryside. Although the end of summer was near, most of the fields were green, but some were changing to light brown as grain ripened. Here and there gatherings of brightly colored wildflowers added contrasts. Hedgerows, long lines of vines and shrubs, intersected to create geometric designs on the sprawling earth. Flocks of sheep roamed freely in some meadows while cattle populated others.

Five passengers traveled with Patience. Two women were completely silent but three men were having a heated discussion about the king. They were not pleased with business conditions, blaming their ill fortunes on Charles 11. "Taxes are too heavy. They are enough to drive a man to crime. The king needs to give more attention to the welfare of the country, promote business and cut taxes. Business people need incentives and taxes do not provide incentives. If he and his ministers would give more time to running the government instead of spending so much time with the Lady Castlemaine and ladies of the stage, they would serve us better. It is enough to make me think about cheating the government."

Patience gazed through the windows. This time the vista was down a dale to a collection of cottages. Smoke curled from one chimney. Above the dwellings on a high hill were the ruins of a castle. She squirmed a bit to find a softer spot on the portion of thin cushion allotted to her. Annoyance was felt on the part of the woman to her right who moved in response and glared.

As night fell a feeling of guilt about her decision to flee was bothersome. Then she though of Patty, dead because of that man. She recalled looking into the face of her carefree sister, once so full of smiles, and saw again her head reclining on the death pillow, her skin cold. Hatred mounted, and the more Patience considered Wyatt's heinous act, the greater became her loathing for the man. "He took her life and he paid with his. I was merely an instrument in a divine plan that provided for him to pay the supreme penalty for the life he took. He had the gall to laugh. Well he has had his last laugh. He deserves to die in hell."

She remembered the Framsdens. "My running away is no way to treat them. What will they think when they return home and find me gone. And poor Mrs. Battey. She will be accused of not taking better care of me."

Her soliloquy was broken by a man's voice. "We are almost to Plymouth." Immediately anxieties induced nervousness. "Where am I to stay? How do I find out about a place to sleep? How much does a bed cost? Be brave. You are on your own."

The coach began to slow, in the darkness buildings appeared, some with candlelight glowing through windows. The horses changed from a trot to a walk, turning the coach and rolling it slowly under a square arch. Cobblestones covered a courtyard enclosed by buildings and walls. The coach stopped in the enclosure. Patience watched the other passengers get out so that she could see what they did and how they did it.

A tall burly man appeared, a huge apron covering the entire front of his person. In a big friendly voice he greeted the arrivals. "Welcome to

Plymouth, travelers all. And a special welcome to the Captain's Helm. A full tumbler of ale awaits inside and a healthy supper follows. Clean beds are ready. Welcome one and all."

"'The ladies and I are off to the good ship WESTWIND. Thank you, sir," one man responded. "I need to pay the coach fee and hire a laddie to take our bags to the ship."

"They started with us in Falmouth, Gov'nor," alerted the driver now atop the coach after the innkeeper gave him a questioning glance. "I am getting their bags."

"For you, the ladies, the bags and the cartage to the harbor will be one pound, ten shillings," announced the man with the apron.

While the traveler reached for his purse, the innkeeper in a lusty voice called out, "Tom!" Almost at once a boy appeared. He looked at the scene, turned and fetched a two wheeled cart. The cart being loaded, the innkeeper directed Tom to serve as a guide to the harbor for the ladies and gentleman. "And be careful of puddles!"

Without waiting, the host returned to the inn leaving Patience standing by her portmanteau. She gave the remaining man a questioning look and he smiled. "Come with me, girl. We shall have a bite from the joint." He picked up her bag and she followed him across the courtyard, through a door and into the inn. The large room, heavily beamed and lined with wooden panels, was aglow with candle light. There were so many candles that scarcely a shadow was cast by any one of them. Smoke filled the room and the atmosphere was dense. She wanted to get back to fresh air, for the mingling of strong odors, mainly of beer and ale, almost gagged her. A smell of burning wood became apparent, and she looked across the room to a huge stone fireplace within which a large beef joint was turning on a spit. About the room were tables and benches occupied by men. Some were smoking and talking while others were drinking from pewter mugs. A few were eating. The only woman Patience saw was a bar maid delivering mugs, holding several in each hand. It was a happy, noisy group with everyone talking at once. The maid made several verbal quips and laughed with the men when she made deliveries.

Patience followed the man with her bag to a counter along the wall opposite to the fireplace. Behind the counter was the innkeeper. He gazed at her with a look of horror on his face. "What are you doing here?" he questioned in a big voice, his large eyes glaring.

"I need a place to sleep this night." she replied meekly, her heart beginning to pound in fear.

"You should be heading for the WESTWIND with that gentleman and those ladies. Aren't you with them?" he asked with astonishment on his face.

"Oh, no sir. I am traveling alone."

"Ah!" he shouted, slamming his hand on the counter. "I charged that man for your coach fare and drayage." Then he broke out in a laugh. "No matter. He seemed to have a full purse and he didn't complain. So you don't owe me for the coach ride. Now for a place to sleep. Mmmmmmm. I can't put a girl like you in the big room. How about sleeping with my young uns. I'll put Tom in the shed. You can have his bed and you'll be company for Grace and Jem. Let's see. That will be ten pence."

Patience reached for her portmanteau to get a coin, but the man from the coach did not release it to her. Instead he said, "I shall pay the lady's lodging, and she is my guest for supper. I shall need my regular room, but I want no one else put in it."

"Oh no, sir! Please! I have my own money!" Patience pleaded with him, shocked at the man's offer. "And I am not hungry. I had a sizeable lunch before I took the coach."

"Nonsense," he smiled. "I enjoy helping young ladies and your company will be appreciated at table. Come now. You can wash up if you wish and return here immediately. I am as famished as a suckling pig. Hurry along."

The man gave the publican Patience's bag and she followed him through his office then into a small room which had a second door and a window with shutters closed. There were three pallets on the floor, each covered with bedding. The room was dimly lighted by one candle. Two girls, each younger than Patience, were sitting on the floor looking at the stranger.

"What is your name, girl?" the innkeeper asked.

"Jill," Patience replied, announcing the first name that came to mind.

"Well, Jill, this one is Grace and that one is Jem, my young uns." To the girls he added, "Jem, when Tom comes back, tell him to sleep in the shed, and Grace, get Jill some water for a wash."

Quickly Grace arose, went to the door, and then hesitated. She was a sad looking little girl. Her hair was uncombed and her soiled dress hung sloppily to the floor. "Get it in the kitchen this time," her father directed in a brisk voice. Fearfully she went out the door.

The innkeeper left the room. Patience took off her coat, put it across the pallet in the corner, shook her hair, adjusted her dress and put the portmanteau next to the pallet. She sat down with her back to Jem so her actions could not be seen. She opened the portmanteau, retrieved her purse, then slipped it inside her bodice as she had seen Mrs. Framsden do. She then fastened her mother's necklace around her neck and placed her father's watch in her pocket. "There will be no temptation for thieving," she decided.

Grace brought water in a pitcher and handed the guest a serviette. "The toilet is out there," she announced, pointing a finger at the door. Outside was a cobblestone passage way. Beyond was a shed.

On her return, Patience bathed her face. Although the water proved to be cold, it was refreshing. She enjoyed the tingle it created on her skin. Ablutions completed, she left for the public room.

The innkeeper smiled as Patience appeared. He guided her to a dimly lit, small, doorless alcove off the main room. "May I ask your name, Miss?" the man from the coach queried as she entered. He was standing on one side of a table drinking from a pewter tankard. He had removed his coat and hat and now appeared in a long sleeve frilly white shirt covered by an open vest.

"It is Jill, sir."

"No need for 'sir.' My name is Chris. Let me hear you say 'Chris.'"

Shyly she said, "Chris."

"I like the way you say my name," he smiled. "You say it sweetly and with a lilt. A touch of Cornish brogue. Would you like some ale?"

Patience declined with a turn of her head.

She watched as a bar maid placed food on the table. The sight and smell of it aroused her hunger. Each pewter plate had a generous cut of beef swimming in brown Juice. A few boiled potatoes and a large slice of bread completed the serving.

Chris sopped his bread in the juice and bit into it ravenously. After eating several bites of meat, some of which were almost raw, he began talking. "I suppose you are off to visit friends."

Patience nodded, continuing to eat.

"I sail tomorrow for France. I go often. In fact, I sometimes make two or three trips a month. I am in the business of trade."

"How long will it take you to get to France?" she asked even though she was not really interested. She talked more to keep him conversing so that she could finish her plate then leave. She was beginning to get nervous being with a strange man.

"It depends on the weather, the sea, and if the ship stops at ports up the English coast. Sometimes a storm will hold us in port. Sometimes a fog sits right on the water and not one captain will cross the Channel. But I allow for difficulties and usually plan on a few days."

His explanation was spoken between bites. He was eating rapidly and noisily. Juice dripped from each cut of meat he raised from his plate. He was still hungry after eating all he had been given, for he called out loudly, "Girl!" and ordered a second full meal.

As he continued talking about his business trips and eating, Patience studied his face. He appeared to be in his middle to upper twenties. He had heavy eye brows and long lashes which protected his pale blue eyes. He had an appealing smile that revealed a small space between his upper front teeth. Perhaps it was the moustache that made his smile attractive.

Mr. Chris' coloring was dark, probably from being in the sun. He was not so handsome as Mr. Wyatt, but he was attractive in his own way. Most noticeable was a scar that began about the middle of his forehead, stretched over the left brow, then curved downward to end at a point even with the left eye. Above all he had dark brown, wavy hair which he wore long.

"The goods I buy in France are brought to England where they are sold at a profit. Even after taxes I do well. Ha!"

"What kind of goods are they?"

"A variety, depending on what my orders are and what I can find that is cheap enough. Where will you be going tomorrow, Jill?"

Patience hesitated. She wanted to say London, but that would be too brazen, and she could not think of the name of another large town that would sound reasonable, so she merely said to the north.

"Ah, Exeter, perhaps?"

She nodded.

"I know Exeter. Fine place. The coach leaves for Exeter at six in the morning. I wont be able to see you off. I shall be up long before you, for my ship leaves Plymouth at five in the morning."

"I wish you a fine and successful voyage, Mr. Chris, and I do thank you for my supper and bed." She started to get up, but he reached across the table and took her hand.

"No, Jill. Not so soon. Let me enjoy your company. I like you. You are sweet. All innocence. I like to look at your eyes. You have beautiful eyes. They enchant me."

"Please, sir. It is getting late. Six o'clock comes early in the morning." The look in his eyes and the loudness of his voice were beginning to terrify her.

"What is my name?" he asked. "Come. Say it. I like to hear you say it."

"Chris."

"If it is sleeping you are worried about, do not fret. I bet the bed his lordship gave you is not canopied. 'Come with me and be my love' as the poet says. For just this night. You and I both will be refreshed and ready for all the tasks of tomorrow."

As he talked the fingers of his left hand began moving up her bare forearm ever so lightly, ever so slowly. Her flesh began to tingle and she felt giddy.

"Please, Mr. Chris."

"Please to do what, little Jill." With that, before she could build a defense, he rose, leaned over the table, and cupped her face in both hands. "Your eyes fascinate me. What do you do with them? You make me wild. I want to put my hands on you, clutch you," he whispered as he looked fiercely into her eyes. Suddenly he kissed her hard on the mouth. She could feel his tongue darting along her lips.

"What is this?" Patience thought. "It is so violent!" Her lips ached. "Get away," she urged herself, but his grip was strong, and seated as she was, her kicking did no good. She put her hands on his forearms and tried to pull his hands from her face, but she could not budge them.

Finally he withdrew his mouth, but he kept his face close to hers and his hands stayed on her cheeks. "There, Jill. Come with me. My bed is warm. I shall teach you to return my kisses and more."

He placed a soft, light kiss on each eye and then on her lips.

"Come, Jill, come," he whispered with intensity.

Patience rose and stood next to the table. "I must go to my room first," she mumbled as she looked at him. Then she turned and rushed to the innkeeper who was behind his counter. "Good night, sir, and please wake me at half after five in the morning. I need a coach for Exeter."

Tom's pallet was hard and uncomfortable. There were no sheets and the worn blankets had not been changed for some time. They had a musty odor. As she lay stretched out, she thought of the day just past and that last awful experience with Chris. "Is this what men do? Paw. Attack. Kiss! In one day two men tried to make love to me. Both were aggressive, determined, violent. My lips still feel bruised from the pressure so long forced on me by Mr. Chris. Is this what a girl must put up with when she is alone? Is every man going to treat me this way?"

Patience's thoughts were interrupted by a sound at the outside door that made her think of feet on cobblestones. She instantly became alert. Only her eyes moved and they became fixed on the door. Slowly, quietly it opened. A candle held in a hand appeared first, then a face peeked around the partially opened door. "Chris! What if he tries his love tactics again!"

A child's gentle voice broke the silence. "If it is Tom you want, he be in the shed. If you want my father, he be in his office. He will be here shortly for bed."

Quickly Chris' head disappeared into the darkness outside. The hand holding the candle pulled back. The door closed.

Patience relaxed here tense body and in silence thanked the dear child. "Here I thought both girls were asleep. Which one spoke I don't know. Little does she know she saved me from another violent attack."

# Chapter Three

"It's half after five, Miss. The coach leaves at six." It was Jem's voice. "Here's water for a wash."

"Thank you, child. You are a great help." Patience gave consideration to remaining in bed but immediately decided against it. Her sleep had been fitful and she felt tired. She arose quickly, washed, then dressed. Her jewelry went into the portmanteau. From her purse she selected a coin and gave it to Jem. The purse went into her bodice.

The courtyard was in dull morning light as she cautiously opened the door and peered out. Chris was no where in sight. Horses were being backed into position for harnessing. The driver took her bag, placed it on top of the coach in the rack then helped her mount two high steps to gain the interior of the coach. She took a window seat facing forward. Two men and a woman became fellow travelers and off they went.

The Exeter road was just as bumpy as the Plymouth road. Sometimes they had all they could do to hang on, but there were beautiful vistas presented to them, rolling hills covered with forests, quietly flowing streams meandering at times along the road then passing under a bridge for the coach to cross and quaint villages with thatched roofs.

Patience was giving more thought as to what she was going to do. The grown up feeling of self importance she had yesterday had vanished, smothered by the reality of the situation, alone, no friends, very little money, no promise of work. She decided she would start looking for a sewing job, probably in Exeter if that town was of any size.

She could feel the coach pitch down a steep hill to cross a stream at the bottom of a ravine. It looked very peaceful in the morning sun, trees and bushes creating a lovely garden. The horses slowed considerably as they crossed the stream and began an arduous pull up the opposite side.

As the top was crested, the travelers heard a commotion, felt the coach roll for a short distance, then stop. They became aware of several voices, but one voice dominated the others. It commanded, "Get 'em out! Now!" A look out the window found a man on horseback waving a gun. He wore a mask over his eyes, leaving his mouth free to speak. The driver appeared at the door, opened it, and told everyone to get out, quietly and peacefully. "We are being greeted by highwaymen. Do as they say and no one will get hurt," he pleaded. The ladies were assisted in descending the high steps and all gathered together at the side of the road in a group.

When Patience looked about she saw two more men on horseback, one at the end of the coach and one in front of the horses. Each had a gun pointing at the travelers. All three wore hats pulled over their ears, the same type of masks, hip type riding boots and long coats.

The two male passengers started to protest, but a nasty threat from the leader and a wave of his gun quieted them. He tossed a leather pouch to the coach driver and commanded loudly, "I want your jewelry and your money. Fill the pouch with what you have on you. Quick!" His tone was forceful and direct and his gun was kept in readiness.

All started to obey. The men reached into their pockets, removed leather folders, pulled out paper notes and put their money in the pouch. The lady unhooked her locket from her neck and contributed it to the pouch, a steady mumbling emanating from an angry face.

Patience was reaching for the coin purse under her bodice when she became aware of someone standing next to her. She thought it was the driver, but when she looked up she saw it was a highwayman, the one in charge, a gun still in his hand. She opened her purse and took out the coins.

"Is that all you have?" he asked in surprise.

"Yes, sir," she responded meekly.

"Well now, little girl," he smiled, showing bad teeth, "the money is still yours for a price." He bent down impulsively, kissed her, then added, "That is the first time I ever paid for a kiss. It's worth it." He stepped back instantly and again became alert to the business at hand, the gun helping him keep charge. His action embarrassed Patience, and she could feel her face redden.

"The nerve of that man," the lady traveler said disgustedly, "but at least you have your money."

The lead highwayman grabbed the leather pouch from the driver, mounted his horse and rode off, the others of his band following. The entire holdup could not have taken five minutes. The male passengers instantly vented their wrath, complaining about the lack of protection on the road, the increasing number of highwaymen who live off decent people and make travel dangerous, the mounting losses to thieves in general and the blame authorities must accept for all of it.

"I fooled those bloody holdup men," one man said. "I kept only a little money in my folder. Most of it is in false soles of my boots. I carry no jewelry of any kind. They didn't get much from me."

"I was warned at the inn that this is a bad stretch of road," the other man added, "so I distributed my money in unlikely places like the lining of my coat. It puzzles me why they didn't have us take off our boots and have one of them go through our coats. That is standard procedure. With three of them they could have searched us good."

"It is possible they could have been beginners," commented the first man. "They appeared to be young and nervous. No seasoned highwayman is going to stop and kiss a girl."

"Well, I hated to lose that locket. This is the worse place on the run between Plymouth and Exeter. Horses have to slow to make the rise, and it is easy for highwaymen to catch us at a snail's pace. We've asked authorities to post protection here but they refuse." It was the lady passenger joining in.

"Maybe they are in with the robbers." The two men kept up their complaints, but the lady looked at Patience and asked, "My dear, would you mind changing places with me. I get such a headache riding backwards"

"Of course," Patience replied, happily agreeing to the request.

"That is sweet of you, dear. Young ones can get by no matter how you sit." She gave Patience a big smile after they moved about gingerly. "Now tell me, what is your destination?"

"I shall get off in Exeter."

"You are going to visit family. How nice. You are on holiday."

"I hope to find work in Exeter. I have to find a way to make a living."

"Oh, poor child. You have no family. You have no one in Exeter. Ah, let me help you. I know just the place for you. My sister has a little business. I will speak with her. She may need someone like you. Stay with me when we alight the coach."

It was almost dark when the coach entered Exeter. "Get ready, dear," the lady directed. "My sister will have a lackey for me. When we get off, ask for your bag then join me."

The coach stopped in the courtyard of an inn. A man with a push cart took the lady's bag and Patience handed him her portmanteau. Both followed him into the street. Patience was surprised by the number of people about, particularly at this late hour. The cart cleared the way, but it was a chore avoiding slimy puddles and piles of filth.

"Here we are, dear." The footman had stopped in front of a brick building. Steps led up to a door with a heavy, highly polished knocker. "Get your bag and we'll speak to my sister."

After a heavy pounding by the knocker, the door was opened by a girl who showed Patience to a room. "Wait there, dear, and I'll get my sister." Presently a large woman who used an excessive amount of paint on her face appeared. It was obvious she wore a wig. "Ah, my dear. Sit down. I am Mrs. Dawes. And may I ask your name."

"Anne."

"My sister tells me you are without a family and looking for a position in Exeter."

"Yes."

"Good. I have a very fine establishment and I think you will fit here nicely. I know you have had a tiring ride and a disturbance from highwaymen, so let us see about supper for you and a good night's rest. Then tomorrow morning we can talk about your duties and your pay. Nell will show you to your room. Ta. Ta."

Nell led Patience to a small room with a bed, a table with a candle holder, a pitcher and a bowl. A towel rack was above the table. A small window at the end of the room was closed. Patience opened it slightly. Nell had told her that the facilities were at the end of the hall and outside, so she used them.

When she returned she found hot water in the pitcher. She bathed her face, changed clothes and sat down to wait. Soon she was asked to supper and was guided to the kitchen where she was served alone. The soup was delicious and she ate all that was placed before her. She returned to her room, undressed and went to bed.

During the night she was awakened by the sound of raucous laughter. Several people were having a jolly time, for she could make out different kinds of laughing, both men and women. At first the hilarity appeared to be beyond the window she had opened, but then a sudden burst of riotous mirth directed her attention to the hall beyond her closed door. She heard doors open and close followed by a quiet period. Then more laughter.

Curiosity got the better of her. She arose, donned a robe, quietly opened her door a small crack and peeked down the hall. No one was in sight but she could hear talking beyond the door across the hall. As she stared, a man, a farmer he appeared to be, and a young woman dressed in a tight fitting white dress with a low cut neck and a feather in her hair came suddenly into view. They disappeared through a door.

Quietly Patience sneaked down the corridor toward a well lighted room from which came singing. She tiptoed slowly until she could stretch her neck around the open door. Men with young ladies were talking and singing and drinking, and all were having a noisy good time. Patience was reminded of socials at Castelamer when everybody dressed up and laughed so merrily.

"This is a happy, friendly place," she thought as she returned to her room. "Maybe I can sew for the ladies. It was such good fortune meeting that traveler on the coach." As she drifted off to sleep, she wondered how that lady knew she wanted a sewing position, for she could not recall mentioning it.

Mrs. Dawes met Patience the next morning. "My dear Anne," came her enthusiastic greeting. The wig was absent and so was much of the face paint. "I hope you slept well and are ready to start your new work. Our business day begins in the evening and carries on to about midnight, sometimes later. But your hours will be from four in the afternoon to about ten until you learn all the skills. After you do learn, we'll talk about a percent of the business earnings. You will keep the room you have and eat with the other girls. You may eat breakfast whenever you get up, but all of us eat our mid-day meal together. Your pay will be eight shillings a week, and if you do a good job, you will get more later. As for your duties, you will meet with the other girls in the social room, greet our guests when they visit us, see that they are made comfortable, and when one invites you to meet with him alone, you will take him to your room and see that you meet all of his requests."

"When do I begin my sewing duties?" Patience questioned, a bit bewildered after hearing Mrs. Dawes.

"Sewing? But my dear, this is not as dressmaking shop. This is a highly honored, indeed respected, social club. The dress we give you may not fit exactly so you may use your needle to alter it it you wish. Come, dear, let us get a dress for you."

Patience tried several dresses then chose a light pink frock. Mrs. Dawes commented happily, "It should show off your figure which is too slight now but it will fill out later. Use your needle to tighten the waist and shorten the length. And keep the neck line low and the bodice loose."

Alterations were made as suggested and at one o'clock Patience went to the dining room. Several girls were chatting together. "Sit down, girls," Mrs. Dawes directed. "Meet Anne who will be working with us. I want all of you to help her. This is her first job. Rosie, I want you to take Anne under your wing and be her big sister. Rosie has her room next to yours, Anne. Ask any questions, dear. Rosie has lots of experience. She will give you good answers."

Most of the girls were dressed in robes. Some had pieces of paper tied in their hair which Patience learned was to encourage waves and curls. There was a lot of laughing caused by one girl who was relating details of a meeting she had with a man in her room the previous night.

Patience did not understand all that was being said but she thought, "With all this happiness, my job will work out just fine."

Following lunch, Rosie put her arm around Patience's shoulder and suggested they talk. "This is not such a bad place to work. The meals are so-so, we have some free time to walk around town, but Madam Dawes doesn't want us out too much. You have to ask her when you can go. The customers are jolly good at times. If you treat them friendly like, you get some shillings in your hand. Madam Dawes lets you keep that. I'll help you with your face paint."

"Paint!" Patience exclaimed aghast.

"Sure. You have to put paint on your face. It helps show you off and our guests like it, particularly the older ones. It makes them feel giddy, like they were younger."

Rosie put paint on her own face as Patience watched. The change was remarkable. "Sit down here, Anne, and I will fix your face." Her hand dabbed into some red with a piece of cloth and put the bright color on her cheeks, rubbing it in. Next she put a different red on her lips and blotted them with a piece of paper. A white powder was patted on her face then buffed with a cloth. "Now for combing your hair and adding some bows. Take a look."

A mirror was held up. "Why, I can't believe the change!" Her newly reddened lips smiled brightly in disbelief. She was like the other girls, a bit wicked. "I am not sixteen. I am more like twenty."

"You'll make 'em stand up. They will be waiting in line. Come on. We need to be in the social room."

Patience listened to the chatter of other girls as the six talked about the best ways to use paints to get the most effective results. They appeared to be in their early twenties with attractive faces and figures. All were jovial, seeming to be talking all the time. They were dressed in a variety of colored gowns, ankle length, cut to emphasize attractive curves, very tight at the waist, and all had low, loose fitting bodices that showed a generous part of cleavages and a goodly portion of ample breasts.

"This could be a slow night. No one has come yet," one girl commented.

"There'll be enough to go around," came a reply. "Anne should do alright, being a new girl."

At the mention of her name, Patience half smiled. "You'll do fine," one girl encouraged. "Just be friendly and let him take the lead. Here. Let me add a bow to your hair. A nice touch makes 'em more interested." She moved to place a blue bow at the side of Patience's head. "There. You look prettier."

"Listen. The door! Get ready for our first guest," some one warned.

A man, a worker he appeared to be, dressed in dirty clothes, entered the room. "Ah, Mr. Keen!" The greeting was warmly given by one of the girls who went to him, wreathed her face in smiles, put one arm inside his, and walked him to a sofa where she pulled him down next to her and began a quiet chatter. In a moment a little girl brought in two tumblers of ale.

Patience's puzzlement must have shown for Rose asked, "What is the matter, dearie?"

"I always saw men dressed up for socials or even when making a social call."

"Oh, it's different here. It's come as you are. Look at that one. He likes Millie. Many of our guests have their favorites among us."

A better dressed middle aged man came through the door. He, too, was greeted warmly, seated, and served ale. In time only Rosie and Patience were without a man to "cheer up."

Millie got up with her gentleman friend and left the room. Then Mr. Keen left with the girl who had greeted him.

"Don't women come here?" Patience inquire, a bit bewildered. Rosie had the strangest look on her face when she turned to reply. "My dear, don't you know?"

Before another word could be spoken, a man appeared at the door whom Rosie recognized and hurried to greet him.

Patience sat by herself but not for long. An older man walked into the room. Rosie must have seen the terrified look on Patience's face, for she appeared at her side, walked her to the man and said, "Welcome. This is Anne. She'll see to your comfort."

Patience put her arm in his as she had seen the other girls do, sat him down and smiled.

"You new?"

"Yes, sir. My first day."

"Good luck for me. I enjoy a new filly."

"Are you a horseman" she asked. "I used to ride."

"Yes, maam. I have a barn of horses." He proceeded to tell her about his horses as he drank ale. Patience noticed Millie coming back to the room alone. Then Rosie left the room with her friend.

"How about getting better acquainted," he suggested, and before Patience could say a word, he took her by the arm, had her on her feet, steered her out of the room, directed her down the hall then stopped at the first door. "Occupied," he commented as he opened then closed it.

"Good," he smiled when he opened the next door. He sat down on the bed and pulled Patience to him. She managed her fall so that she ended up sitting at his side. "I like to start with 'em sitting on my lap," he said, staring in her face, his eyes misty, fierce looking.

"Why, sir, I can be just as social sitting here.'

"We'll start your way and then end with how I like to do it." He turned to face her. She felt a hand on her knee and saw his other hand come up to fall on her breast. It felt rough.

"Lovely," he murmured, his eyes glowing. Quickly he removed his rough hand and buried his face on her breasts, kissing and nipping. His hands began roaming about her body. Suddenly one hand began pulling at the back of her bodice.

Frightened, Patience tried to stand but he held her back. He started to rise but fell backward. "Get that bloody thing off!" His command was sharp.

"Very well, sir, but I must stand to do it." He allowed her to stand. She deliberately fiddled with the back catch. "Oh, me! I must get help. Do not go. Stay here, please. I'll be back before you know I have been gone."

She flew to her room, tossed her belongings in the portmanteau, threw her coat around her shoulders, ran down the hall and out the back door. All was dark. Because of previous visits, she knew the backyard was fenced and that it had no gate. She quickly climbed onto some ale kegs piled in the corner, looked over the fence and saw an alley filled with debris of all kinds. She dropped the bag over the fence, pulled up her skirt and climbed over.

Hearing noises behind her, she quickly looked about, spied a pile of trash, grabbed her bag and huddled behind it. Voices grew louder. She heard the fence being mounted as she had done and a man's voice said very clearly, "Can't see a soul. You look. I'll go around and check the alley."

"The alley! He will see me! He will see this white dress. Get it off!" As fast as she could, she dropped her coat, removed the dress, put the coat back on and ran down the alley, plodding through puddles, slipping in slop and dodging what debris she could see.

The top of the alley opened onto a street. She stopped. In the darkness she could see no one in either direction. She straightened her coat, shook off her damaged shoes and rearranged her hair. The bows! Off they came.

Feeling more presentable, she started walking. As fear from her escape left her, Patience was sieged by a different fear "What if I am caught out at this late hour! What would they do to me!" She walked faster not knowing where to go, what direction to take, what to say if she were stopped.

She passed several shops, crossed streets then decided to go straight ahead. "If only I could find a way out of town I could hide among trees and wait until morning."

Suddenly the street ended. Ahead of her was an open area and beyond it the front of a church. "A church! Who would ever think to look for me in a church?"

Quickly she ran to the front portal and tried to open the door. Locked. She ran around to the left side hoping to find another door. She did. Locked. To the opposite side. Quick! A door. A sign. "All who enter here find peace."

# Chapter four

Patience stepped into a world of darkness, a vast cavernous darkness that allowed no light except for a minuscule glow emanating from a single candle sitting on a table some distance away. The light, although it identified its most immediate surroundings, had the effect of creating total blackness beyond its perimeter. It was possible to distinguish only shadowy details of a few objects in the space about the door where she stood.

Almost at once the frightened girl experienced a sense of security, and in the darkness she gave a sigh of relief. "It must have been divine guidance that directed me here." Candle glow drew Patience to the table, and as she approached the faint light she could feel the first surge of courage. She stopped in front of the table, placed her portmanteau under it and turned to look towards the altar. The center nave led abruptly into an ebony cavern to which she could see no end. She entered a pew closest to her, descended to her knees, and in humbleness returned thanks. She recalled childhood prayers and recited those fervently.

She stayed on her knees feeling more consoled and refreshed from her terrifying ordeal. The reality of her situation sobered her, and she gave thought to her financial condition.

"Tomorrow I shall learn where dressmaking shops are located and ask for employment. I must work."

Her body tensed as new thoughts came to mind. She shuddered at the recollection of ways men had treated her. "In two days four men, only one of whom I knew even remotely, have either clawed, pawed, pulled, kissed, ripped clothing, or physically manhandled me, caring nothing for my dignity, treating me as a thing, a bauble to juggle then toss away. All men are alike. How else am I to think after this kind of treatment. They are animals. No. Less than animals, for animals have caring for their fellows. No. No man must be allowed near me."

In time she rose, and as she did so, her coat fell open. Shocked, she realized she wore no dress. And the paint! She seized her portmanteau, hurried to the edge of candle light, and in darkness removed her coat and put on a dress. She used a bit of cloth to wipe paint from her face. Reentering the darkened pew, she placed the portmanteau under it, lay down on the bench, spreading her coat over herself and tucking the sides under her prone body. She closed her eyes and fell asleep.

Rest was short lived. A thunderous sound filled the church, rumbling mightily as reverberations caromed off the walls. Patience bolted upright, almost sliding off the pew, unaware for the moment of her location. "What is that?" she cried out fearfully. The sound clamored, resounding in gathering crescendos around her. She searched her experiences to identify it. "Yes! A peel of bells! Brixton Village church has bells, joyous bells that fill the church on Sundays. But these bells are tumultuous!"

Having determined the source of the noise that had awakened her, she lay back on the pew, fully awake, and enjoyed the crash of harmonies. The clang and clash of clappers in rapid rotation on a variety of pitched metals produced metallic melodies that fell gloriously about her. "This is the morning curfew," she thought, "announcing to all people of Exeter the beginning of a new day."

As if exclaiming this feeling of confidence, a blaze of color appeared in the high reaches of the church as first rays of a rising sun filtered through stained glass. Slowly as the sun rose upward more glass glowed until one side of the nave was covered with a myriad of blended colors, a spectrum, glowing vibrantly, brilliantly, like pastels in a garden, soft and light.

Patience sat up and looked into the vast openness of the church's interior. Revealed was one of man's greatest creations, a cathedral. She was in the Cathedral of Exeter.

Leaving her coat and portmanteau on the pew, she wandered down the nave looking up at the soaring vaulted Gothic ceiling, the ribbing reminding her of spreading branches of giant trees whose trunks found life through massive supporting columns rooted below the nave floor.

Singing was heard somewhere in the distance. As the voices came closer a procession of men and boys entered the chancel led by a crucifer carrying a pole topped by a simple cross. The choir filed into beautifully carved stalls on either side of the chancel, and the following priests took places next. To Patience it was the familiar service of morning prayer.

Greatly refreshed both in body and spirit after the service, Patience passed through the door she had entered the previous night and walked into sunshine. At the edge of the cathedral close, she turned to see the great west front. Now in morning light appeared a host of figures carved in stone, apostles, bishops, prophets and angels. One figure brought her particular joy, for an apostle, hand raised in blessing, was looking at her, bestowing, it seemed, his protective guidance.

With determination, Patience mingled with other pedestrians, everyone eager to be about the business of the day. Many were women, shopping baskets in hand, collecting food for their family's needs. Shops were opening for business and she entered a bakery. Carefully she selected what appeared to be the best value after watching other women buy and after learning prices. "That will be tupence," a sales girl asked as she handed Patience two rolls.

On the street she came to a chocolate shop where she ordered a mug. The hot, sweet liquid warmed her insides and she ate the rolls. In a matter of fact manner and feeling very much grown up, she asked the serving girl for directions to the nearest dressmaker's shop. The girl thought a moment and with a gesticulating arm explained very carefully what turns to make.

The shop was found, a sign over its portal declaring, "Madame Robair, Dressmaking, French Style." Patience flinched at the word "Madame," but she entered, and still feeling grown up, asked to see Madame Robair. A portly lady with fuzzy hair dyed red and wearing a good deal of paint on her face, reluctantly came into the room.

"What is it you want?" came the doleful greeting in a husky voice emphasized by a squint from puffy eyes.

"I am in need of a seamstress job, Madame Robair. Do you need help?"

"You disturb me with that kind of question! I barely have work enough to keep flesh and limb together. If I need help a sign goes in the window. Get on with you and don't come back unless you need a dress." An arm was raised and an outstretched finger pointed to the door.

"Could you direct me to another dressmaker, please."

"I don't pay attention to my competition. Get out with you."

Patience walked about the streets without direction, afraid to ask for help. More people were moving about now, and after covering several blocks she began to realize that Exeter was a sizeable city. Horse drawn wagons filled much of the road space, and horse droppings were left to rot where they fell. Boys pushing carts had to be avoided. Sidewalks were narrow or not at all. Slop was left on the streets and befouled puddles were everywhere.

At one turning she found a busy market organized in a large open area bounded by shops. Stalls had been set up in the center and men and women were hawking their wares.

A hanging sign attached to a scrolled wrought iron arm extending above a shop attracted her attention. It said simply, "Dressmaking." Patience walked inside to be greeted by a pleasant lady working on a dress. "This would look fine on you," she smiled. Let's try it on."

"I could not pay for it. I am looking for a job. I could finish it for you, though." It was stated almost as a plea.

"Dear child. Business is not good for anybody in this town. I do my own work without help. But hurry along to Mrs. Hardy. Go to the top of this street and take a turning to the left. You will see a sign like mine as you walk along. Hurry now."

In her haste, Patience tried to avoid puddles and slippery cobblestones. The portmanteau became heavy and she bumped a lady who reacted angrily. Making the turn as directed, she soon saw the sign. "Dressmaking - Ladies Fashions"

She entered a little shop as a bell tinkled. "Hello, young lady." Mrs. Hardy came from a corner behind hanging drapes with some goods in her hands.

"Do you need a helper to make dresses, Mrs. Hardy?"

"Bless me, love. I do indeed." Mrs. Hardy's voice changed from matter of fact business to enthusiasm and her face beamed. "You are the answer to my prayer. Bessie turned sick yesterday an she's abed today. And me with two rush orders and only these two hands to make my promises good. Tell me, where have you worked before?"

"I have not worked before. I just came on my own and I have to work. I am good with a needle. Let me show you."

"How old are you, what is your name and where do you come from?" Her tone returned to businesslike directness and it had some suspicion in it.

"I am sixteen, my name is Victoria, and I am from the west country." The name just bounded out. Why she chose it she did not know. It was the name Mrs. Battey gave her cat, the one that had a litter twice a year.

"Do you have a family name?"

"It is Tatham. My parents are dead." Patience caught her error and inwardly she shivered. "The authorities could trace me with that name."

"Well, can't be too careful." Mrs. Hardy's tone softened, but she was still serious. "I can't care for a pregnant girl and run a shop. Here. Give this frock a hem, then let me see your work. In here."

The drapes were pulled back and Patience entered under Mrs. Hardy's arm. It was the work area and cluttered with material. She removed her coat, selected a needle and thread, sat down and went to work. The light was dull but adequate, and she was especially careful to make good stitches.

Mrs. Hardy worked nearby, and Patience could feel the older woman's eyes on her assessing progress. She said a little prayer asking for a chance to work, even for Mrs. Hardy.

"Done? Let me see," Mrs. Hardy ordered when Patience raised her head. The frock was given to her. The stitching was examined with a critical eye, then came an evaluation. "Average like. But I need a needle, Victoria. Now one more question and I'm through asking. Are you in trouble?"

"No." The reply came quickly. She had her fingers crossed as she and Patty used to do when they told little lies.

"I've had girls with problems and they were a constant source of headaches. Alright. I'll take you until Bessie returns. At first you get

44

your bed and food. When you learn you will get some pay depending on how much we earn. Who knows when that will be. Business is slow now, but I have regulars. Some of the town's proper ladies come to me and some of the improper ones, like the ladies from Madam Dawes social club."

Patience heart dropped. "The social club! What will they do if I am discovered here?" She forced a smile and said aloud, "Thank you. I shall make you proud of me."

"Let's get you settled then we'll get back to work." They went to a tiny lean-to type room off the kitchen. In it was a bed, a bench, a small chest of drawers and a dinky, fuzzy white dog. "Unpack your things and return to the sewing room. Be careful of Rags. He's over friendly."

Patience arranged her clothes, left the locket and watch and the remaining coins in the portmanteau and pushed it under the bed. Rags watched every move with a wagging tail and a cheerful grin on his face. He was a chummy little fellow sending his wet tongue upward to lick her nose. With a final squeeze of his shaggy body, she returned to work.

"We need to get this dress finished today even if we must work after supper," Mrs. Hardy warned. "How are you on fancy stitching?"

"The lady who taught me said I was very good. 'A natural pupil and a born seamstress,' she called me. I want to learn, Mrs. Hardy. Teach me and I shall help you. I have to earn a living."

Both worked through the rest of the day, and even with the few minutes taken to eat at noon, both were tired. While Mrs. Hardy prepared supper, Patience sewed and listened to her employer talking in the kitchen. "I took on a girl this morning to fill in for Bessie. She works a good needle, but she has a lot to learn. I'll make money on her. We'll eat first then I'll fix something for her. Can't give her meat the way prices are."

The man said he would go to the pub for the evening. He sounded as if he wanted to get away.

Mrs. Hardy checked Patience's work then directed her to eat supper. Afterwards both sewed by candle light until the girl could keep her eyes open no longer. "On to bed," she was told. "We'll continue in the morning."

Rags met Patience with a greatly agitated wagging tail. He lifted her tired spirits with his joyous behavior, jumping on the cot and licking her hand with his tiny tongue. She prepared for bed quickly and when she pulled the covers up, Rags settled down at her side. Sleep was immediate.

The first promised dress was completed the following morning and a lady called for it. She was admitted to the fitting room. Mrs. Hardy called for Patience to make alterations. As she pulled back the drapes, she recognized instantly the lady as one of the girls from the social club. Millie! She dropped the drapes until she could recover from astonishment. Hurriedly she tied a cloth around her head and put a paper of pins in her mouth. Mrs. Hardy called again. Millie watched the seamstress enter then faced a mirror to continue the fitting. Patience followed directions, pinning here and there.

"Now dear," Mrs. Hardy said to Millie, "slip this off and Victoria will finish your gown immediately. You will look lovely in it. Victoria, only the best stitches. Hurry!"

Patience, working in fear, hurried. When she returned the dress she kept her head down. Millie slipped the dress on and was delighted with what she saw in the mirror. "This is your fee," Mrs. Hardy. And, Victoria, this is for you. Mrs. Hardy has been very complimentary of your work. When Bessie returns, come to the social club. The girls there always need help with sewing"

"Millie is right," Mrs. Hardy beamed. "Your work on that dress was excellent, and I like the way you kept at it when I had to keep a promise. You are going to be a big help to me."

Mrs. Hardy's compliment helped and so did the coins. "If Millie didn't recognize me, I can feel safe. There should be no trouble from the social club and Madam Dawes." Patience smiled confidently to herself as she started on the next gown.

The following morning Patience awoke early but found Mrs. Hardy already at work. They sewed together then had breakfast. Patience asked about Mr. Hardy and was told he always ate early then left for duties at Lord Covington's estate. He had been with his Lordship many years, had charge of the stables and often stayed at the estate for days on end, especially if Lord Covington was preparing for a horse show. "Too bad we didn't have children. I could not carry a baby to full term." A forlorn look appeared on her face.

"Bessie isn't doing well I heard today, but even so when she does return I'll keep you on, Victoria. Right now there is not enough work for three of us. It will be crowded in the sewing room but we will manage."

Patience sighed in relief for Mrs. Hardy had promised a job only until Bessie returned. By the end of the second week Mrs. Hardy gave Patience some coins with the comment, "You helped me make money, Victoria. You earned it. I like your work and your willingness to get a job done."

Thanking her, Patience went to her room to add the coins to those in the portmanteau. As she stepped into the kitchen she saw a man sitting at the table. He looked at her and she looked at him. Both glared. Patience hesitated. A feeling of shock covered her instantly. His face reddened. "This is Mr. Hardy," she heard Mrs. Hardy say in back of her. Patience nodded then hurried to her room, falling across the bed since her jellied legs could no longer bear her weight. It was the same man who had accosted her in the social club.

She lay for a while on her cot, numbed. She began to think. Her thoughts were not good. "I am finished. He will tell Madam Dawes, they will come for me, and I shall have to return to the social club." She cried a bit. A knock on the door startled her. Fear made her body tense and she could not speak. The door opened. Mrs. Hardy spoke. "I am going to visit Bessie. Mr. Hardy wants to talk to you."

She added something else but Patience did not hear. She was too terrified. "He knows me. He got rid of Mrs. Hardy. He sent her away so he can finish what he started at the social club," she convinced herself. "I cannot run without going through the kitchen. I am done for."

Rags bounded on the bed, his little body twisting side to side as the pumping tail generated action. He snuggled close to Patience and she patted his furry coat. She advised herself to put on her coat and leave the shop. "Just pass by him and ignore his presence." She was about to do exactly that when she was disturbed by a rustling noise. She held her breath. Immediately she had visions of Mr. Hardy opening the door and coming in to assault her. After some minutes she decided to face him. She got up, straightened her clothes and hair, and feeling more assured, she opened the door. The sight of him sitting at the table brought back fears. The look he gave her told her he was scared, too.

"Sit down there," he directed. Patience went to the appointed chair which was opposite to his across the narrow table, but she stood in back of the chair starring at him.

He stared back.

"So it is Victoria, is it?" He broke the silence with a slur in his voice. "So you didn't like my advances. You ran. What is the matter with me? I could finish what I started. She's gone. You can't run now.

I want to do that right now. Only this time I intend to finish what I start." He gave her a sneer and reached out sharply as if to grab her. She stepped back. He rose then sat down. "Did you tell my woman about that night?"

Patience shook her head. Unexpectedly he reached over the table and grabbed her hand. "You ruined that night for me. I was ready to enjoy you. You had me excited. You do the same now. It's those eyes. The way they look at me. I could take you. I will take you." He got up, still holding her hand, gripping, hurting.

She looked at his face. His eyes appeared the same as they did that night. Watery. Anxious. She tried to squirm out of his grip. He led her around the table to him. An arm, strong and determined, went around her waist clutching her tightly against his heavy frame. A hand grabbed her chin forcing her face upward until she peered into his soggy eyes.

She spat in his face and screamed knowing no one would come to aid her, but it was all she could do.

As she glowered into his face, she felt his tight vice relaxing. His head rose above her. He let go of her. Patience spun around to find Mrs. Hardy standing in the kitchen doorway, a cutting shears in her hand.

"So this is what happens when I am gone. This is how you use my young seamstresses. I did visit Bessie. She is not ill. She is pregnant because of you. You had her so scared she could not tell me. Her father is out for you. You swine. Just like the floor of your stable.

"I know about your comings and goings at the social club. I am no longer good enough for you, so you sleep with paid-for girls. Anyone will do.

"Victoria. Get my carving knife out of the table drawer. Bring it to me. He wont touch you now."

Patience did as she was told.

"Take these shears. They have just been sharpened. Open them. If he comes at you, just push the points right into his stomach and turn the handle.

"As for you, Mr. Hardy, get out! Go to the stables. Enjoy the paid-for girls. Tomorrow you will find your clothes on the street."

Mr. Hardy spat at his wife, turned and went out the back door without a comment. Mrs. Hardy went to the chair he just left, sat down and cried bitterly. "I kept that man," she sobbed, "all those years. Now he can take care of himself."

The sobbing eased and then stopped. Patience stayed in the doorway not knowing what to do.

"Come here, Victoria. Sit down."

She did as she was told. A tear filled face looked at her. Mrs. Hardy was suddenly an old lady, made aged by a puffy face broken with emotion.

"I learned about you, too, Victoria. Only Mille called you Anne. She recognized you even though you covered your hair and put pins in your mouth. She told Madam Dawes and Madam Dawes told me. It's alright, Honey. Rose told Madam Dawes about your questions and the girls agreed you didn't know about the social club. It all started with Madam Dawes' sister who thought you wanted that kind of job. That led to a lot of misunderstanding. The girls liked you, and Madam Dawes says you can return to do their sewing. We'll see about that later. Off to bed. I must see to Mr. Hardy's things."

# Chapter Five

Bessie returned just after her baby was born, and Mrs. Hardy treated her wonderfully, just as if nothing had happened. Mr. Hardy tried to come back but Mrs. Hardy would have none of it. Bessie's father threatened him so he was forced to provide money for the child's care.

Bessie was an excellent seamstress. She taught Patience a variety of skills and Mrs. Hardy instructed her as well. Proficiency improved, she worked faster as time went along, and Mrs. Hardy was pleased with results. Patience was earning a pound a week and still getting room and board.

One day Madam Dawes entered the shop and asked to see Victoria. Since no customers were present at that time, Mrs. Hardy invited her to sit in the kitchen. It was the first time Patience had seen Madam Dawes since she ran from the social club, and even though she knew her former employer was no longer interested in her, apprehension was evident as the three talked casually. After Mrs. Hardy announced she had to return to the fitting room, Madam Dawes spoke. "Victoria, the past is forgotten. We want you one day a week to help us with gowns and other sewing. Mrs. Hardy is agreeable. Would you like to come?"

Patience sat soberly. "Is Rose still with you?"

"It was Rose who told me of your innocence, and I was embarrassed that you were hired for a job you should never have been offered. But, as I say, the past is long past. We need you every Thursday. The girls asked for you."

"Of course, Madam Dawes, I shall come. I want to see the girls again, particularly Rose. I shall be there Thursday."

Shortly after Madam Dawes left, Patience spoke to Mrs. Hardy. "Of course you can go. I want you to go." she encouraged. "It is another opportunity for you to learn and, Victoria, the money you earn there is yours to keep."

The following Thursday Patience entered the social club. Rose greeted her with a big hug, calling her Anne. Both laughed at that, and Patience said, "It is really Victoria. We can forget Anne. She never was."

"She was for a time," Rose smiled. "She was the girl I met and she was the girl I liked. But I like Victoria, too. Anne gave me quite a start though when she asked me if women came here. Tell me, didn't you know what you were getting into?"

"Not at all. I expected a sewing job."

"Do you know now?"

"I understand that men only come here. I know Mr. Hardy started pawing me, and I did not like that. I know I did not make him happy. He was getting angry."

Rose gave Patience a puzzled look then asked, "How much do you know about a man and a woman when they get together, alone, in private?"

"I have seen them together holding hands or arm in arm and sometimes I have seen them kiss."

"Well that is a beginning. Do you know about babies, how they are made?"

"No." She hesitated. "I have never really thought about it. I have never been around babies. My sister died giving birth to a baby."

"Have you ever been around horses?"

"Yes. At Castel......At home I rode horses."

"Do you know the difference between a stallion and a mare?"

"Yes."

"I never thought I would be telling anyone about birds and bees. I understand, Victoria. This is a subject that is never discussed. It is the year 1662 and we are still afraid to talk about it. Yet it is the most basic act of life. Alright. Here goes. Let's start with horses since you have been around them. Do you know how a colt is created?"

"Yes. I know that."

"A man is built the same as a stallion. He has an organ that makes him a man the way it makes the male horse a stallion, only praise be it isn't so big as a stallion's.

"Now, when a man and a woman share their deepest love, the highest emotion between a man and a woman, they place their bodies together and he places his organ inside her. When they are in love this is a beautiful occasion, almost holy, for they become one person, experiencing the greatest joy two people can have in sharing their lives. Sometimes as a result of this act of love a baby is born."

"But a girl can have a baby without being married, even when there is no love."

"That's true. You see, Victoria, some men and women get together even though they are not married. That is why some men come to this social club. They want to get together with one of us."

"Do you like getting together with a man?

"Sure I do or I wouldn't be in this business. And it is business. Men pay Madam Dawes when they come here."

"So that was what you meant when you told me to make a customer happy. But, Rose, I wasn't happy. I did not like all the pawing and clawing. I did not want their hands on me."

"You are not made for this business. I do like to be with men and that is a difference among women. Some like men and what they do more than others."

"Why is it that married men like Mr. Hardy come here?"

"Lots of married men come here. Most of our business is with married men. Sometimes their wives are sick, or sometimes their wives don't want to be with them often, or sometimes they are not happy with their wives. They may want a woman frequently. When their wives can't please them they come here."

Millie appeared at the door. "Hello, Anne. Come on, Rose. Bring Anne with you. Time to eat."

Time to eat! Patience did not realize time had gone by so quickly. She had questions to ask, but she joined the other girls and they were pleased to see her. Rose explained her name is Victoria and they laughed, but no one teased her about running away.

After the meal, Patience continued on the sewing Madam Dawes had given her. She had to be out by four o'clock when the club opened and there was much to do. Rose returned. "You had a question then I must rest and get ready for tonight."

"I guess I have a lot of questions. You have been so wonderful taking time and being so patient to tell me what I need to know. I wish you were my big sister. A question. A man where I lived and a man in an inn were mean to me. They pulled at me, kissed me, one tore my dress and one took me to the ground. I had to fight. I was frightened. They had strange looks in their eyes. Why did they do that?"

"Sounds as if you had some bad experiences. They wanted to take you, to join with you as if you were man and wife. Some men think girls are made for them and that the innocent are for the taking. When you resist them they fight. That look they get in their eyes is what we call lust. It is the need they have to take you."

"Does getting together mean fighting, struggling and hurting?"

"No, Victoria. That happens only when men lust for you and you refuse them. There will be a time when you will meet a man who interests you, who is appealing, who makes you tingle, makes your heart flutter and you want to be near him, even wanting him to put his hands on you. That is not hurting. That is the beginning of loving. It happened to me once but he was a married man with children. I would not be here if we could have married. You must save your questions. Big sister will answer them,"

"Thank you, Rose. Little sister needs you."

The dressmaking shop closed on Sundays. Patience arose a little later than usual and went to the cathedral. She enjoyed communion services with its lovely ritual and beautiful singing. She continued to give thanks for the help she received there. When the weather was good, she walked along the river to watch men repair boats and mend nets or she walked to the castle to enjoy the medieval ruins with its gatehouse and decaying walls.

Mrs. Hardy always roasted a joint for Sunday dinner, and it was always served at three o'clock. After dinner they went window shopping, frequently meeting customers on the street, chatting with them and on occasion attending evensong at the cathedral.

Patience was happy. She had an excellent job, met and talked with customers, and she had Rose to enliven her life with discussions about the social club's activities. She was aware of time going by, but it was a pleasant passing. She was also growing older. During the three years she had been in Exeter, she had become a young lady with, thanks to Rose, a greater understanding of life.

Women from the higher social classes were coming to the shop in greater numbers and they were ordering better dresses made from finer materials. Mrs. Cleeve, a lady of the highest social class, a visitor at Lord Covington's Dunston estate, came in one day for emergency repairs on a gown she had damaged. Mrs. Hardy called for Victoria and in the fitting room the necessary repairs were made while the two chatted.

"My dear, you do excellent work. When I have more time, I want to return to see the gowns you make."

In a few days her carriage stopped. Mrs. Cleve announced she would like to see some representative gowns made at the shop.

"All of our gowns are made to order. I could show you one that has not been completed and a couple that are well advanced toward completion." Mrs. Hardy brought the gowns from the sewing room and displayed them with a flourish.

"You do have an accomplished seamstress. I should like to speak to the girl who helped me last time I was in. I believe her name is Victoria."

Mrs. Hardy called for Victoria. "Your work is excellent, my dear," Mrs. Cleeve addressed her. Then to Mrs. Hardy she said, "I am in need of two gowns. The materials I have already. I would need your seamstress to work at Lord Covington's house. Would you release Victoria for the time required?"

"I could do that. We do have immediate commitments, however."

"We need not start at once. But I shall be leaving Dunston for Kensington House in Cornwall at the end of the month and the gowns must go with me."

"Victoria can do your work by then but Dunston is some distance from Exeter. It would be difficult for Victoria to make the long trip each day to and from the city, and in stormy weather the trip would be almost impossible."

"That is no problem. I can arrange lodging at Dunston for Victoria. Let me know when she is ready and I shall have her picked up."

"This is a nice opportunity for you, Victoria," Mrs. Hardy encouraged after Mrs. Cleeve left. "You will be around people of means, you will learn refinements and the pay will be good. When do you think you can complete the gowns you are working on?"

"I can work a couple of nights and with Bessie's help they will be ready by the end of the week. I could go next Monday. But I shall have to return to Madam Dawes next Thursday."

"Good. We'll get a traveling case ready for you on Sunday. I'll make an arrangement with Madam Dawes for you to skip Thursday next week."

"Mrs. Hardy, Mr. Hardy is at Lord Covington's estate."

"He is no worry. He is no longer employed there."

Patience saw Rose at the club and told her the news. "Good for you, honey, but be on the alert. Men with means are no different from bums. They make offers with attraction because they have money, but they can't be trusted. They'll take you and then leave you, promises be damn. Just be careful."

On Monday morning a buggy arrived. It was to be a drive into the future, part of which Patience would learn to regret and part of which she would remain forever grateful.

# Chapter Six

Patience traveled some distance before the driver turned from the main road onto a dirt lane that twisted through a small forest, around a hill grazed by cattle, then through a long stretch of green meadow bordered on either side by English elms. The lane became an esplanade of crushed gravel outlined by low clipped hedges to Duston in the distance. It was a great stone rectangular building, three stories high, with a severe entry portal. She was driven to a side entrance where she was greeted by a servant who took her bag and showed her to a room on the second floor. "You will be called shortly by Mrs. Cleeve. Please be ready," she was told.

She arranged her belongings in a chest of drawers and in an armoire then gazed out the window which had a view to the east. Not far off was a young man trotting a horse, a beautiful bay with head held high.

Turning from the fetching scene, Patience wandered about the room, casually inspecting it and being impressed by ornately carved woodwork in the white molding and by a deeply embossed off white plaster ceiling. The bed was full size covered by a canopy of highly carved oak with light brown velvet hangings trimmed in white fringe and tassels. She was aware that this was not a servant's room and speculated as to how she was to be treated.

A knock interrupted her musing. "Mrs. Cleeve will see you now." she was told by a girl dressed in a uniform, black skirt falling to her ankles, white starched blouse tight at the neck and a white cap. Patience gathered her pencil, sketch pad and pattern books and followed the girl. At the opposite end of the building, the maid knocked on a door then guided Patience to a sitting room where Mrs. Cleeve rose to greet her.

"How good of you, Victoria, and Mrs. Hardy, too, to arrange your schedule to make my gowns. I would like them made from these." Displayed were two bolts of material, a gold satin and a dark blue velvet, both costly.

"Oh, Mrs. Cleeve!" she gasped, "how beautiful! These are the finest materials. I have never worked with anything of this quality."

"Both are the latest from France. My husband brought these to me. I want gowns that will do justice to me and the materials. I must look just right in them." Her face lit up as if she were already dressed and monopolizing the social event for which they were intended.

Mrs. Cleeve then proceeded to describe in detail what she wanted. Patience made sketches of the ideas and when finished the drawings were studied. Changes were suggested and approvals given. "Let us start now," Mrs. Cleeve proposed enthusiastically. "The room next to mine has been readied as a dressmaking shop for you. Ask for whatever you need."

A glance around showed that someone had brought together everything needed. "I must take measurements first, Mrs. Cleeve." A maid appeared and helped remove her gown, and Patience recorded the statistics needed. "After I cut patterns, I shall need to see you again, perhaps tomorrow. It will help to have two gowns you consider to be best fitted to your figure to use as models."

Patience worked diligently measuring paper and cutting patterns. By next afternoon she was ready for Mrs. Cleeve to review her work. Quietly and quickly patterns were placed on Mrs. Cleeve's trim figure and then a few alterations were made. Mrs. Cleeve talked freely. "It is important to be seen and talked about at the royal socials. I need impressive gowns. I intend to be out shown by no one. Not even by the king's ladies."

"Where are the socials held?"

"Of course some are held at Whitehall, the king's palace, and others are in the stately homes of Chelsea, Westminster and other fashionable sections of London. Often it seems that someone is giving parties each night. Some are small suppers or evening soirees and others are banquets. There is dancing and sometimes entertainment, but always there is laughter and gaiety."

Patience guessed Mrs. Cleeve to be about twenty-eight years of age. She was tall for a woman, but she carried her height with dignity. Her back was straight and erect which gave a squareness to her shoulders and an impression of statuesqueness as she walked, allowing her skirts to fall in straight folds. Her tiny waist was emphasized by a swelling hip line that gave interesting curves to her figure.

Her face was beautiful, soft features touched lightly with pastel colors to enhance light blue eyes and a small mouth. Her nose, the most prominent highlight, was slightly aquiline. Natural wavy brown hair was brushed to give a reflection of changing lights as the sun shown through the windows on her moving head.

Her speech was noticed immediately for it was in sharp contrast to English spoken in the west country. Words were delivered with preciseness demanded by the culture of London's upper class.

"I must keep up," she was saying. "I have been away from London for a little more than a year, and I do not want my friends to think I have become a country dame. Christopher, my husband, owns Kensington House in Cornwall, and he wants me there with him. After living in London until I married, I miss it dreadfully. We entertain at our Cornwall estate, but that is not like London with its constant whirl."

"I hear the king attends parties but I do not hear mention of the queen," Patience commented.

"Queen Catherine is from the royal court of Portugal, and she brought with her the archaic and reserved customs of Lisbon. Even her gowns are more like those worn in our Elizabethan times. She has found it difficult to accept our ways. Our gay parties are not to her liking. And then she has been ill, one an unsuccessful pregnancy. No, she does not attend many parties."

"Who sets the styles for the gowns?"

"Certainly not Catherine as one would expect the Queen of England to do. Most of the ladies of the court vie to be the fashion leader, but no one person is looked up to for setting styles. That is why some of our gowns are outlandish, each lady trying to out do the other. French designers are brought to London to help some of the ladies. Part of the entertainment in going to parties is to see what is being worn by whom."

Work progressed faster than Patience expected since no one interrupted her, and she was able to make first fittings on one gown by the end of the week. Mrs. Cleeve was pleased with what she saw and began coming to the sewing room just to chat.

In answer to questions, Patience explained that she was from the west country, going on eighteen years of age, and that her parents were dead. "But you speak English so well. You use grammar and vocabulary as if you came from a background of means," Mrs. Cleeve commented.

"A tutor was provided in my home and my teacher drilled me on English. He was demanding."

"I did not suppose you came from the lower class. But tell me, how did you manage to be a seamstress with that kind of background."

"My parents died and I was left on my own. I had to support myself, and since I had learned sewing and enjoyed creating with a needle, I found a job with Mrs. Hardy. She taught me the finer skills of the craft."

"I was born in London of a titled family that found favor with the king. As a reward for my father's role as an avid royalist, he was knighted and became very wealthy, mostly through grants of land. I was presented to King Charles. As a result I was invited frequently to court socials. It was through these activities that I met my husband, a dashing young man whose love overwhelmed me. He carried me off to Kensington House and away from the excitement of London to the quiet, uneventful life of the country" The last statement was spoken with a touch of forlornness.

"Sometimes I want to run to London. My husband is absent frequently, often to France on business, but he is thoughtful of my loneliness. He brings back lovely perfumes, exquisite jewelry and fabrics like these. He brought me here while he conducts business with Lord Covington, but regretfully he was called away on business last week. I am staying on until he comes for me."

On one of her afternoon visits, she said, "Victoria, you are too long at your needle. Let us pretend we have an invitation to a court soiree and we must prepare for it. Come."

Patience followed Mrs. Cleeve to her room and sat down at her dressing table. "First, let us take down your hair and see what we can do with it." Down came the hair and Mrs. Cleeve exclaimed, "How beautiful! Such lovely color. Its shine tells me you keep it brushed. Let me see. Let's try this." She went to work, skillfully combing, pinning, carving a wave with the side of her hand, peaking a tuck here, placing a clip there and brushing a lock until she was satisfied.

Patience was amazed at what she saw in the mirror. "I never thought to dramatize my hair, but I never go anywhere that requires a change from the usual pulled back bun tie. Mrs. Cleeve, it does look lovely. Thank you."

"But we are not finished. Let me study your face. It is a lovely face, and one to be enjoyed by some young man. Now for paint." She opened a tray and began applying colors. Patience thought of Rose. "Ever so lightly, so subtle," she heard Mrs. Cleeve say in a whisper. "A little red, a blue. A young face needs only highlights to compliment the natural features. A little powder to your fine skin."

As Patience watched she became transformed. A new person appeared, alive, attractive. "There! The new Victoria." Mrs. Cleeve beamed.

"With no place to go." Patience laughed.

"Oh, yes. I have been thinking. We may not be going to King Charles' court, but we shall go to Lord Covington's court. We shall join him for supper. Come. Let us choose our gowns."

What started as a happy jest ended in serious preparation for supper. Mrs. Cleeve's enthusiasm mounted as she proceeded to make all the arrangements. She hummed a tune, smiled in satisfaction when she made a decision and glowed when her plan turned out well. It was evident she was in her element as she worked intently, completely involved in the activity.

There were four for supper, Lord Covington and his grandson, both in evening dress, Mrs. Cleeve and Patience. Mrs. Cleve introduced Patience as her companion. Lord Covington presided with dignity, making light talk, and reporting on some of his horses. He was a distinguished old gentleman with wavy hair, white beard and white flowing mustache. He was energetic, conversing with enthusiasm, flashing his eyes with excitement and laughing vociferously at a small joke. Patience was able to ask a few intelligent questions about horses and thus enter the conversation.

"Yes, I have been developing my stables for years," the old gentleman explained with pride. "My horses are considered to be among the best in England, if not the best. I am training young Edward here to continue my work."

Edward sat across from Patience, and she was aware of his long stares. When she looked at him he smiled. He asked about her interest in horses and when she told him she rode, he proposed a meeting the following morning. She looked quickly at Mrs. Cleeve and received an approving nod.

Later when the two ladies walked upstairs to their rooms, Mrs. Cleeve complimented her on the way she handled herself and added, "Enjoy the ride with Edward. He is a good catch and you are worthy of him although his Lordship might prefer a union with a titled lady. He is a dashing young man with a reputation in London."

A proper riding habit was found for Patience and off they went. The Devon landscape was beautiful in morning sunshine with new greens glistening luxuriously. A gurgling escaped from shining rivulets bouncing between gentle hills, and wild flowers were adding color.

The two young people rode together for a while then walked their horses, talking mostly about the estate with its prized stables. Edward told of particular horses and their attributes. On the return ride they raced, but neither Patience nor her mare was a match for the stallion and Edward's skill as a horseman. Her long absence from riding was evident, but she enjoyed watching him. He seemed to be one with the horse as he leaned forward and paired his rhythm to the beat of his mount. She complimented his performance, and he beamed his pleasure.

"Tomorrow again, please," he urged and she accepted, pending of course Mrs. Cleeve's approval.

Patience worked diligently on the gowns over extended hours so she could enjoy horseback riding. Not only did she appreciate the opportunity to be out of doors in the invigorating air, but the exercise was good for her. It was the very activity she needed. She had to admit also that she enjoyed Edward's company.

Riding became almost a daily routine. On one occasion during a walk between sprints, Edward turned suddenly to Patience and said with boyish enthusiasm, "Victoria, I like you. I like to be with you." He turned his head and kept walking, his horse beside him.

Patience stopped momentarily, more to assess his sudden outburst of feeling but also to look at him. She became aware of a feeling she never before had experienced. She felt a need to be wanted. No, it was more than that. She wanted to possess someone, a person who was part of her, someone she could touch, no, more than someone, a man who was hers.

To this point Edward had been a riding companion. He was someone with whom Patience shared a common interest in horses. Now he was more than a companion. His simple statement aroused in her an awareness of her feelings. She walked up to him and said, "Edward, I like you, too." It was an honest confession expressed in sincere simplicity.

Both kept walking. Patience felt fulfilled for having spoken, but she wanted to do more to seal her statement, like putting an exclamation mark at the end of an important sentence, but she did not know what to do.

No more words were spoken until they reached the stable. He placed a hand on hers and said, "Please. Tomorrow."

Patience nodded and they went their ways.

One gown was completed and Mrs. Cleeve was joyous in her praise. "Soon you will have finished your work and you will be off to

Mrs. Hardy's. I shall miss you, Victoria. I have enjoyed so much having you with me."

As she worked to complete the second gown, Patience's thoughts were about Edward. At night she wondered what his presence had done to her. No man had ever interested her. Instead of fear such as she felt toward Mr. Wyatt, she wanted Edward to put his hands on her. "Why doesn't he?" she asked herself.

The next day the ride was particularly lovely. Rain during the night had put a sparkle on all vegetation and delicious odors permeated all the outdoors. Edward suggested a run and off they galloped, his stallion taking the hedgerows in graceful leaps. Her mare was equally elegant, letting Patience feel her muscles as she tensed in anticipation of a jump then springing into a rising glide over a barrier, landing in full stride to continue the run.

Next she knew she was flat on her back, Edward kneeling over her. "Victoria, dear, don't move. Let me feel for broken bones." His face looked so young, so caring, full of anxiety. Gently he felt along her legs, her hips then her arms. "You fell, dearest. She must have bolted before that hedgerow and you went sailing. You were ...," but he did not finish his explanation. Gently his arms slipped under her shoulders, and he raised her slowly until his face was directly over hers, his eyes exploring her face as she ascended. "You have such beautiful eyes. They captivate me. You enchant me," he whispered. Slowly his lips curved over hers and he kissed her with tenderness, expressing his loving quietly. Her arms glided over his shoulders and pulled him closer, returning his kiss in an expression of joy.

He lowered her slowly to the ground following her head downward with his face just above hers, his lips saying sweetly, "Lovely." His mouth moved to her chin then to her neck for warm brushes and on down to her cleavage where he allowed his lips to settle. His hands roamed about her body, ever so lightly, her eyes closing as she felt a tingle mounting within her. She felt her bodice being released, and he buried his face between her breasts. She was aware of one hand terminating its exploration, and opening her eyes, she saw he was unbuttoning his shirt. She wanted him to hurry. She lifted her hand to give the shirt a jerk, pulling it free as he stretched arms out of the sleeves. His naked torso rose above her, and she let her hands roam about, feeling well developed muscles. He moaned and she felt a hand on her leg moving about. Patience pulled at her skirt to move it upward then raised her hips so the gathering material would be under her. Her head fell backward, and she closed her eyes after she saw him loosen his belt.

Gently he came down to her again, his weight spreading across her anxious body, and she received his mouth on hers. She could feel him searching for her. A sharp unexpected pain startled her for a moment. Then joy unbounded filled her. Together they thrilled to their loving, ecstasy rising to heights supernal on wings of glorious flight.

After, they lay next to each other expressing in silence their gratefulness to one another. "I have never known this love," he whispered, clutching her closer. "This is the first time I......"

"Shuuush, my heart's love," she murmured, covering his lips with her finger tips. "Let the enchantment last without words."

"But you must know," he pleaded, pecking at her finger tips with his lips. "I want your loving. I want you, Victoria. I want you for my wife. Will you marry me?"

"You are my love, sweetheart. Of course. I shall marry you."

When they returned to the stables, he kissed her warmly and they parted.

Patience was jubilant as she climbed the stairs to her room. She felt fulfilled, wanted. Here at last she had someone to treasure, to care for. She was now a woman, deeply in love. It had happened so suddenly and she had wanted it to happen. This is exactly how Rose said it would happen. The pleasure of her love mounted as she thought about it, and she wanted to run to him, to be next to him, to love him more. Such elation she never felt. "This is what my father and mother must have experienced together," she speculated.

A knock at the door broke her musing. Mrs. Cleeve entered. "My dear, I need to talk with you." There was concern in the statement. "News from London is not good. The plague worsens. The royal court is moving to Hampton Court and all who can are taking leave of the city. I must return to Kensington House to care for refugee guests my husband has invited. Can you finish the second gown immediately?"

"Of course, but I shall be very sorry to see you go. You have been wonderful to me. It will be necessary to return to Mrs. Hardy's, however, for the last alteration you requested requires material I do not have here."

"That will be fine. I shall arrange for a rig." As she moved to call a servant, Patience spoke. "Please, Mrs. Cleeve, may I take time to speak to Edward?"

Edward was just entering the house as Patience opened the service door. "Why are you rushing, my sweet?" he questioned, smiling, as he put an arm around her.

"I am hastening to tell you I cannot ride with you tomorrow. Mrs. Cleeve is leaving for Kensington House, and her gown must be completed at once at the shop in Exeter. I leave Dunston immediately."

"That is no problem. When do you think we can ride again?"

"Give me at least a couple of days, just to make sure I can complete the gown."

"Very well. This is Tuesday. How is Friday? On Friday morning there will be a rig at your front door to whisk you away, away and into my arms."

"Edward, you are sweet. Until Friday then."

Patience packed her few things and hurried downstairs to the waiting rig. As soon as she arrived at Mrs. Hardy's, Bessie filled her in on all the local news, and she in return told of all her experiences at Dunston, all except Edward. He was still her secret to hold.

Mrs. Cleeve arrived the following morning, and after speaking to Mrs. Hardy, called for Patience. "My dear," she explained, "I have spoken to Mrs. Hardy and she will agree if you agree. Will you come with me to Kensington House?"

Patience stood aghast. The new pronouncement completely overwhelmed her. She thought immediately of Edward. "This is so sudden. May I have a few moments to think?"

"Of course, dear. I shall wait."

Patience went to her room and sat on the bed. Rags jumped up and found a place on her lap. As she stroked him and looked into his upturned face, she reflected on her predicament. "How can I leave Edward? I have just found him. I cannot leave him now. I cannot bear to be away from him for who knows how long. I must talk to Edward. But first I must tell Mrs. Cleeve I cannot go with her."

Patience returned to the fitting room. In front of Mrs. Hardy she said to Mrs. Cleeve, "I cannot leave Mrs. Hardy. She has been very good to me and with Bessie we have built a fine business." There was no way she could include Edward in her explanation.

"Now child, don't think about us," Mrs. Hardy said softly. "Bessie and I shall manage until you return. You will not be gone forever. It is just so you can help with all the guests."

"Mrs. Hardy is right, Victoria," Mrs. Cleeve encouraged. "You can help me entertain refugee ladies by making dresses. We can use the lovely fabrics from France and you will be paid well. When the plague is over, whenever that is, the guests will return home and you can return to Mrs. Hardy."

"When do you leave, Mrs. Cleeve?"

"Friday morning."

Friday morning! My ride with Edward! "May I give you an answer Friday morning? It will be early."

"That will be fine. Until Friday morning then."

Both Mrs. Hardy and Bessie encouraged Patience to go, and she came to the conclusion that she would let her meeting with Edward decide. If he said no then her reply would be no.

Patience slipped a shawl about her shoulders and hurried along to the social club. Rose as always greeted her warmly, and instantly she was told about Edward. She giggled in approval. "I told you you would know when you met the right man. But be careful, Victoria. Like I said, the rich and the titled can be bums, too."

Then Patience told her about Mrs. Cleeve's request. Rose thought a moment then said, "Sounds like you are stepping up in the world, Love. Go ahead. If it doesn't work out, you can come back. But remember, think about Victoria first." They gave each other a hug and said their goodbyes.

Early Friday morning Edward's rig was at the front door as promised, but he was not driving. She rode to him in silence considering what she would say and wondering how he was going to react. As soon as the driver stopped, she hurried to the stables where she found Edward. She explained her plight after he welcomed her and kissed her affectionately. "There is no need to be concerned, my sweet. If you go to Kensington House, I shall send word to you of our wedding date, and then I shall bring you here. If you decide to stay with Mrs. Hardy, I can retrieve you more easily."

"With your loving assurance, dear Edward, I shall go with Mrs. Cleeve."

He pulled her to an empty stall in the barn and covered her with a profusion of kisses. She said goodbye as he brushed away a flow of tears and promised their separation was only temporary and of short duration.

"My answer is yes, Mrs. Cleeve."

"Wonderful, my dear! I am so pleased. I am ready, only awaiting your word. The coach will stop at Mrs. Hardy's and then we will be off to Kensington House."

Patience had no way of knowing at that moment what far reaching implications her trip with Mrs. Cleeve would have on her life.

# Chapter Seven

Patience's traveling case and portmanteau were placed on top of the coach while she said goodbye to Bessie and Mrs. Hardy. Tears flowed especially when she picked up Rags and tried to explain to the little dog that she would return before long.

"My dear," Mrs. Cleeve sighed, "These coaches are never comfortable but we do our best. Use a pillow if you like. You will find that after all the hours of riding you will have sore muscles that will remain so for a week."

Patience placed a pillow at her back and smiled at the luxury inside the coach. It was nothing like a public coach except for the four wheels. Thick padding on seats and at their backs cushioned bumps, and an arm rest gave support for each pitch and roll. Foot stools could be moved to relax tired legs. Windows were large and clean providing clear views of the always interesting countryside.

"It will take two days to get to Kensington House. We must stop at noon to rest the horses, and tonight we shall have another rest in Plymouth," Mrs. Cleeve explained. Always when I travel I think of our court socials to make time go more quickly."

"Would you tell me something of the court."

"Of course, my dear. If I shed tears in the telling, it is only because I get lonesome for all the activities. I have just heard more gossip about the king's doxie, but there is always interest in the Lady Castlemaine and much chatter centers around her. Castlemaine has borne the king children, and one child the king openly acknowledges. The boy has been given a title and an estate. Some say the king will legitimatize him so he can succeed to the throne. However, the Duke of York is wary of that because his own succession will be in danger. As the king's brother he is next in line for the throne. Should the queen have no child by the king, the duke will become James 11

A shout was heard from the driver's seat. "Oh, dear!" Mrs. Cleeve cried out, frightened. "That highwayman! He has been so busy on this run. Lord Covington insisted on sending a second man with a gun to provide protection. Feel the coach? Are we going faster?"

The coach was going faster. The shouting was of short duration, however, and Mrs. Cleeve relaxed as the sudden emergency ended. "I have some valuable jewels hidden in the coach, and I would not like to lose them. Maybe that was just a scare. I hope we are not submitted to the indignities of a holdup. There is one highwayman who insists on kissing the ladies. At first, it is told, he kissed instead of taking coins from a lady. But now he takes both, the coins and the kiss. Imagine!"

By late afternoon they were in Plymouth where Mrs. Cleeve arranged for a room in a private inn. "How different," Patience thought, "from the night three years ago when I stayed at the public inn and the man with the scared face paid for my bed, bought my supper, then invited me to his room. Three years ago."

The remembrance brought a smile to Patience's face. "I ran away with a few coins, no place to go, found a job, met wonderful people, developed a fine skill, and now I am going to a big house with considerable cash riding in my portmanteau."

The night brought thoughts of Edward. "He surely went riding this morning. Even now he must be thinking of me as he gets ready for bed. I miss him so much already. Before long he shall come to me."

"Victoria, I want to tell you about Kensington House before we arrive," Mrs. Cleeve said the next morning as the coach was well along the Plymouth-Falmouth road. "You need to have some background so everything wont be completely strange to you.

"The house itself is big, not so large as Dunston but large enough to care for the number of guests we expect. I want you in a room near me, for I have decided you will be my companion. I grow fond of you, Victoria, and I need your company. We shall have a good time. You will see.

"Now to the people who work there. You will meet Mrs. Tubby, the housekeeper, and Osborne, the head of servants. Mrs. Tubby has been with us the two years we have lived at Kensington House. She manages very well, relieving me of tedious tasks. I want you to get acquainted with her, for as you learn the comings and goings, she will more and more be reporting to you.

"We have a complete service staff for the estate. Mr. Evers is in charge and an excellent man he is.

"Another person you might meet is Mrs. Tatham. She is an old lady who came to us last year saying she wanted a place to stay. She said she lived in the house as a child and as a young lady, but she married and came on bad times in later life. My husband in a moment of weakness gave her a room at the top of the south tower."

As Mrs. Cleeve spoke the name Tatham, Patience balanced. "Tatham. Strange, that. I don't recall another Tatham family, but there could be one in the west country."

Patience prepared herself mentally to pass Castelamer and Brixton Village, warning herself to give no sign of recognition and hoping they would not stop at the village inn. "How do you spend your time at Kensington House?

"I do some entertaining, inviting people in the neighborhood for supper, and we have some dances. I enjoy walking in the garden.

Most of my time is spent managing the big house. We are planning to redecorate some rooms, and I am considering how best to do that." She indicated no enthusiasm in the recitation.

"Do you ride?"

"No. I do not ride. I don't care for horses. Christopher, my husband, wants to teach me, but I have no interest in the sport. I am an indoor person."

Patience concluded that Mrs. Cleeve must indeed be lonely at Kensington House.

"We are about to enter the house precincts."

Patience looked out a window in time to see a metal plate on a pedestal reading KENSINGTON HOUSE. The drive passed a stretch of trees that reminded Patience of Castelamer. Clearing the trees the coach followed a curve of the road that presented the first view of the house.

"You can see our home now." Mrs. Cleeve did not appear to be excited.

Patience gasped. "It is Castelamer!" she shouted to herself. She felt faintness overcoming her and fought to recover her senses. A knot appeared in her stomach, and she became aware of perspiration covering her forehead. She searched for a handkerchief and dabbed her face. She was still fighting sickness when the coach slowed then stopped at the main entrance. The door opened and out came a woman and a man, both dressed in livery. "Welcome home, Mrs. Cleeve," they both said at once and the woman added, "How good to have you back. Mr. Cleeve sent word that he has been delayed but will be here for supper. Come. A nice bath will make you new again."

"Mrs. Tubby, Osborne, meet Victoria. She is my new companion and will occupy the rear south guest room. And thank you for greeting me so warmly. I have missed you and Kensington House. Please show Miss Victoria to her room then arrange baths for both of us."

Patience continued the struggle to control her emotions. The sight of her girlhood home shocked her, and she was afraid that if she spoke she would say something that would reveal her past. Even after three years she feared arrest for the murder of Mr. Wyatt. She was fearful, too, that the sight of familiar surroundings would evoke memories and induce tears which would be difficult to explain. She quickly made a decision to say nothing, look directly ahead when taken into the house, see as little of the interior as possible and go directly to the room.

While Osborne and the drivers began unloading luggage, Patience picked up her portmanteau and followed Mrs. Cleeve and Mrs. Tubby into the house. Her plan to be indifferent fell apart the moment she stepped into the entry. The warm, heavy grey granite stone work that was part of the original house remained untouched. Even the two wall hangings, one on either side, were in place, beautiful Flemish tapestries that were at least two hundred years old. She did follow the others up the stairs, keeping eyes straight ahead, struggling not to look about. She heard Mrs. Cleeve say, "Rest, my dear. You will be called for supper," as she entered the master bedroom.

Mrs. Tubby turned left and Patience followed, feeling emotions building up again. The housekeeper stopped near the end of the hall, opened a door and motioned for her to enter. The girl held together long enough to say, "Thank you, Mrs. Tubby," stepped inside, heard the door close behind her, then fell apart.

After almost three years, she was back in her own room. It took a little time for her tears to dry so that she could see clearly. "Furnishings are in the same place, but the window hangings are new and so is the bed coverlet." She walked to the bed, placed her portmanteau on top and opened it. After removing one item, she stopped, looked about the room again, then stepped to the paneled wall. Her hand traced lovingly the finely carved linen fold of which she was so fond. As she walked to the window, she noticed that all of her keepsakes were gone.

"It is home and it is not home." she thought. "What was is gone. I left the past when I ran away. My home went with the past. I come as a stranger. In the short time I am to be here before Edward comes for me, I shall forget about Patience and be Victoria. My name is Victoria. This is the present. I am a companion for Mrs. Cleeve. But be alert! You, Victoria, have never been in this house. One slip and the authorities could be on you. Murder is never forgotten."

A knock interrupted her intense thinking. She went to the door and opened it expecting Mrs. Cleeve. Instead a young lady in uniform smiled at her, the traveling case, a hip bath and a container of water behind her. "A bath will refresh you, Miss Victoria. I am Pall, your upstairs maid. I shall be helping you."

"Pall," Victoria reflected as she stood for a moment facing the girl. To herself she wondered, "Where is Nancy? She must have a new assignment, perhaps serving Mrs. Cleeve. Nancy will surely recognize me. How shall I handle that meeting?"

Recovering, Victoria smiled, "Come in, Pall. I would like to remove the contents of the traveling cases and put everything away before bathing." Pall opened the cases and put all contents on the bed while Victoria selected a place for each item. Pall left the room but returned quickly with towels, placing them on a rack above a low chest on which were a bowl, pitcher and soap dish. She brought in a hip bath, filled it with water then helped Victoria bathe. The water was indeed refreshing. She rubbed briskly when drying herself, put on a robe and spoke to her maid. "Thank you, Pall. I shall rest and please call me in time so I can dress for supper. Oh, one moment, please. Do you serve Mrs. Cleeve?"

"Yes. Until the guests come, I am the only maid."

The girl removed the bath and towels, brought in a pitcher of fresh water and announced that supper would be served at seven o'clock. "Madam dresses formally," she added as she left the room.

Victoria lay on the bed. One thought after another came and went, action she must take, find out about Nancy and Mrs. Batty, items she must get for sewing, clothes she must make for herself and on and on. When her eyes opened someone was tugging at her shoulder.

"Time to get ready for supper, Miss," Pall was saying. "I'll help you dress." Victoria arose and went to a table on which she had placed the face paints Mrs. Cleeve had given her. She leaned a hand mirror against the wall and used directions she had been given. She made her face. "What dress, Miss?" she heard Pall ask.

"I don't have a supper dress. What dress do you think I should wear? Look in the armoire and make a selection for me."

Pall looked at the few hanging in the armoire and lifted one out. It was the dress usually worn on Sundays. "This should do." Expertly Pall slipped it over Victoria's head then adjusted it. "Stand before the mirror, Miss. My, you do look attractive. Come. I'll take you to the dinning room."

Candles in sconces on the walls were prepared for the evening. They lighted steps down the stairs to the receiving room, through the large room where socials were held then into the dining room.

"There you are, my dear. Come meet my husband." Her mistress was standing in front of a fireplace in which a blaze was giving off sputtering sounds. As she spoke, Mrs. Cleeve came forward with a warm, welcoming smile on her face, extending her arm to take Victoria's hand and lead her companion to the fire. "Christopher, this is Victoria."

The fire placed the figure of Mr. Cleeve in shadow as he turned to face her. The outline was of a tall frame, square at the shoulders, tapered at an angle to the hips. The boots he wore emphasized his slimness. His hair was dark and wavy. "Elizabeth has been telling me about her plans for you. Let me welcome you to Kensington House but warn you quickly that you must not be so busy that you cannot enjoy this lovely estate."

"Thank you, Mr. Cleeve. I so look forward to wonderful experiences. The view from my room is enchanting. I do accept your kind offer."

"Victoria rides wonderfully well, Christopher. Perhaps you could arrange a horse for her."

"Jolly good idea, that. Stand nearer the fire, near me, Victoria. There is a nip to our Cornish night."

As Victoria moved to the right side of the fireplace, she commented, "It is an invigorating air, spiced with salt from the sea." Mr. Cleeve turned with her movement and as she looked up, the front of his figure was reflecting the full glare of the fire. A gasp tried to escape. Quickly she raised her hand to her face in reflex to smother the look of shock she knew was evident. The face she looked up to was accented by a scar crossing the forehead and curving around the left eye! The smile on his face revealed white teeth made noticeable by a space.

In a flash, memories of that night in Plymouth's public inn, the tightly gripped shoulders, the hard kiss, the bedroom door opening with a candle in hand illuminating that face darted through her mind. Aware that all eyes were on her, she struggled to cover her astonishment, and to prevent questions she knew would come, she continued to move her arm upward forcing her hand to adjust a lock of hair. Immediately she added, trying to renew the conversation, "From my window I can see the Channel waters crashing along the coast. Thank you for placing me in that enchanting room." She wondered if her voice was shaking.

"Other rooms have lovely vistas, too, But you will see all the rooms tomorrow," Mrs. Cleeve said, giving no evidence of having noticed Victoria's alarm.

Mr. Cleeve apparently noticed nothing for he asked, "Where did you learn to ride so well?"

"Why doesn't he recognize me," she pondered silently to herself. "I am older, my hair is different, my face is painted. True, but then he saw me only that one night, and he had been drinking too much ale." Aloud she answered, "As a girl who grew up in the west country, I was taught to ride and I love horses. Edward very generously took me riding. The sport is so relaxing and so enjoyable." At the mention of Edward she thought of her lover with great pleasure and wished he were here to be her partner at supper. Inwardly she assured herself, "Before long he shall be here, and we shall share all this before we return to Dunston."

Conversation stopped when a voice at the far side of the room announced, "Supper is served, Madam."

"Thank you, Osborne. Victoria, let me place you here, to Christopher's left. We seem to be dwarfed by many empty chairs, but no matter. When our guests arrive we shall have all filled."

Victoria was seated by Osborne and Christopher seated his wife. "What a pleasure to be in this room with so much beauty in candle light." Victoria beamed. Except for new drapes at the window, no changes had been made in the furnishings. The table, providing for eighteen guests, was still lighted from above by a familiar, beautiful brass chandelier. The same six tall candlesticks were placed at intervals along the length of the table.

When food was served, the Framsden china appeared, white plates, two circles of gold trimming on the circumference, a basket holding a formal bouquet of colorful flowers decorating the depressed center.

"It is ideal, isn't it? Christopher and I give supper parties in this room when he is home."

"Tell me about France, Mr. Cleeve," Victoria requested. "Where do your travels take you?"

"I get to the wine areas, Bordeaux, Burgundy, along the Loire. Of course Paris is necessary for the capitol is the center of trade. And since I arrange for shipping from the Channel ports, I get to Brittany. Regretfully I don't travel for pleasure and therefore I do not see all the places of interest. I keep telling Elizabeth that one day I shall forget business and take her abroad so we can see what travelers should see." His energetic comments reflected the interest he had in his work.

As they talked, Victoria calmed herself, the scar on his face seemed less noticeable, and confidence grew in her ability to control emotions.

"What does your business entail?"

"The purchase and sale of wines, mostly. But I deal in fabrics, tobaccos and other goods that will provide a profit."

"Then after all that traveling in France, he must get about in England, up to London, off to Plymouth, down to Falmouth. All this takes him away from home, and much too often." Mrs. Cleeve pouted.

"You know, my dear," he sympathized, "I must find markets for my goods. And after all, it was on one of my travels about London I found you, my greatest reward and biggest profit."

The evening passed quickly and Victoria had to admit she enjoyed Mr. Cleeve's company. Finally Mrs. Cleeve announced she was tired from the trip and need to get to bed. "Sleep well, dear. Tomorrow I shall have Mrs. Tubby acquaint you with the house. Do you recall how to get to your room?"

Victoria nodded, wished her hosts a good night's rest, then went to her room. She did not feel tired, the pleasant evening having stimulated her, but she removed her clothes, put on a robe and gazed out the window. A last quarter moon shed enough light to outline the ever changing surf in the distance. Familiar objects rose about the landscape. High fog clouds made an appearance as she watched the scene, gradually shutting off the moon's shine on the sea and graying the landscape. She found herself remembering that night some three years ago. "It began the same way, only this is fog moving, not storm clouds."

She thought of the scratching noise that night of awful recollection and began listening alertly for it. She walked to the linen fold paneling and began tracing her hands over the surface. "There must be a space behind this paneling where a person could hide, perhaps in the linen closet next door. Maybe there is a peep hole a person could use to look into this room. Tomorrow I shall search."

Little did Victoria realize at that moment what would result from her inquisitiveness.

# Chapter Eight

After breakfast the following morning, Victoria and Mrs. Cleeve met Mrs. Tubby. "Victoria will be assisting me with our guests when they arrive from London, Mrs. Tubby. Please acquaint her with the house. Little by little I want her to assume most of the house management."

As Mrs. Cleeve talked, Victoria glanced about the sitting room and through an open door into the bedroom. Memories from the past darted through her mind as she recalled her frequent visits in these rooms as a child. Then as now this had been the master bedroom suite occupied by the Framsdens. The sitting area had been redone completely and of what she could see of it, the bedroom had been redecorated as well.

"Let us start as if we are entering the house," Mrs. Tubby proposed as she led the way downstairs. Visitors are shown to this reception room to await the mistress or master. As you can see it provides considerable comfort.

"Smaller social gatherings are conducted here." Mrs. Tubby guided Victoria into a large room decorated in dark woods with warm autumn colors in the drapes and various pieces of upholstered furniture. Tables and straight chairs were of dark oak. She recalled that the Framsdens entertained their friends here, mainly neighbors and business associates, and often Penny and she were asked to participate.

They progressed through the next door with Mrs. Tubby commenting. "When the guests from London arrive, we shall be using this room for entertaining."

They had entered the great hall. A beautiful hammerbeam ceiling soared mightily two stories above, heavy dark wooden rafters spanning the width of the room topped by angled spars to form arches. A huge natural stone inglenook fireplace dominated the north wall, while on the east wall, three quarters of the way up, was a gallery which extended slightly over the room. "Musicians play for entertainments and dancing from that balcony." Three walls were constructed of large, sized polished granite stone rectangles, part of the original medieval building. The south wall was covered with exquisite linen fold paneling from the Tudor era.

Mrs. Tubby noticed that Victoria was looking at two large tapestries. "They are new to the house as is this smaller tapestry on the south wall and these two fine Brussels carpets. Mr. Cleeve brought all from Flanders. When dancing is planned, the carpets are removed in favor of the hardwood floor."

Passing through the library and music room, they came to the west part of the building. "Our live in staff has these rooms. We wont enter but we shall walk through the pantry, buttery and kitchen." At once odors evoked for Victoria wondrous recollections of venison on spits, soups in pots, cakes, biscuits, flan but especially fresh bread. The same great quantity of pots, pans, skillets, ladles, forks and bone saws hung from a wrought iron frame attached to the ceiling above a large work table. Many of the utensils were of polished copper. Two large fireplaces with ovens were being attended to by a char woman.

In another corner were hanging a collection of freshly killed, unskinned rabbits and a brace of wild pheasants still in their colorful plumage. Nearby were hanging strings of onions and garlic.

A blackened kettle sat before a low fire in one fireplace spewing quiet puffs of steam, while over coals, hanging from an iron arm, was an equally blackened pot making muttering sounds. On the large table below the hanging utensils were set a large mutton joint, vegetables and carving boards. "You can tell cook is preparing soup and she does a delicious soup. We are blessed with water coming into the kitchen, there, to the sink. Mr. Cleeve had it installed only recently. He said if London houses can have this luxury, so can we. It is such a time saver and cuts down on labor, too."

They climbed the back stairs to the south wing. "On the second floor are bedrooms. In this wing they are for the family while those for guests are principally in the north wing. The Cleeves have no children, but in former times, children of the house had lessons in this room." Victoria took a glance through the open door. She saw the tutor's desk and the table where she and Penny once did their lessons.

"The only rooms occupied are the master bedroom, the study and your bedroom." As they continued down the hall, Mrs. Tubby touched a door adjacent to the master bedroom. "This is the master's study. No one enters this room unless directed by Mr. Cleeve."

The housekeeper paused and opening the next door said, "Of great interest to all visitors is this chapel. It is not used since we attend Brixton Village church, but in Tudor times this chapel was used by traveling priests." It was a small, narrow room with a simple altar and chairs for ten persons. "Builders of the Tudor parts of the house were Catholics, and they maintained their religion despite suppression of that faith. Services were secret except during Mary Tudor's reign."

They proceeded to the long gallery, a room that stretched the length of the front of house, from one wing to the other. "You may want to use this room when our guests arrive." Immediately Victoria recalled the long gallery as a source of great fun, for during cold or inclement weather, she and Penny would run the full length and back again then be completely out of breath.

"This gallery is from the Tudor period as well," Mrs. Tubby continued. "In those days, people would use this as a recreation area, especially during the cold season or on rainy days. I can just imagine them walking up and down on this hardwood floor as if were a street. Not one thing has been done to it since I came here, and it will need a lot of attention if you decide to use it. Look at the pictures. Staff wonders who these people are."

Victoria started to identify the portrait across from them, but quickly realized her error after the first syllable slipped out. She coughed and covered her mouth. "Excuse me, Mrs. Tubby. I started to ask if I could remain here for a few moments."

"Of course. If you know the way to your room, I'll just leave you. Oh, yes, I forgot to show you the linen closet. Pall can do that. Noon meal is served at one o'clock."

Victoria watched Mrs. Tubby leave the room then she walked down one side of the long gallery, halting before each portrait to identify the person. On the return stroll she looked out the many windows that perforated the east wall. She began considering ways she could use the room to entertain the London guests. "I'll discuss these with Mrs. Cleeve, perhaps now, before we eat."

Mrs. Cleeve called for her to enter. "How was the tour? This house is so large. It will take some time to learn your way about."

"Mrs. Tubby was very kind to show me all the features. It is a gigantic house, indeed, but there are so many beautiful rooms and so many treasures. I was taken with the great hall. It is truly magnificent and the long gallery is equally intriguing."

"I was just making an activity list. It is not a long list and it is only for ladies. Christopher will have to plan for the men. It is all so overwhelming.

There is not only entertaining to consider, but feeding the group will present problems. Mrs. Tubby has not dealt with a large group of guests. Would you mind meeting with us to give us your ideas?"

"I am afraid I am classed with Mrs. Tubby. But maybe something good will come out of three heads knocking about some ideas. How many guests do you expect?"

"Dear Christopher. He is so generous. I think he has invited half of London, maybe even the royal family. He is trying to recall the names of people to whom he spoke. Let's plan on twenty. If more come we shall change the name of the house to Brixton Public Inn and sleep four and five to a bed."

"I have an idea. We can use the long gallery for entertaining. During the day we can keep the ladies busy playing games, and I can use one end for a sewing area. The many windows provide excellent light and morning sun should warm it comfortably for the day. We shall need more chairs and tables."

"Excellent idea! We could do a card tournament and maybe a little gambling. We shall just transport London to Kensington House. Let's make a list of the games to be played then we shall list what we need as accessories. We shall buy everything in Plymouth."

"Pall mentioned a fair in Brixton Village. We could take our guests to the fair one day," Victoria suggested.

The two continued to discuss their ideas and plans through the meal and into the afternoon. They chuckled over considerations for games and thoughts for making gowns. "You must see the materials we have for your sewing projects," Mrs. Cleeve proposed. "Come."

Victoria could not refrain from expressing a series of superlatives as her hands strolled across varieties of fabrics. "I have never seen such silks and velvets, this taffeta, and what lovely lace. I could never do justice to these materials."

"Of course you can. And I want you to make some gowns for yourself, too. Look these over and make a selection. When the plague is over we shall return to London in glory."

Victoria returned to her room happy but thoughtful, her concentration centered on patterns, ideas for color combinations, styles, all a seamstress considers in dressmaking. The sight of Pall provoked a thought that superseded all others. "Pall," she called. "Do you mind showing me a linen closet."

"Of course. Mrs. Tubby said you would be asking. There is one next to your room." The two entered and Pall explained the organization of linens. "This closet serves rooms at this end of the hall. There are three other closets, one down the hall and two more in the other wing."

"Thank you. You go ahead with your work. I'll stay and get acquainted with this closet." Immediately Victoria began searching for a peep hole, moving the stacked linens and towels to examine very carefully every portion of the now exposed wall adjacent to her room. She ran her fingers over surfaces, along seams and into spaces where shelves were attached to the wall. She pressed corners, tapped, stood on a footstool to reach above eye levels. Nothing suspicious. She tried pushing but nothing gave. She stood back and considered every possibility for a peep hole. Feeling convinced she had tried everything, she returned the linens to their proper places and went to her room.

"He said he watched me. If he did, he did not use the linen closet. He would have had to use the south wall. But how?" The question puzzled her. She sat on her bed and directed her eyes all over the paneling. "I believe if there is an opening it will have to be at eye level or near it. It probably is in a fold or at a seam for best concealment"

She stepped deliberately along the paneling checking ever so closely, looking for imperfections that might reveal a moveable portion. Nothing. Next she guided her fingers to move gradually over panels, concentrating on the feel of a rough spot. She came on a few. At these she paused and examined them carefully with eyes and fingers. Nothing of promise.

"Maybe if I pressed, something might give," she considered. Choosing a panel, she began pressing her fingers and her palms on every area then moving on to the next panel. At the fourth panel she became aware of a scratching sound. Scratching! "It sounds the same as the scratching I heard that night," she gasped.

Quickly she paused in her task and listened intently. No more noise. After a wait she started her examination again, moving to a fifth panel.

Scratching! "There it is again!" She listened, pressing her ear against the wall. It appeared to be to her left. She moved back to the fourth panel. The scraping stopped. How much time she had taken to do the searching she did not know, but the light of day was fading. Ready to give up in disgust, she gave vent to her irate feelings by jabbing the tips of all ten fingers at the center panel. Immediately the bottom panel to the left began to move. Victoria stepped back, her right hand clutching her throat, her heart beating rapidly. She gasped in disbelief. She starred as the panel opened slowly, sliding to the left until it disappeared, leaving an opening. It stayed open.

Gradually calmness returned and with a little confidence, she slumped to her hands and knees and looked into the opening. Light from the room revealed an immediate space beyond. Hesitatingly she crawled into the space. It appeared that she was in a passage way that continued beyond the darkness. She considered continuing but heard noises in the hall. Quickly she crawled back into her room. "Close the panel!" She screamed to herself. "How!" She was confounded. Panic overwhelmed her. "How did I open it?" Putting her hand on the third panel, she pressed. It did not close. She struck the panel with her fists.

Nothing! She jabbed furiously with her fingers. Nothing! Fear made her breath come in gulps, in desperation she turned and leaned back on the panel. She felt a movement. Looking down she saw the opening starting to close.

"What did I do? I opened the panel. I closed the panel. But what did I do?" Still leaning against the wall and still in shock, she heard a knock on her door. Pall entered.

"Miss Victoria! You look so pale. Do your feel ill? Come, lie down."

Victoria was more shocked at almost being caught with the panel open than with her own discovery, but she let Pall help her onto the bed. "Suddenly I felt weak. I'll be alright."

"A bath and rest and then supper. All will do you good. Mr. Cleeve will not join you for supper so Mrs. Cleeve has asked that it be served to the two of you in her sitting room. You will not need to dress. I'll call when supper is served."

Victoria thought and planned far more than she rested. "If Mr. Wyatt saw me from the other side of the south wall, he must have had a way to get there. Where did he come from to get behind the wall? Should I try exploring the passage? Where is the peek hole? Tonight after supper I shall try again to make that panel open."

During the supper conversation, Mrs. Cleeve proposed a shopping trip to Plymouth. "It is too much for one day with all we have listed. Let us stay over to the next day and enjoy the shops. Is Wednesday too soon? We need to talk with Mrs. Tubby. She may have some special needs. I shall call for the coach to be ready at nine o'clock. Now, dear, join me for a walk in the garden. Our summer evenings are lovely."

The evening was indeed balmy with a soft breeze blowing in from the Channel. A moon, just passed the full, brightened the garden and easily lighted pathways. The two, arm in arm, turned about geometric miniature hedgerows guarding beds of flowering plants. They walked along the brink above Hythe Haven, and as they turned back toward the house, Victoria noticed a dim light in the top of the south tower. "Mrs. Tatham must be up," she thought as they continued walking.

Still arm in arm, Mrs. Cleeve suggested they watch the surf from the top of the palisades. Victoria paled as they approached the site of Mr. Wyatt's attack, and Mrs. Cleeve felt the shudder that ran through her companion's body. "We should return to our rooms, dear. I have kept you too busy today. You need your rest. Come."

They separated at the top of the stairs, each wishing the other a pleasant good night.

"My room is dark!" she exclaimed as she entered. "Moonlight should be lighting this room through open shutters. I did not close those drapes. Pall would not close them unless I told her to do so." A tiny light pierced the darkness! It was on the south wall. It disappeared instantly.

Victoria walked directly to the spot on the wall where she had seen the miniscule light, her eyes fixed on the site. Carefully she took a mental reading of the area, left the wall, found the candle holder next to her bed, opened the drapes and the shutters covering her window and returned to the spot on the wall. Slowly she ran her fingers about the panel. For some time the search went on but she could detect nothing. Giving up, she started to prepare for bed. She slipped off her gown, removed her underclothing and for a moment she was entirely nude. Scratching! She froze, listening. Scratching! Quickly she slipped her nightgown over her head and blew out the candle. Silently she glided to the wall and listened. Nothing. Her eyes went automatically to her door. It must be the door, expecting to see it open. She considered what she would do when it opened. It did not.

She stood where she was for some time thinking then said half aloud, "I must know! I shall know!" She walked to the door and slipped the bolt to lock position.

As she lay in bed, she continued to be puzzled by the scratching and considered who could be doing it. "Of course. Mr. Cleeve. This is his house and he knows about the passage. But then it may be Mrs. Tatham. She has her room directly above me. I must meet her."

# Chapter Nine

Mrs. Cleeve, Victoria and Mrs. Tubby met to discuss the preparations required to feed, house and entertain their plague refugees. It was decided that two full time maids would be necessary to care for the rooms. The long gallery would be cleaned thoroughly and sofas, comfortable chairs and game tables would be placed there to make it a recreational area. Potted plants would be brought in from the garden to improve its attractiveness.

"Here is a list of furniture needs for me, Mrs. Tubby," Victoria said, handing the housekeeper a paper. "I shall be making gowns. I would like a sewing area arranged near the south door since I want to use as much natural light as possible, but a large candelabra would be helpful."

"What about serving meals to our guests?" This was Mrs. Tubby's greatest concern.

Mrs. Cleeve answered, "I believe serving sit down meals three times a day requires too much effort. Let us have the sideboard prepared for breakfast and noon meals then we can sit down together for supper at seven o'clock. That schedule will give our guests some freedom. Oh, yes, warn cook that we shall need picnic baskets from time to time. I am sure we should plan some outings on particularly nice days, perhaps on the beach and in the garden but surely at some of the lovely spots on the estate. Work with cook to plan meals a week at a time, and bring plans to me for approval. Mr. Cleeve must have an inventory of what food is on hand, and you must give him an idea about your needs for mutton, lamb, beef, pork and ham. Alert the fishermen at Hyath Haven that we shall need more fish for a time. Cook will need additional help. When she knows how much, tell Mr. Cleeve so he can arrange for some women in the village. Maybe cook knows of some women. We have talked already with Mr. Evans about vegetables from the garden. He will have to buy from neighbors."

"There is a problem about bread," alerted Mrs. Tubby. "We have limited ovens for the expected number of guests. We will have to buy in the village."

"Talk with Mr. Cleeve about that, too. Bread will go quickly at every meal."

"I hope not everyone will want to bathe at the same time," cautioned Mrs. Tubby. "We could have a problem heating water."

"That is a thought," agreed Mrs. Cleeve. "I shall have to talk to our ladies. I am sure they will understand." After a pause she added, "The banquet room could stand some decoration. I must ask Mr. Evans to bring in some potted plants, and as flowers are blooming, some nice arrangement would be colorful. Also, Miss Victoria and I are going to Plymouth day after tomorrow. If you think of anything you need, Mrs. Tubby, tell me and we shall shop for you."

As they concluded their planning meeting, Mrs. Cleeve asked that some boxes of the French fabrics be moved to the long gallery. "Now, Victoria, as my companion I want you dressed in the grand style for our special events. The Londoners must not outshine us. It is as I said, they are not to think we are country dames, and you are not to be working all the time. I have asked Pall to place a riding habit in your room. You may have to make some alterations. Speak to the stable master about a horse and do go riding."

After she arranged her sewing area in the long gallery, Victoria went to her room. On the bed was the riding habit. A note had been placed on top of it. "Join me for a ride tomorrow morning at seven. If you are not in the stables, I shall call for you at your room. Chris."

She stood next to the bed, note in hand, pondering the invitation. "Mrs. Cleeve did not include her husband when she suggested I ride, but she may not mind. He still may feel free enough to get brazen with me as he did that night at the inn. Of course he was not married then, but he still may enjoy a flirtation. I shall have to be careful. I shall meet him, but I shall be alert to any advances."

She tried on the riding habit and found it too large. She immediately went to work on alterations. Satisfied, she slipped it on. An excellent fit. When the hat was placed on her head, she decided her hair would have to be done differently to make it look right. She tried a few settings, looking in the mirror, then made a decision.

The next morning, Victoria was up early. She took time to arrange her hair, first brushing vigorously, followed by a braiding into narrow strands, then she formed it all into a bun at the nape of her neck. The narrow brimmed hat was perched on top, the plaited ball showing at the back.

Carefully her face was made up using soft coloring. "A sunny day does not require much paint," she cautioned herself. The riding costume went on last. Before the mirror she made final adjustments then surveyed the picture she made. "Mr. Cleeve cannot possibly recognize the girl at the inn. But be on guard, Victoria."

The stables were active at the hour of seven. Stalls were being cleared, horses were being exercised and two were saddled. "This horse is for you, Miss Victoria," a voice said. She turned to face Mr. Cleeve. "Thank you for accepting my invitation. It is a beautiful morning for riding, but it can in no way match the beauty you bring to it. Come, let me help you mount." He placed locked hands to form a step low enough for her raised foot and lifted her expertly to the saddle. "Where shall it be?"

"You suggested I enjoy Kensington House estate. Would you be my guide and introduce me to its wonders." There was a challenging glint in her eyes.

"You say that as if we have not much to show. Very well. I am your guide, our wonders to behold." His broad smile evidenced acceptance of her challenge. "Follow me. But be careful I do not lead you astray." He mounted, took the lead and walked his horse around the north side of the house. "Come next to me. The path is wide enough."

She joined him and together they went through the garden to the brink overlooking Hythe Haven. "It is a small harbor, Victoria, but it has a history, in the early days of this house, raiders from Normandy crossed the Channel to hit our coast. They pillaged, robbed and sometimes stole our women, but we fought them off. That is why the original part of the house was built as a castle. It has known skirmishes. Of course our Cornish men attacked the coast of Normandy in retaliation and brought back spoils, including women. Just think, Victoria, since you are from the west county, you could be part French."

His look at her was facetious and she laughed at his jibe. "You say that was when, the Middle Ages? In generations since, the French tinge should be very well washed out. Tell me, aren't you affected, too."

He pulled on the reins and his horse stepped along the path leading to the harbor. Victoria's followed and then drew next to him. "I'll show you where your ancestors landed. I can't claim them." Cleeve's voice took a mirthful lilt. "I am a newcomer to these parts. Perhaps you haven't heard London speech enough to identify me as a Londoner. The business of trade brought me to Cornwall, and I took a fancy to Kensington House."

"Why is it you would choose this estate for your home when London is the center of trade? I would think you would want to be near your business."

"I wanted to get away from the city and try country living. London is crowded, dirty and the lack of sanitation has undoubtedly contributed to the plague now ravaging the city. As for business, London is not the only port. Plymouth and Falmouth are very capable of receiving goods I ship from France, and I do have customers throughout the west country. It is much easier to serve them from our southern ports than to deliver out of London."

As they talked, the horses continued walking down the hill until they came to the dock, in retrospect, she conjured family outings on the sea and other times when she came here to watch fishermen unload their catch, clean fish and fill carts to make deliveries to neighboring farms and villages.

His voice brought her back to the present. "You may want to come here, get one of our boats and go sailing. At this hour men are still at sea fishing or probably on their way in, but there usually is some one about to prepare sails and take you out. I have learned to handle a sail very well.

"Thank you, Mr. Cleeve."

"Now, Victoria. Since you are Elizabeth's companion, please call me Chris. May I hear you say 'Chris'"

"Chris," she said softly. His request was the same he had made at the inn.

"Good. Now I want to show you the beach." He spoke to his horse and directed his mount to the left, onto the narrow path skirting the water at the base of Bodacombe Bluff. Victoria followed.

Before them stretched the familiar strand where she and Penny used to roam on warm summer days such as this, enjoying the sun, wadding in the surf, climbing rocks, examining tide pools and stretching out on the sand to take the sun. The palisades rose sharply, almost straight up, to tower above her, seeming from this view much higher than the one hundred feet they were. At the base was a border of boulders that had formed through the centuries. As soil gave way on the face of the cliff, and no longer able to stay within the grasp of the earth, they lost their hold and fell onto the beach.

Victoria instantly looked away, not wanting to see the place where Mr. Wyatt's body had struck to break on ragged boulders. Her eyes searched the sea instead, looking for an interest to take her thoughts. Sure enough, fishermen were returning, heading for Hythe Haven.

"How would you like to walk along the sand and get your feet wet?"she heard Cleeve say. She hesitated replying for she would much rather move on, getting away from this place of terrible remembrance, then he added sharply, "You will feel like a child again with your feet in the water." He was already off his horse and coming to help her dismount. "Put your shoes and stockings on that boulder."

While she followed directions, he took off his boots and stockings leaving his legs bare below the knee pants and placed them beside hers. He then dropped his shirt on top, leaving his torso naked. He offered his hand and she accepted it, raising her skirt with her free one. Together they laughingly approached the surf, gentle in the ebbing tide. As he predicted, the sensation of cold water rushing about her toes, the joy of splashing and kicking about, the sheer delight in racing from an incoming wave made her indeed feel like a child again. They both laughed boisterously. He called attention to a stone made smooth by constant licking of water, and she wanted him to see a beautiful anemone in a tide pool.

Together they were inspecting a shell when they heard a disturbance, like the cracking of a board. Their eyes sought the source along the escarpment above them. From high up they saw the fall of dirt from the face of the palisades. Without other warning, a huge boulder broke loose and began its heavy plunge, creating a roar as if in fear of falling.

Victoria dropped the shell and grabbed for Cleeve, throwing her arms about his waist and burying her face in his chest. He sought her to give protection, his arms enfolding her shoulders and drawing her to him, tightly, his eyes anxiously following the boulder in its noisome cascade. Fear had taken him, for there was no escape from the danger the boulder created. He anticipated that the tremendous rock could bounce in any direction once it struck others that had suffered a similar fate.

A horrendous crash was heard and Cleeve felt Victoria shudder within his shielding arms. He saw the boulder strike, shattering some pieces from those it struck, then rebounded in their direction. As it made contact with another boulder, it caromed away, coming to rest with others, its echo lingering along the bluff.

Cleeve made no move to release her, the trembling still evident in the body he held closely. He felt her head move, and he looked down as she searched his face, his eyes staring into hers. After a time he said gently, "You had a scare, Victoria. Don't move. Let fear go away."

She stayed, her head raised looking at him, eyes still seeking his protective shield, admitting shock from the ordeal. Slowly he lowered his face to hers, brushed his mouth across her forehead then found her lips. He first was gentle, but as the sweetness of her kiss incited his ardor, he pressed harder on her lips and drew her more tightly into his strengthening arms. He held her imprisoned, then tenderly released her, raised his head and beaming at her he whispered, "Forgive me, Victoria, it is your eyes. Blame it on your eyes. I could not help myself."

She half smiled and to relieve the situation he suggested, "Let's take a look at that boulder." It was a huge one, larger than its neighbors. "Had it hit us we would have been flat as a Cornish pancake," he laughed.

Victoria shivered, thinking Mr. Wyatt must have had the same fall, imagining the noise when he struck the receiving boulders, and the bones that must have been crushed when he hit. To get the thoughts out of her mind, she said, "Look how pieces were broken from it," then added quickly, "The horses! Where are the horses?"

When they dismounted to go wading, the horses were left untethered. "There they are, down the beach, near the spit. Come on!" Victoria challenged. "I'll race you! Off they darted, she holding up her skirt, he teasing her to greater effort. "They must have heard the noise and ran off. It is good they did. They were in the same danger."

The steeds were led to where their clothing had been left. Both dressed and mounted. Instantly she darted off, urging her horse to greater speed. He was left standing, surprised by her sudden departure, but after a moment he took chase, letting her keep the lead, watching her horse kick up sand in its flight.

A touch to the ribs enlivened his mount, and he caught up with her, motioning her to slow. "We need to leave the beach," he yelled and she slackened the pace. Now at a walk, he explained that Philruan Stream flowed to the sea a short distance off. "The cliffs lose some of their elevation to hills and at that point we can go inland easily."

A bridle path was well marked where the waters of Philruan Stream crossed the sand and emptied into the Channel. "This stream drains the western part of our estate. It is never dry. Natural springs keep it flowing all year. It spills out of the Vale of Strothern, a lovely stretch of trees, bushes and ground cover, and provides water for cattle and sheep. It is a boon to all nature."

The two rode side by side except where the path narrowed, and at those stretches she fell behind. There was a rich fragrance on a breeze that only occasionally strengthened enough to disturb leaves. Victoria was on familiar ground. Often she guided her horse here in past years, waded in the stream, collected wild flowers and sometimes brought a book to read. She liked to gaze across the landscape of rolling hills, spotted by copses and stands of trees, and watch cattle graze.

The sun warmed and Cleeve asked if he might remove his shirt. She did not mind. When she followed his horse, she watched ripples of muscles on his back as he moved in rhythm to the steps of his horse. When he was next to her, she noted strength in well developed arm and chest muscles.

Her gaze, noted by Cleeve, brought thoughts of Edward and his movements following her fall at Dunston when she guided her hands over his chest. "Edward cannot call for me too soon," she thought. "I need him now. Were he here I would provoke a fall and let him take me gently as he did that day. But he shall call for me soon, very soon, and I shall return with him to Dunston to share our lives evermore."

Cleeve noticed the far away look on her face and interpreted it as a longing for him. "She did not object to my embrace or the kiss I gave her while on the beach," he reasoned. "Removing my shirt is having the effect I want. I do believe she grows more interested in me." He adjusted his position in the saddle to give her a fuller view of his nakedness and began figuring a pretense for alighting his horse and making love to her. This is a secluded area, no one is likely to see us, and I know this is what she wants."

Victoria noticed the manner in which he had turned to present his nudity more completely. "Careful. Remember his violence at the inn. He thinks I accepted his kiss on the beach. Admittedly I did enjoy his embrace, but I was frightened, and his protection was comforting. The kiss was meaningless. He is a married man and I am promised. Watch him."

She watched as he reined in and dismounted, then he came to her. "The horses need a drink and so do we. I'll help you."

"I am fine, really. I can guide him to the stream and let him drink while seated."

Disbelief and then disappointment were revealed on his face. "Very well," he muttered and returned to his horse to lead him to the stream. Hers followed. "One lost," he sighed to himself, "but if not today, there is always tomorrow. I did at least get a kiss out of this ride. That is a beginning."

The tour continued along Philruvan Stream until a road crossed it. "How would you like to see Brixton Village?" The question was a cover for his defeat.

"Oh, fine."

"Good. Let's go for it."

On the road the two took off in haste, each horse given full freedom to run. Victoria felt carefree, exhilarated as her mount created a fresh wind in her face. "A free spirit!" Suddenly she remembered her circumstances. "What if I see villagers and I am recognized? What if someone calls me Patience. The vicar! I cannot meet the vicar. He surely will recognize me. And Claire! She will call me by name. Turn back!"

The run covered the distance quickly and already the first buildings of the village were in view. Victoria slowed her horse to a walk, brought her hat lower on her head to cover more of her face and became alert to examine faces of people she might know.

Cleeve waited until she caught up. "I thought you lost, Victoria. Trouble?"

"Why, no. A village means people, and I do want to look presentable. Do I?" She noticed he had donned his shirt.

He laughed out loud. "Of course. A lovely girl. Come on. I see the vicar just ahead. Let's meet him."

The vicar! Just beyond was a man on horseback approaching at a trot. Recognizing Cleeve, he slowed to a walk. "Hello, Christopher," he called. "This is one of God's finest days."

"And this is one of God's finest children, Miss Victoria. Victoria is Elizabeth's companion. The two are planning wonderful things for Kensington House."

Victoria looked away expecting the worst, but she could not avoid a head on confrontation. She saw a face unknown to her.

"Welcome to our midst, Miss Victoria," she heard him say. "Please join us for worship on Sunday."

Relaxed now, she replied, "Thank you, vicar."

"Excuse my rush," he apologized. "Mrs. Poole is ill and I must visit her. Good day to you both. It is a pleasure having you with us, Miss Victoria."

"What happened to Claire and her father?" Victoria wondered as the vicar rode off. "Perhaps he received another living."

"This is an old village," Cleeve explained. "I am told it was established several centuries ago when nearby Eyton St. Mary's Abbey was founded. The inn is one of the oldest in Britain. In the old days it offered shelter and food to pilgrims visiting the abbey where it is said a holy relic brought comfort.

Victoria knew the story. She knew the village well, too, a large collection of single story stone and plaster homes with picturesque thatched roofs, the angles of some almost touching the ground. A stream, spanned by a single arch stone bridge, was dammed on the north side of the village to form a pond for some noisy ducks, geese and swans. There were modern houses as well, for the village was the largest population center for miles around. Its size qualified it to be called a town, but tradition being strong, it was called a village.

"Let's see if we can get a bite to eat," Cleeve suggested. The two walked their horses over the bridge and entered the main street, dirt surfaced, wide, with expanses of land separating the cottages. All had vegetable gardens. Nearer the center a few shops, closer together, lined either side of Plymouth Road as the villagers called it. Here was more activity with horses and horse drawn wagons moving about as well as people, mostly men, conducting business. Victoria remained alert for familiar faces but none was identified.

The inn was found easily, for it was the only two story building in sight, and over the entrance a wrought iron sign carried the identification THE BELL AND CROSS. Hanging immediately below was a board with a painting of a cross superimposed on a representation of a bell. The building was constructed of rectangular cut granite stones placed together in various sizes. Lichen had formed in some places, and a flowering vine covered a portion of a wall.

The interior was a combination of stone and Tudor wood and plaster construction, the wood being irregular and unfinished. Along one wall was an inglenook fireplace.

"Good day to yuh, Mr. Cleeve," greeted the host. "The Cornwall sun is hot today. What would it be, double cream and strawberries?"

"Wonderful idea! For two," gleamed Cleeve. To Victoria he added, "I don't suppose many travelers fill his rooms, but villagers and those in the neighborhood come here for an evening and they have a jolly time of it"

Victoria recognized the innkeeper instantly. "Three years have not changed him. He is still a heavy, robust man." He gave no indication he recognized her.

"The strawberries are fresh from the garden," he smiled in delight, "and the wife says the double cream is fresh, too."

"First strawberries of the season for me," Cleeve acknowledged, "and after the first bite I declare it is manna from heaven. There is nothing like west country double cream. This is one of the reasons I came here. How is yours, Victoria.?"

"Delicious! Like you, I enjoy the treat. I am so pleased you brought me here. Thank you."

"It is a pleasure for me. I like your company and you ride well for a woman. Where did you learn?"

"My family made a horse available, men at the stable gave me instruction, and Edward invited me to join him at Dunston. Now there is an excellent rider."

"And excellent horses to mount. Ah, Edward. There is a fellow for you. If it were not for the plague, he would be high tailing it for London."

"How well do you know Edward?" Victoria was surprised by Cleeve's comments and showed it in both her question and the look on her face.

"Does that surprise you? Yes, I know Edward but not well. Lord Covington is a customer of mine, and on business trips I see Edward either in London or at Dunston. One day he will inherit the title, and he will be the catch of London. Women are after him by the minute." With that he let out a suggestive laugh.

She felt her face become flushed and wanted to change the subject but Cleeve went on. "I trust he kept his interest on horses when you were with him. Would you like more strawberries?"

"No more, thank you."

"Shall we head for Kensington House?"

"I am ready, but first, why did you select Kensington House for the name of your estate?"

"That was Elizabeth's choice. When I asked her to marry me, she wanted to stay in London but I could not. I suggested she bring London to Cornwall, even to renaming the estate. It was called Castelamer when I took charge. I liked the name but Kensington was more pleasing to Elizabeth. It is the name of a favorite house in London."

"Yesterday as Mrs. Tubby gave me a tour of the house, she said you had plans for redecorating it. May I ask what you plan to do?"

"It is a grand house and I do like it. I want it to be the show place of the west country, not only for Elizabeth, but I want to be proud of what I create. I want to restore the structural parts, particularly wood being damaged by the death beetle. That is a constant battle since those creatures eat wood as we eat strawberries, but you know that, Victoria, being a west country girl. Perhaps you could advise me on redecoration schemes to bring the interior up to modern times. And maybe you could make some window hangings for me." Cleeve became excited as he talked, impressing Victoria that he had developed a deep feeling for the house, and his enthusiasm began to rekindle the love she felt for Castelamer before she left that day some three years ago.

"I shall be glad to help you with the hangings, but I do not know about redecorating houses."

"Of course you can. Look about the house with an eye to new ideas then we shall get together for a talk." His eyes were on her as he spoke, a bit too anxious, she thought.

"I noticed you have a music room. Do you play an instrument?"

"No. Since I first heard music I have wanted to learn to play an instrument, but I needed other things first, like money to buy what I wanted. I kept saying as soon as I have some time I'll learn. London has a lot of music. It is one of the joys I have going to London."

"Were you born in London?"

"No. I was born in Surrey. My parents are farmers. They hold a fief to a lord. Just like the Middle Ages. As a boy I saw socials at the great house, and I made up my mind I would have the same. Of course I couldn't have that life as a farm boy so I went to London, took a job in the shipping business, learned all I could, inherited the business, enlarged it and obtained government contracts. That brought me into court contacts."

Is that how you met Mrs. Cleeve?"

"Yes, actually. I did some work for her father. The more I made money, the more I spent and the more I spent, the more I moved up in social circles. You must know that the upper classes thrive on money. I met Elizabeth when she visited her father on the docks. Her interest in me resulted in invitations to parties, first to the big houses and then to court. Those parties led to a close association with Elizabeth. We married."

Victoria watched his face as much as she could as he talked. Sometimes he looked directly at her, but mostly he looked straight ahead as if in a pensive, contemplative mood, his statements being made in a matter-of-fact recitation, lacking color or enthusiasm. "Strange. I would expect more eagerness, more emotion when speaking of Elizabeth. Do I detect all is not complete devotion? Is she a step in his struggle to achieve? Does he feel a social class difference in their marriage?" Aloud she praised him. "You must have worked arduously to achieve so much in your youth."

"Yes, I did but fortune at times was good to me. The first years on the wharf were the most difficult. It was a struggle to survive. Fights, intrigue, destruction of a competitors goods. I almost didn't make it in one fight. I was part of a crew to protect goods on a wharf. A knife caught me on the forehead, and I was left to die. The owner took pity on me, helped me recover, gave me a better job, taught me all he knew of the business, then he left it to me when he died."

"And you developed it."

"Yes. Now my associates manage a part of it for me, and I am relieved of much of the tedium. I can do other things."

Their riding took them past fields of maturing grain. "A few days of sun like this will ripen those fields," he commented, indicating he had talked enough of the past.

"Do you plan to do anything with the chapel?"

"Not for some time. It is never used."

"I understand a priest lived here at one time. Do you know where he stayed?"

"I haven't the faintest idea."

"I wonder how a priest would hide since the practice of the Catholic faith was illegal at times." Victoria had considered his reply and decided that if he knew about the passage he would try to avoid speaking about it, but she continued to probe. "There are always stories about priest's holes in the west country Tudor houses. Do you know of any in Kensington House?"

"I have heard those stories, and I believe they are part of the romantic folklore of Cornwall. There may be priests' holes in other Tudor houses, but I do not know of any here. What makes you ask?"

The counter question took her by surprise. "I was hoping there would be one, for I would like the folklore to be real at Kensington House."

The precincts of the house were entered and she gave up probing. They dismounted at the stables. "Thank you, Victoria, for riding with me. Of course we could not cover all the estate, so you must ride with me again. Soon, in fact I wish we could ride every day. You are a joy to be with." He took her hand and squeezed it, looking down at her with a noticeable gleam in his eyes. She stepped back so that he would not kiss her on impulse.

As she went to her room, she considered her meeting with Cleeve. "He is good company, a thoughtful and considerate man. He has a fine physique. And it is strange how the scar disappears as I am with him. But be careful. The kiss he has taken may not be the last he seeks." She smiled at the thought, acknowledging her interest, although reserved.

# Chapter Ten

"Shopping with you gives me much pleasure, Victoria. You know what you want and you take time to select quality. But you wear me out. After visiting so many shops, I am ready to sit down," Mrs. Cleeve complained.

"The shops in Plymouth are a delight, and there are so many compared to Exeter. Mrs. Hardy always says, "Look around before you buy. You can't get the best bargains until you look and make comparisons. I am convinced she is right."

"We are going to make that coffee house or I shall drop," warned Mrs. Cleeve, "and there it is." She led the way to an empty table and ordered coffee and scones. "In London these coffee houses are all the rage. They have taken the place of chocolate shops. It is fashionable to gather in a coffee house, order a mug and chat about all the gossip. It is such great fun meeting in one to hear the latest."

As they talked, Mrs. Cleeve cautioned in a whisper, "Do sit as you are, dear, but as you can, do look about to your left. You will see a lady whom I swear looks so much like you. Of course she appears older and may be a fancy lady, but there are so many similarities."

While they continued to talk, Victoria turned casually. There was no doubt about the person in question. Her hair was auburn, a dyed color, and the neckline of her dress was cut low so that generous portions her breasts showed. Even though Victoria could not see all of it, the gown was flamboyant in design and excessively colorful in flowered patterns. She gaped longer than was polite, but she was fascinated by the resemblance even in a three quarter profile of the face. The woman was talking to a well dressed man who gave every evidence of being interested in her to the point of fascination, and Victoria waited for the woman's head to turn toward her for a full face view. When the woman did, Victoria saw instantly what Mrs. Cleeve meant. The face was indeed like her own. Her laugh revealed fine white teeth with a slightly protruding incisor tooth. The skin looked fresh although a liberal use of paint had been used. The forehead was high like her own. It was evident she was older with harder features and her manner was extreme. She emphasized a laugh that was too loud and her gestures were theatrical. She was making an effort to enjoy the company of two male companions, each considerably older, and they were enthralled with the attention fawned on them.

Turning to Mrs. Cleeve, Victoria commented, "I see what you mean. I have heard that for every person there is a counterpart. That woman is my counterpart. Perhaps she is a cousin, a part of my family I do not know exists. Shall we finish our shopping?"

There were not many items remaining on the shopping list, and in a short time Victoria felt satisfied that she had purchased what she needed or could adapt.

The two returned to the inn where their driver awaited. The coach rolled toward Kensington House, boxes on top of the coach and boxes inside the coach. "We accomplished so much in a short time, Victoria. I am so excited by all we bought, and it will be great sport unwrapping everything, especially game materials. I am beginning to feel almost like a child again, just in anticipation. Our long gallery will make a fine play room, but we must not make our guests too happy or they wont want to go home. We do not want to be accused of trying to transfer too much of London to Kensington House."

Mrs. Tubby opened the front door as soon as the coach came to a stop, and she immediately came to Mrs. Cleeve. "The first guests from London are here, Madam. I have placed them in the front bedroom in the north wing. They announced themselves as being Lord and Lady Arlington."

"Oh!" cried Mrs. Cleeve in horror. "I wasn't here to greet them. It will be all over court that Elizabeth Cleeve has lost her sense of courtesy. I must hurry to see them. Come, Victoria. Let us freshen up a bit then express our welcome."

While assisting Mrs. Cleeve out of her traveling gown, Victoria was told some of their guests' background. "Lady Arlington is an off and on passing favorite of the king, and I am surprised she was not asked to go to Salisbury with the royal court. Maybe her husband said no to that idea if she did receive an invitation. Lord Talbot Arlington is a bore despite his wealth. He does business with Christopher. Of course she married him for money and position. He is much older and is very demanding of her. He tries to keep her in sight but is not very successful. Of course I can't blame her for seeking attentions elsewhere, and the king falls so easily for the least flirtation. She was a nobody at one time but no longer. She is quite influential in court circles. She is a striking person, most attractive. I like her. Now, you freshen yourself and we will welcome Lord and Lady Arlington."

"Oh, Nicky, dear," Mrs. Cleeve gleefully enthused as she bounced into the room. "Welcome to Kensington House. Forgive me for not being home to greet you properly. We had to be in Plymouth and just returned. Are you receiving all the help you need? Meet Victoria, my companion. You must be tired after that exhausting trip from London."

"How lovely of you to take us in." Lady Arlington opened her arms to receive her friend. "Talbot wanted to go to Carlton Manor, but his estate is too close to London, and the plague is spreading to the shires around the city. Kensington House is perfect. So far away from that dreadful plague. How have you been Elizabeth? How well you look. Hello, Victoria. I am not too tired. We stayed in Plymouth last night."

Lady Arlington appeared to be in her early thirties, of medium height, and was expensively gowned with a string of pearls around her neck and an emerald brooch on her bodice. Her face was lovely, a creamy complexion touched lightly with paint, dark eyes, and her brown hair had a fine sheen. "Talbot went to the kitchen with Mrs. Tubby to get a bite to eat."

"Come, Victoria," Mrs. Cleeve called, "Lady Arlington needs to get organized and we have much to do." Once in the hall she continued, "I have asked that all our shopping boxes be placed in the long gallery. You run along and arrange your sewing area then we'll do the game things. The furnishings you asked for should already be there. I'll be with you shortly."

Victoria found the lounging furniture nicely arranged to form sitting groups and the tables and chairs placed for games. "This looks effective," she thought and began creating her area near the first large window. She wanted work tables set up near her and the candelabra placed on a low table. The chair she chose for herself was comfortable for accomplishing all the work she would be required to do.

As she proceeded she thought of Edward and yearned for his coming. "How much I would like to hear from him, but then no one has come from Dunston to bring me word." Pleasure filled her heart as she thought about her avowed, and she worked diligently, humming a tune from childhood. Mrs. Cleeve appeared, completely unnoticed.

"What a happy child. It is a joy to see you work, humming away. You make me feel better, too. What causes this jollity?"

"Just thinking," she smiled in reply, but to herself she added, "You will know my thoughts of love when Edward comes for me."

Her thinking was interrupted further by the appearance of Mr. Cleeve. He was dressed for riding. "You two are working too hard. From all appearances, we are going to have good times in the long gallery. I just wanted to tell you, dear, that I am taking Lord Arlington for a little ride but we will return for supper. Lady Arlington is resting, and Talbot did not want to interrupt. Would you be a darling and tell her."

"Of course. Dress is formal tonight. Enjoy your ride." Then to Victoria she added. "I must see to some duties. Let's stop work here. You have done enough."

"Would you mind if I did not join you for supper. There are a few things I must do."

"My dear, I take too much of your time. Surely. Pall will bring you a tray."

After an early supper, Victoria closed her door, bolted it then placed a chair with its back at the base of the knob. She went to the panel that opened the priest's hole and studied it for operational clues but found nothing. She then placed her fingers on the panel and moved them slowly until the panel opened. She noted carefully the position of her finger tips. "Interesting," she thought. "Both hands must be used and the ten finger tips must be placed in a precise position or the panel wont open." Keeping her finger tips in place, she took a mental picture of the locations, noting every measurement with the panel edges as points of reference.

She then went to the opening, moved one panel to the left and placed her back against it. The panel closed. Mentally she considered her position, reached her arms backward and placed her hands on the wall then moved them outward to the edges of the panel to determine distances. Turning around, she imagined herself in the proper position and made a mental note.

Returning to the panel that controlled the opening, she placed her finger tips in the memorized position and the panel opened. She returned to the closing panel and made it function. Good! She practiced opening and closing the priest's hole until she felt sure she had learned the operation.

Victoria went to her knees to peer inside the opening and let her imagination carry her backward in time to the last century when it was a crime to practice Catholicism. "A priest was in this room. A warning came. Possibly by a signal. He operated the panel. It opened. He crawled through the hole. He closed it. He closed it from the inside! How did he do that?"

Retrieving a candle and again on her knees, she peered into the opening. On her right the light revealed a passage way to the depth of light. On the left the corridor ended abruptly at a wall. On the far end was the brick outer wall of the house. She considered passing through the panel, put half her body inside, hesitated, then withdrew. Rising, she selected a book from a shelf and placed it on the floor next to the opening. Being careful to avoid touching the sides of the opening in fear of springing the panel shut, she crawled through, turned and placed the book on the track, then stood up. Holding her candle high and to one side, she attempted to analyze the corridor. It faded into darkness.

"The peek hole. Find the peek hole." She blew out the candle leaving her in darkness, the only light coming through the panel from her room. She began exploring the wall. There! She raised herself on tip toes. She placed one eye directly over the pin hole and peeped through it. "Oh! He did!" she exclaimed to herself. "He did watch me!"

The opening allowed her a broad view of her room including the bed and the mirror. It was the exact area where she always undressed standing nude before she put on her nightgown.

She lighted the candle and raised it to explore the hole, considering a means for closing it. The light revealed activity of a wood worm, a nuisance insect that devours wood, leaving cavities and tunnels where they munch. Rarely do they eat completely through the wood.

She brought nothing which she could use to seal the hole, but she noted carefully its location with an intent to return and seal it.

She turned and looked down the corridor, slowly took a few steps toward the darkness then decided to go no farther. She turned and retraced her steps toward the opening. As she was about to stoop down to pass through the crawl hole she felt a breeze. Instantly the candle was blown out. The panel sprung shut, knocking the book into the passage. She wanted to scream but could not produce a sound. She felt faint, sick to her stomach. Perspiration appeared on her forehead. She became aware of a noise behind her. "Hit the wall," something told her. Frantically she began striking the wall furiously, working her arms wildly, her lips drying, her mouth parching, panting, sucking for air. The noises took the form of foot steps, becoming louder, slow steps, some with a dragging sound. She sensed a person near her. Blackness took her sensibilities.

When she did come to she was aware of a light. Something cool was on her forehead. Her head was raised, resting on something. She blinked her eyes but the strong light forced them closed. Slowly, very slowly, she raised her lids, letting her eyes adjust to the light. She looked up directly into a face.

"Now, my dear. You have just had a shock. Easy. Rest easy," Victoria thought she heard the voice say. The face, wizened, a landscape of arid earth, furrowed, with low hills and shallow gullies, closely arranged in uneven rows. Above was a cloud announcing a coming storm, grey, fluffy, disarranged. Ponds of blue formed two depressions, a mound rising between them. A piece of land moved and she heard more words.

"Gently. Don't move, Patience. When you are ready, you will go to bed."

"Patience! My childhood name! Who said that name?" She struggled to rise, wanting to look directly into that face, but a hand pressed her back. She was resting on a floor but leaning on the breast and shoulder of a person. The face was unrecognizable as she studied it. After a time she heard, "This damp cloth is no longer cooling for you. Now rise slowly and crawl through the priest's hole. I'll help you to bed."

Victoria did as she was told. Her head throbbed a bit, and she appreciated some aid in rising and crawling to the opening. With effort she crept through it.

"Let me take off your dress, child. Now other things. Slip into this nightgown. Now under the covers."

"Thank you. What happened?"

"As I sat in my room upstairs, I heard noises. As I listened they appeared to be coming from the secret passage. I came down to see what it was. I saw light coming from your room. When I reached the light I found you on the floor, your clothes in disarray, pulled up almost to your waist and you had fainted. I bathed your face with a wet towel."

Victoria glanced at the door. The chair was pushed aside and it was ajar.

"Now rest, Patience."

She heard her old name again. "Please let me look at you."

Victoria viewed a crone, an old shriveled elf, short, thin, almost emaciated, dressed in a grey frock that had no shape, torn in spots, hair that must not have been cleared of knots and tangles in months, and when a smile appeared, it was totally toothless. "You know my name, my childhood name. How do you know it?"

"As a young lady I came to Castelamer to work. I married here. My husband and I worked here. My babies were born here."

"I don't recall having ever seen you."

"You were too young when I went away. There was difficulty, serious difficulty. I returned only when Mr. Cleeve became master of Castelamer, or as he now calls it, Kensington House. He gave me a room. There I stay. Except....." The head cocked to listen. "Shusss. Someone is on the stairs."

The witchlike creature moved like a cat that in its sleekness slithers slyly to a hiding place, disappeared, only the noise of the sliding panel closing giving evidence to the place of retreat.

Victoria waited, apprehension building. Steps with a dragging sound came down the hall toward her door, stopped near it, then after pausing, returned along the hall, quieter, quieter, then silence.

She got up, closed the door, put the bolt in place, then returned to bed, still expecting the door to open. She wondered what she would do if it did. Scream? Attack? With what? Scissors! She got up and went to her sewing box. Recalling Mrs. Hardy's weapon when Mr. Hardy threatened, Victoria felt the sharpness of the cutters with her fingers. "Good," she mumbled, then placed the scissors next to the candle. In bed again, she planned, "I must catch him unawares, before he knows I have them."

She tried to sleep. The chair! She got up and pushed the chair in front of the door, its back under the knob. When the covers were pulled around her neck, she decided to remain awake to surprise the intruder. Sometime during the night she fell asleep.

With dawn breaking, she awakened with a start, instantly alert. She glanced at the door. The chair was moved. The door was ajar. She reached for the scissors. Gone!

# Chapter Eleven

The next several days were busy ones for Victoria. More Londoners arrived, and she was greatly involved with Mrs. Cleeve in making them comfortable and providing for their needs. Not all those who received invitations from Mr. Cleeve arrived, but by the end of the week sixteen persons were in guests rooms. Lord and Lady Arlington were the only titled guests, but it was obvious from conversations, wearing apparel and jewelry that others were of very substantial means and had close associations with the royal court. It was evident, too, that all the men had business relations with Mr. Cleeve. One couple brought their sons, each in his early twenties.

Much of the daytime recreation for women guests was arranged in the long gallery. They frequently gathered around the work area to watch Victoria sew, oh and ah over exquisite fabrics, place orders, take fittings, offer critical opinions to one another, make suggestions and just for the sport of it, take up a needle and try their own skills.

Comfortable furniture on thick carpets created a home sitting area. Game tables were next, but much of the long gallery beyond was left open for group games.

The men were active outdoors, riding, hunting, fishing and generally being absent from the house. On occasions when the sea was calm, Mr. Cleeve arranged for boating excursions for everyone.

All the guests knew one another before arriving so it was no problem getting them together. Their conversations were of the plague, and they were all anxious to relate their experiences. "People are dying by the thousands. Before my sister closed her Charing Cross house, we watched from her window as carts stopped before houses marked with great red exes, and men carried out bodies to pile them higher in the carts. Men moving the dead covered their faces with masks."

"And the living, when they do go outside, walk about with their mouths covered. It is dreadful. Very few people are seen on the streets. Everyone stays inside as much as they can. There is no social life at all. London is a dead city."

"Those who can are leaving. Those who can't face death. My maid said she watched her mother shake with chills and burn up with fever at the same time. Great swellings appeared on her thighs, forming blisters, then they broke open before the lady died. Why, the idea of the girl coming to see me to tell me all that when she was exposed. I sent her off immediately. I packed to come here."

There was absolute silence as all eyes stared at her, each person thinking that she could be a carrier of the dreadful plague.

Aware if the silence and the inference of her innocent statements, she added quickly, "Don't fret, my dears. We are safe. The incubation period, I am told by my doctor, is two to ten days. We are well passed that time."

It took more than a few minutes for the atmosphere to warm when one of the men added a positive note. "It is not all death. It does take time and a great deal of care, but some victims do recover."

"We should give thanks that we could get away to Kensington House otherwise we could be in those carts." A clapping of hands expressed agreement.

"Let me tell you about our coach trip. We stayed at an inn......," and as the conversation turned to another subject, Victoria concentrated on her needle. Her skill had developed to expertise and she made her fingers fly, for Mrs. Cleeve had said that some of the guests would be moving to Oxford where Parliament was to sit. She wanted to have all gowns completed before they left.

One afternoon as she worked alone, she did not hear the door open. A figure moved silently through it and approached Victoria, scissors in hand, pointing it at the girl's neck. In the silence a board creaked loudly, and Victoria jerked around quickly, startling the intruder.

Facing her was an old lady, an arm extended like a stick, clutching a pair of scissors in a gnarled claw. "She is my tormentor!" Victoria exclaimed to herself and prepared to defend her person.

As if caught in the act, the old lady stopped and said, "My dear, I found these in my room. Are they yours?" The voice was deceiving for it was mild, kindly, avoid of any roughness or the snarl of challenge one would expect from a person with gross ill intentions.

Victoria hesitated. "What is this woman's purpose? Why did she come to this house?" The questions were spoken to herself as she took the scissors from the boney hand. One glance told her the sheers were hers, the ones she had placed on the stand next to the candle as a defensive weapon. She tried to cover her shock by saying as calmly as possible, "I believe they are. I thank you," but what she wanted to ask but didn't, "How did you get them?"

Picking up her needle, Victoria began her work again determined not to let her anxieties show. She looked at the face that hovered over her. It appeared less like a witch in the natural light of day, but it was aged and wan, reflecting a life of hard work and much worry. She felt sympathy for the old one and hoping to draw her out said gently,

"Please sit down and chat with me. I would call you by name but I do not know it."

"I am Mrs. Tatham," she replied, taking a chair by its back and pulling it closer to Victoria. She sat down. "You do beautiful work."

"I enjoy sewing and it is even more pleasing making gowns from this lovely material."

After a period of silence, Mrs. Tatham asked, "Why did you run away from Castelamer, Patience?"

Victoria looked up and studied the face before her. "I did not run. I decided it was time to be on my own." She spoke gently and in a matter of fact tone.

The manner of the answer as well as the contents took the questioner off guard. "Yes, I can understand that. Even as a child you were independent. But you had the whole household, the villagers and much of the neighborhood upset for days, and all the men and many women helped search the countryside for you. It was known you had left Castelamer for the vicarage, but you never arrived. It was thought you had been kidnapped or even taken by a wild animal."

Not wishing to prolong the inquiry or getting involved with explanations, Victoria took command by becoming the questioner. "What happened to the Framsdens?"

"That was part of the trouble, serious trouble," came the immediate response. "Shortly after you left, it was reported about these parts that grave business problems developed at Castelamer and the Framsdens departed. What happened to them no one knows. They have not been seen."

"When did the Cleeves take the house?"

"Right after the Framsdens left. He came. Then she came from London."

"Why do you call me Patience?"

"That is your name, child. I knew you before you came to Castelamer. I worked for your mother and father."

It took a moment for Victoria to comprehend the statement. Then her face showed complete dismay. "You did! You knew my mother and father! Tell me about them." She put her sewing aside and looked directly at the old lady, her countenance changing to keen apprehension.

"Why, I was your mother's only servant. I helped her day after day. You twin girls she cared for by herself, so much did she love you. She was a lovely lady, so kind and sweet, a gentle, caring person. I never felt I worked for her but more with her, for I enjoyed her company. She always did so much for others. She and your father were devoted to one another, completely devoted. He used to tell her how much he loved her, any time of the day. He had many friends. Their deaths shocked everyone. Some say it was not an accident, that boat with a hole in it. Strange, isn't it. They were to come to Castelamer. But it was the Framsdens who came. They asked me to help care for you and Penelope after your parents' deaths, but I asked questions and was sent to the village." The statements were clipped as if being produced from a machine, delivered almost like a child's recitation.

Victoria followed the story. The basic facts she knew. She had heard the questions about the boating accident, but the idea that her parents were supposed to come to Castelamer she had not heard. "Why were my parents to come to Castelamer?"

"The will, of course. The old family was dying out. There was only that old man left, your father's uncle. He liked your father. He asked your father to come to Castelamer to stay with him. I heard your father tell your mother that the will had been made and that they would inherit Castelamer. But the old man died, sudden like. No will was found. Framsden was the closest relative, only months older than your father. Framsden and your father were cousins."

Victoria thought about the reply and was puzzled about the will. "The oldest son inherits," she recalled to herself. "That is custom, a hand down from the Middle Ages. Primogenture. But the old man had no children, only two nephews, and without a will the older nephew would inherit. Perhaps the old man said he made a will but didn't. Best forget it."

Aloud Patience complimented, saying, "I want to thank you for helping me out of the secret passage, Mrs. Tatham. I could have died of fright if you had not come."

"Or by some other way," came the sudden comment.

"Some other way?"

"Yes. When I found you, you were knocked out by a blow to the head. That blow was either striking your head when you fell or being hit on the head. And you did not faint. Your clothes were bunched up. They didn't get that way from the fall. Someone pushed your clothes up. Someone with ill intentions."

"I didn't know that, Mrs. Tatham. Who could that have been?"

"Whoever knows about the secret passage. It is not a secret passage for those who know about it. I don't know how many know about it around here. But more than one knows, I fear. When the Tudor wings were added, the passage and sliding panel in your room were made to help Catholics. Old Henry Eighth was after them and so were others. Castelamer was a Catholic stronghold. The priest stayed in the room you have. If trouble was expected, he could escape through the wall and down the passage. I would say it is used for other purposes now."

"Tell me how the panel is closed and opened from the passage side."

"It is simple. I'll show you."

"Now?"

"Come."

Victoria followed her out the door and into the hall then into her room. From the doorway she watched as Mrs. Tatham used the same hand code to open the panel. Victoria closed the door and slid the bolt in place, lighted a candle, then both moved through the opening. Inside the passage, Mrs. Tatham directed, "Watch me." She stepped on a board and the pane closed immediately. Using the tips of her fingers, she pressed on a section of the wall and the sliding panel opened.

"How did you learn about the secret passage and this sliding panel?"

Mrs. Tatham put a forefinger on her lips. "We must speak in whispers. We can be heard. We do not want to be caught in here." Victoria strained to listen as the old one continued. "I knew about the priest's hole from stories I heard. So at night when the Cleeves were asleep, I came to your room to look. That was before you came back. Once Mr. Cleeve caught me in the hall. I told him I could not sleep. Since then I have been careful. It took time, but I found out how to open and close the panel. Now, Patience, if you should forget a light when you use the passage, there is a candle hidden here." Some material was uncovered and a candle was revealed.

"You have been extremely helpful, Mrs. Tatham. May I ask you to do something for me, something that is very necessary?"

"Yes, dear."

"Please call me Victoria. It is important."

"I shall try. Now let me show you the rest of the passage. Follow." The passage stopped where a stairway began. They went down quietly, carefully. At the bottom the old lady stopped, and by using her foot and pressing on a specific spot, which Victoria memorized carefully, a small exterior door swung inward, exposing the out of doors. The door had a facing of very thin brick which meshed exactly with the rest of the exterior, and unless examined carefully, could not be identified.

Also, the exit opened onto some thick, tall boxwood plants that helped shield the door. It was necessary for Victoria to crawl along in the dirt before she found a way to break through the hedge.

"Now to return," Mrs. Tatham directed.

The two retraced their steps up the stairs after Victoria learned how to open the exterior door. She noticed the fine construction of the Tudor brick wall and that the passage way, with smooth wood flooring, was free from debris so that by stepping carefully a person could move the length of the passage without being heard.

"Now watch, Victoria. Look at your room before you enter." At a touch of her finger, a minute portion of the panel opened a peek hole. "Notice the wood. The workmanship is so fine that only this side of the panel is affected. The interior panel does not move. You are looking through gauze-like wood. Even though you were to search and search for it, you could not find it on the room side."

"But I found a peek hole the night you found me here."

"Show me."

Victoria took measurements with her fingers and pointed to the spot.

Mrs. Tatham looked. "Mmmmm. That is only because the wood worm has been active."

"Do you know the names of persons who have learned about the real peek hole?"

Mrs. Tatham thought. "I am not sure. You know the old saying, 'Tell one a secret and three will know.' But I cannot be sure that I am the only one who knows. You must promise on fear of death that you will not tell another soul. I am telling you for I know someone is interested in you. You may need an escape to the tower room one day. I want to show you what to do. I found this panel quite by accident. See. The passage appears to end at the sliding panel to your room. But look." She pressed a point on the wall at the end of the passage. A panel opened. Victoria on hands and knees looked through and saw a stairs. "The stairs go to my room. Learn this so you can open the panel. Don't use it unless you absolutely must. Listen! Listen!"

"What is the matter? What do you hear?"

"Look through the peek hole. If it is clear, get into your room. I'll show you the rest of the secret later. Quick!"

As Mrs. Tatham disappeared through the opening to her stairs and closed it, Victoria looked into her own room through the peek hole. Clear. As rapidly as she could, she entered, closed the panel and made sure it was secure. She paused to contemplate. "Why did Mrs. Tatham depart so quickly? What did she hear? I didn't hear anything. She must be nervous and is suspicious of everything and everybody."

She returned to her sewing in the long gallery. As her needle sped along, she thought about a disturbing comment Mrs. Tatham made. "She said, 'I know some one is interested in you.' She could not know about Edward. No one knows that he is coming for me. That is our secret. Maybe she means Mr. Cleeve. He definitely has shown an interest in me. Could she have seen us on the beach? Maybe she saw him kiss me."

Her face greyed than paled. Her hands turned cold and she dropped her needle. "What if he lived! He could recognize me. Mr. Wyatt could be the interested person. What if he were in the west country and that he learned I was at Kensington House. He could know about the secret passage. He had complete access to the house when the Framsdens were here. He said he watched me. If he used the peek hole, he would know about the passage.

"Oh, Victoria," she cautioned herself. "You are being foolish. You are letting your mind run rampant. Mr. Wyatt could never have survived that fall. One blow on his head from that fall would have done him in. Look how that boulder struck the others and splintered itself. No human body could have taken that kind of beating and survived."

Her face sobered. "Oh, Edward. Hurry!"

"What is that, dear?" Responding in fright to the unexpected voice, Victoria turned to see Mrs. Cleeve standing in the doorway. Trying to control herself and forcing a smile, she replied, "I must have been singing to myself. Did you have a good outing with your guests?"

"Oh, Victoria! All our guests are so happy with their visit. In a way it is like London with all the activities, and people and good times. You made it possible with your ideas. You are a dear, such a delight to me. But you have worked all day. Get to your room. Rest. Tomorrow I want to talk about a special event. No, two special events."

In her room, Victoria found herself considering further the person who might be interested in her. "However, I must remember to dress and undress carefully. If I remove the scene there will be no need to use the peek hole."

As she began to bathe, she was startled by the sound of scratching. Her fears returned instantly.

# Chapter Twelve

"Please join us for supper this evening, Victoria. We would like your company, for I want to wear your latest creation. You must hear first hand all the accolades the ladies will pile on you when they see my new gown. Come. You can enter with Christopher and me. I want to make a grand entry." Mrs. Cleeve presented an entreating look at her companion as Victoria worked in the long gallery. "Remember, I said I did not want our guests to think I had become a country dame? Well, with this gown you make me look regal, as if I were at court." A broad smile complimented her words of praise.

"Very well, but I must do a final fitting before you wear it. Shall we try on the gown now?"

"Yes. Bring it to my bedroom. I don't want the ladies to get even a glimpse of it before tonight. What will you wear? Would you like the gown you wore for our little escapade at Lord Covington's? You captivated Edward in it."

"Thank you, Mrs. Cleeve. You are thoughtful. That gown is indeed beautiful, but I have been putting a gown together. If I can finish it this afternoon, I'll wear it."

"Take time, dear. Now let's get into my new gown."

Victoria worked quietly during the fitting then directed, "Let's see how it looks in the mirror."

Looking at her reflection, she beamed, "Why. Victoria. It is beautiful, truly beautiful. I do thank you for your fine work."

Victoria smiled in satisfaction. She had used blue satin to form a tight fitting bodice in the form of a V that ended in a point at the waist. The neck was cut low to emphasize her breasts which were thrust forward and upward by a tiny boned corset fitted below the bodice thus revealing an enticing cleavage. Shoulder straps barely touched the extreme shoulder points where began tight fitting sleeves made of golden taffeta which burst into a cascade of gathered lace reaching the wrists. The taffeta was repeated in a billowing skirt gathered around the back and sides of the waist. Down the front Victoria had placed a generous piece of light weight multicolored damask outlined on either side by gathered folds of Flanders lace which continued around the bottom of the skirt to touch the floor.

"Lovely, Victoria. It is lovely. I have just the jewels to set it off perfectly. Really, Victoria, I should take you to London. We could open an exclusive salon. Christopher would supply French fabrics, you could create, and I could provide customers. Why, we would have as our clients all the royal court. What do you think?"

"Oh, no, Mrs. Cleeve. You are making a joke of it. I have too much to learn. The competition would be too great to overcome."

"Well, keep it in mind. I think you would be a sensation."

The idea prompted Victoria to think of a dress shop in London, and the idea became intriguing. "Imagine sewing for the ladies of the court." A smile formed as she allowed herself the luxury of a daydream.

All dreams burst when she pricked her finger. "Anyhow Edward would not permit it. My place will be with him as he manages his estate. What sewing I do will be just for me and perhaps shirts for him."

By seven she was dressed and had made a final review of herself. Her hair had been brushed to a sheen which in candle light appeared burnished. It fell in waves down her back, held off her face by small gold satin bows, producing a child like effect. A further touch of youth was added when she fastened her mother's simple gold locket about her neck.

She was about to blow out the candle when she heard the scratching sound. In her turn to face the south wall, her eyes caught the reflection of the paneling in her mirror. She held her position, her back to her antagonist. She became aware that she was not experiencing a nervous reaction. She felt in control. A thought burst, a smile revealing a clue to its content. "Whoever it is, this person is only trying to annoy me. Well let him or her think of success." With that she blew out the candle and left the room.

Pall was assisting Mrs. Cleeve when Victoria was admitted to her mistress' bedroom. "Why, Victoria! What a captivating aura of loveliness! What have you created for yourself? Let me see."

Victoria had made her gown of blue velvet. A square necked bodice streaked with vertical lines of gold embroidery ended at the waist. Sleeves were puffed at the shoulders narrowing to close at the middle forearms while gold slits of the bodice material were repeated in puffs. The skirt, made of gold silk, was gathered at the waist, falling in folds to the floor. A second skirt of three quarter length Flemish lace was placed around the back and sides leaving the front of gold silk open to full view.

"It is as I said, dear. You should have a shop in London. Let's do it! Come. We'll pick up Christopher and make our grand entry." Mrs. Cleeve's face was aglow as she guided Victoria through the door.

As was the custom, guests were already present in the banquet room when the hosts entered, the Cleeves first, Victoria following. Applause greeted them, partly as an expression of grateful appreciation for accepting so many refugees from London, and partly to recognize the attractive group.

Mrs. Cleeve was right. All the ladies and even the men ogled at the gowns and contributed a variety of complimentary comments about them. The hostess gave full credit to her companion, and all agreed with Mrs. Cleeve that she should open a London shop. "It must be a fine salon, and I will guarantee you the ladies of the court will patronize you," Lady Arlington announced. "We are always looking for new talent to make our gowns something spectacular. You can certainly do that. You make this London gown of mine look like a rag. With your skills I could make you the star of next season."

At one point in the predinner conversation, Mr. Cleeve appeared at her side. "Your dress is lovely, Victoria, a tribute to your skills, and I, too, believe you should open a salon. I shall bring you the best fabrics I can find. I can help you select a location and get you started. I shall appreciate the opportunity to see you. We can enjoy London together. You wont have to work all the time."

Guy and James, the only young men among the guests, appeared before her, cutting off any opportunity for a reply and from that moment the two tried to consume Victoria's time. "We had no idea a jewel like you was shinning in this waste land." It was Guy, unable to keep his eyes off her. "Why do you hide in the long gallery. Stop working so hard and spend time with us."

James even breached etiquette by changing place cards to sit Victoria between them. Then fascination grew as the three talked during supper. By the time the young men were forced to say goodnight, they had enticed a promise from Victoria that she would meet them for riding. But her promise would not be fulfilled the following morning, for as she prepared for bed that night, the scratching noise was heard.

Victoria stood where she was and listened, her back to the peek hole. She knew he was well within the range of view. "Since he or whomever it is who uses the peek hole, certainly knows how to operate the sliding panel. Why doesn't he open it and come in? Why doesn't he do whatever he plans to do?"

Now convinced that the noise was being made to annoy her, she ignored it, and as she planned, moved out of range of view. She blew out the candle leaving her room in darkness.

Her escape from view took her near the window. She breathed deeply the balmy air that bathed her face as she opened the shutters, and the freshness calmed her. "How refreshing," she murmured, thrusting her head and shoulders through the shutters to feel the salt air. She let her eyes roam casually about the countryside, and she subconsciously identified faint outlines of familiar physical features on the landscape.

She caught what appeared to be a glow of light in the south garden, and it attracted her attention. It lasted only a minute. She made no effort to account for its presence. Again she saw the light. It seemed to fade, not a strong light, more of a glimmer. "Someone must be in the garden. But who would want to be there at this time of night? It could be one of the guests or a staff person. Why does it go on and off? The wind is not strong enough to blow out a candle constantly."

The corner of the south wing of the house cut her view from the remaining portion of the south garden. Victoria stretched farther over the window sill, but the leaning increased her range only slightly. The second light made her more alert to possible activity and aroused her curiosity.

"There is a window on the south side of the tower room," she recalled. "If I were there I could see the source of those lights. That is Mrs. Tatham's room. At this hour she would be asleep. Should I awaken her? Now, Victoria. Have patience. It is not your business. You are a companion here. Mind your station."

Withdrawing from the window, she slowly made her way to the bed, thinking. She sat down. The stimulation from the lights on her curiosity removed any feeling of sleepiness. Quietly she went to the armoire, reached for her robe, put it on, and stepped to the door.

She listened intently. Nothing. Slowly she opened the door slightly, put her head into the hallway, and looked about. No one. Opening the door wider, she slipped into the hallway, closed the door, and in bare feet tiptoed to the long gallery and opened its door. How long and uninviting it appeared at night. At the far end she opened the door to stairs that would lead her to Mrs. Tatham's room. Tapping lightly on the door, she waited. Silently it opened. Victoria entered into complete darkness, only the dim light of night passing through the window to give it some life. Her body shuttered in fear. A hand went to her throat. "I have walked right into her hands. She could do me in right here. If she makes a threatening move, grab her. You can overwhelm her easily."

"You saw the lights," Mrs. Tatham whispered. "Come. Look out the window." Victoria hesitated a moment to let the old crone move ahead of her. The shutters were open. She was motioned forward. "Look straight ahead, near the brink. There it is!" The ancient voice was serrated, almost staccato as whispered, but it was full of excitement.

Victoria saw a light glow briefly then cut off.

"I have seen those lights on some nights since I returned to Castelamer." The old voice was more direct, less excited. "They are always in the same place."

"How often?"

"Off and on, but never on a foggy night. There is no pattern as I can tell. I don't see anything but the light. No person."

"Do you think it is a signal light? I would guess it is a signal. But why isn't the light on Signal Bluff across the bay. It should be. If it is a signal for boats, the signal should be for Hythe Haven. Not here. Except!" A thought flashed across Victoria's mind.

"What?"

"Did you ever hear stories about contrabanders who lighted boats onto rocks below Bodacome Bluff?"

"Of course, but that was always on foggy nights. This is a clear night. No captain would make a mistake on a night like this."

"That is right, but let us watch for a time."

The two waited patiently. At times the light blinked two, three or four times in rapid succession. But no person was seen. "Whoever is making that light must be standing beyond the high hedge," Victoria guessed.

"I have watched all night at times, but never have I seen any person or anything move."

Victoria tired. "I must to bed. Tomorrow I shall walk along the brink to look for evidence. I do not know what to look for, but maybe I shall see something that will help us decide what is going on."

"You must be careful. Remember what I told you."

Victoria turned and faced the old lady. "Do you know who it is? A man. A woman."

"I doubt it is a woman. It is a man." The voice became mysterious, almost ethereal in quality, hyphenated by hesitations as if she were trying to recall clues before she made a judgment.

"Is it someone I know?"

"Yes, it must be."

"Is he interested in me to do harm?"

"I do not know, but you must be careful. I saw a man looking at you through the peek hole. More than once I saw him. He knows about the priest hole and the sliding panel. I saw him open it and go into your room. When I am sure who it is I will tell you."

Victoria returned to her room, thoughts caroming about her mind as to the identity of the person using the peek hole and the sliding panel. She saw her door ajar as she approached it. "Why, I definitely closed it. Someone in this house is trying to antagonize or frighten me. Well, I am not going to give any one the satisfaction of knowing the efforts are being successful. I am disturbed. But I shall fight it!"

Gingerly she stepped into her room and looked around in the muted darkness. Nothing appeared to be disturbed. She placed her robe across the foot of the bed and slipped under the covers. She lay awake considering a course of action to learn about the lights.

The next morning was grey with heavy clouds covering the sky through which no sun could penetrate. From her window, Victoria watched a wind blow leaves about the garden and bend branches on elm trees. "Looks like we are in for a good blow. Best be about my plans before the rains come."

She rolled a heavy woolen cloak over her shoulders and thrust her arms through slits on either side of the warm garment. She looked for a hat but decided against it believing the hood on the back of the cloak would serve the purpose should rain strike before she returned.

As soon as she entered the garden, the wind caught her cloak and tossed it free. Quickly she gathered it tightly about herself and tied a belt securely. Leaves were being thrown about angrily. They gathered in clusters, but dryness made it easier for them to be battered furiously by the playful wind. Victoria pushed aside some low branches being whipped as if they were a conductor's baton.

The closer she came to the crest of the bluff the stiffer the wind became. Angry gusts slammed into the face of the cliff, fought their way upward to spread over the brink, then run wildly through the garden. Victoria bent over, putting her head and shoulders into the blasts to push against the invisible force. "The wind will have erased any evidence of foot activity," she concluded as she inspected the walk next to the lip of the bluff.

Determined to continue her search anyway, she crawled to the edge on her stomach then stretched out to look over. Huge angry waves forming on a slate grey rough sea rolled landward, dashed against boulders on the beach, and thundered against the bluff. "The sea is washing over the sand, and like the wind, it has wiped away any sign of activity."

As she lay prone, she continued to watch the sea, fascinated by its violent action. "I was in this same position three years ago," she recalled. "The sea was not so active that day. I was enjoying the play of the surf on the sand and the wanning sun on my back when he came. He towered over me saying pretty words. Then he held me close. I was drawn to him, mystified, wanting him to smother me. We scuffled. He fell off the cliff. Onto the boulders. Dead."

Her eyes continued to scramble along those same rocks, watching waves beat then wash over them, leaving foam to form within separating spaces during the ebb flow.

She raised her head, alert to a sound like a rhythmic crush on gravel. Pushing the thunder of waves aside, she concentrated on a new sound, decided it could be footsteps, only there seemed to be some kind of dragging with the steps. The noisy wind kept interfering, interrupting any chance of definite identification. "What if it is another Mr. Wyatt!"

As she looked, a figure broke through the hedge immediately before her. Victoria gasped in fright then smiled, relieved. "Good morning, Mr. Cleeve."

"I thought I saw you walking in this direction. Don't you know it is dangerous to be on these palisades with a storm breaking," a half smile showing the space between his two front teeth. He was dressed in a heavy coat that fell below the tip of his riding boots, his head uncovered. In his hand was a heavy walking stick, almost club like in appearance. As he stepped free from the hedge, it dragged on the ground. "What takes your attention?"

Having already considered what she might say should she be accosted, she answered with, "I enjoy walking on a blustery day. There is something about the strength of wind that fascinates me. What brings you out?"

"But you can't be walking stretched out as you are. What is on your mind?" He ignored her question. "Are you looking for something?"

"Yes. Last night I heard the surf and I wanted to see it this morning."

"You are on very tenuous territory, young lady. There have been very serious accidents on these cliffs, even deaths. Remember the boulder we saw fall onto the beach?" His tone was serious and she detected concern. "You could be another boulder."

"But lying like this does not put much weight on the edge and the view is so spectacular."

She saw the look in his eyes change. He took a step forward and instantly he was prone next to her. "Show me what you think is so spectacular."

When she turned to look over the brink her body touched his and she reacted strangely, quite opposite to the feeling of abhorrence she felt that night in Plymouth when he kissed her. Instead she felt exhilarated. She wanted him next to her. There was a wish rising inside her that he might touch her. "It is like the feeling I had for Edward when he held me. Careful. He is a married man and you are avowed to Edward."

"Look at those waves, so forceful, so relentless in their charge against the boulders. They make me feel strong, too, as if I can win battles." She made herself talk about the surging of the sea to stop the surging taking place within her.

"Do you have battles, Victoria?"

"No, not in the same sense of fighting people, but building courage to help me face some issues."

"Tell me."

"They are not ready for discussion, Mr. Cleeve."

"Why do you persist in saying Mr. Cleeve. My name is Chris. I want you to call me Chris. Let me hear you say 'Chris.' I like you, Victoria."

She ignored him. What of Elizabeth? She became tense. There was a period of silence. If he expected a statement from her, he was disappointed.

"We were talking about some issues you face." He renewed the conversation. "Let me guess what they are. Is one the idea Elizabeth gave you about a shop in London?"

"No."

"Is one your job here at Kensington House?"

"No."

"Is it because you are a young lady with no young man to take your fancy?"

The question shocked her and she turned her head to look into his face. She remembered his eyes that night in the Plymouth inn, fierce they were, and threatening, a warning just before he grabbed and kissed her. They appeared that way now, tense, determined. She felt strength grow back in his arm as it moved down her back, then his arm gripped her side.

A moment ago she wanted him. Now fear was the only emotion. She rolled away from him and stood up, a blast of wind forcing her to take a step away from the edge.

He rose, too, legs akimbo, looking handsome despite the scar, his hair tumbling all about in the wind. "Do I frighten you?" He spoke gently.

"You are a married man, sir." She spoke with conviction.

He stared at her, defeat inscribed on his face. "But an embrace, perhaps a kiss, is no breach of my marriage vows, particularly when I have enjoyed them before."

"Ah, the day on the beach when the boulder fell. I was frightened that day and you protected me. I let you kiss me, for I was still in fear as you held me."

"You enjoyed that kiss, Victoria."

Rain started to fall, first a few drops, then quickly a steady fall. Victoria broke through the hedge, raised the hood of her cloak over her head and ran for the house, upset with her last statement and disturbed by the truth of his statement.

He remained as he stood, his lips forming a tormenting smile.

# Chapter Thirteen

The center of the storm struck later in the morning. Rain pelted down in torrents from a leaden sky, wind blowing it in swirls to pommel window panes. Mostly it fell in transparent curtains at a thirty degree angle. "It looks like a fall of grey spaghetti so constant it is," described one guest looking out a window in the long gallery.

"All living things stay home on a day like this," another guest commented. It was true at Kensington House at that moment, for all guests had forsaken their outdoor flings and were in the long gallery. A number of women were around Victoria as she put the final touches on a cloak.

"Will you be able to get to my gown next, Victoria?" asked a lady with a hopeful tone filtering through her question. "I am sure you are next. Have you chosen your material? Do you have an idea for the design of your gown?" Victoria was pleasant in her questioning although she knew most of the women had no idea at all of what they wanted and left the designing to her.

Other women were playing cards, a new game that was becoming popular in London before they left. It was mainly a quiet group seated around a table, for the shuffling of cards could be heard. It was only when a game was over that there was a discussion about cards held and the manner in which they were played.

Most of the men were gambling, talking loudly and getting angry when they lost. Money was on the table, and it was obvious they all wanted to win. Guy and James stood at a window moaning about their ill fortune at not being able to ride, and occasionally they looked at Victoria trying to get her attention. "I think I'll go over and break up that nest of women. It isn't fair that they take all her time when she should be entertaining us." Sconces of candles lined the west wall providing only passable light to the large, long room. A candelabra sitting on a low table in Victoria's sewing circle made it possible for her to do her work on the dark day.

Mrs. Cleeve walked about making sure her guests were as comfortable and happy as possible, chatting here, laughing with someone there, requesting something from a staff person. It was evident she was enjoying her role as hostess and she was skillful at it.

"I can imagine her entertaining in a London home," Victoria envisioned. "I can just picture a lovely room beautifully decorated, men attending women, women dressed in the latest styles, a hubbub from happy chatter filling the room, and Mrs. Cleeve keeping the party moving so expertly. She is showing her happiest luster when she is with people, amusing them, feting them, providing for them. Her charm shows through every courteous gesture. She is vivacious, so alluring when she is in her element. Her face beams from the excitement. She is the perfect hostess."

Mr. Cleeve had not made an appearance.

"That is their void," Victoria recognized. "She likes people to be around her. He prefers to be alone. Perhaps it is their different backgrounds shinning through. He is not used to the social whirl, and he may not feel comfortable in the glitter. I would guess he thinks it to be artificial or affected, even deceitful. I, too, wonder how genuine some of it is. Their differences add to the conflict they must suffer."

She gave attention to the conversation she heard on every side. It was the usual light banter she had been hearing since the women began collecting near her, who went to parties, what they wore, what men were cheating on what women, wives and mistresses, playing the social game. It went on incessantly.

A flash of lightning lit up the gallery for just a moment, flooding the room with intense light. A mighty clap of thunder directly overhead shook the entire house rattling windows. Everyone froze. There was complete silence. It took a moment for the tension to pass then all started talking at once. The din of voices was calmed immediately by a tremendous battering on the windows. Guests crowded quickly in groups to watch a cloud burst slam into the earth and to listen to the wind dash rain in terrifying cacophony against the panes.

"Here comes a rider!" Guy called out. All eyes went to the horseman, his head and shoulders bent over his black horse's neck, driving against the force of the whirling rain. Down the road approaching the house he came, passing in front, then turning out of sight as he headed for the service area.

Announcement of the noon meal cleared the gallery of all guests, but Victoria kept working, deciding to complete a cloak. The door to the tower room opened and Mrs. Tatham passed through it. "What did you learn about the lights, child?" she asked instantly.

"Nothing. The strong wind had obliterated any foot marks and the sea had washed the beach clear."

"I saw Mr. Cleeve walking in the garden. At first he was with a man who drags his foot. I couldn't see his face well enough to recognize who it was. Their conversation seemed serious. When they separated, Mr. Cleeve walked in your direction. What did he say to you?"

Victoria reflected on the information a moment then replied. "He wanted to know what I was doing. I said I was just enjoying the surf." She paused then commented, "I wonder about the man with the handicap. I have never seen a man of that description about the estate."

"What do you think about the lights?"

"I am not sure. I think they were signals of some kind."

"Tell me when you go searching. I will try to watch out for you. You could be in a graver position if you learn something you shouldn't know."

Victoria looked at the old lady, in a silent voice she asked, "What are you doing here, Mrs. Tatham? I wonder about you. Why would Mr. Cleeve place you in the tower room? From that vantage point you can see most of what goes on and you can report to him. Is it his purpose to have you as a spy?"

"Nothing more is likely to happen for a time. This rain isn't going to let up for a day or so." She turned, opened the door, and passed through it, closing it behind her.

Victoria was left wondering. She sat and contemplated. "Mrs. Tatham is not letting out what she knows, or perhaps she doesn't know a thing and is just making statements."

Mrs. Tatham was right about one thing. The storm continued as she said it would, the wind blowing with a high velocity at times, and the rain falling heavily, rarely letting up. Fortunately the long gallery was proving a boon. Victoria thought that this scene must be similar to those of the past when ladies in farthingales walked up and down, their extended skirts taking up so much space.

Following lunch Mrs. Cleeve was able to make a special announcement. She clapped her hands to get everyone's attention then when murmuring ceased she spoke loudly, "We have a unique treat for you. We know you miss the London theaters, so Christopher has brought London to you. He has invited a troupe of players from

Plymouth to present Mr. Shakespeare's HAMLET to us right here on the stage of the Kensington House theater. We can't tell you the exact night the players will be here since our weather will determine that. As soon as travel permits, you will be entertained.

There was a clapping of hands at the announcement. Anticipation of a play created immediately a new interest, and conversation turned to the theaters of London, the popular playwrights, actors, actresses and experiences the guests had attending plays. "I am so glad the king returned to his throne. It was dreadful during Mr. Cromwell's Commonwealth," one lady expressed herself. "Puritans would have nothing to do with the stage and they closed our theaters. I understand, though, that some troupes went to the shires where they presented plays in barns. Of course the whole troupe ran the risk of being put in prison."

"Now even women are appearing in roles written for women," Lady Arlington reported. "In former days, remember, boys took those roles. I like the idea of women on the stage. It is about time we grew up. After all it is 1665 and we need to be modern."

"I agree," spoke a voice in support. "Some of the actresses as they are called are quite good."

"And some end up in the king's boudoir," a man quipped. "Look at those we see invited to court. Nell Gwynn for instance."

"Maybe they are trained to do more than act," someone called out. The jibe stimulated laughter.

"So be it. I always enjoy very much going to the King's company in Drury Lane on an afternoon, seeing a play and watching the audience," a man expressed himself with conviction.

"And pinching the buttocks of orange girls. Tell the whole story," a voice rang out. There was more laughter.

"I always want to see who comes to the theater," said a lady patting her hand on her knee. "The king so often brings Lady Castlemaine, and she is perturbed when His Majesty shows interest in any other young lady. Everybody wants to be noticed by the king."

"I am for the king sponsoring the Royal Theater. I do believe it has the best company and the best presentations," another man offered.

The great hall was selected by Mrs. Cleeve as the playhouse because it could be warmed and the acoustics were better than those in the long gallery. It was given a good cleaning, chairs were set up, and the Cleeves invited some neighbors.

On the morning of the second day, the rain let up, and by afternoon the sun was shinning. Puddles did not last long, and Kensington House drive was clearing. "The Plymouth road will be drying, and I am sure the troupe will arrive tomorrow. They can present the play after supper," Mrs. Cleeve informed everyone.

Victoria was happy with the prospect of attending a play. "It will be a special occasion for me," she informed her mistress. "I have never seen a play."

"It may be the first for this old house, too, I do believe. Come, guests are gathering in the great hall."

"Oh, it is beautiful!" Victoria exclaimed as she entered. A fire burned in the huge fireplace, and candles in brass sconces and hanging chandeliers made stone walls glow with warmth. Mrs. Cleeve was introducing Victoria to some neighbors when Mr. Cleeve appeared. It was the first time she had seen him since their meeting on the bluff. "Good evening, Victoria. I have a friend for you to meet." He gave no sign that he recalled their brief encounter. "He has had eyes on you since you entered the hall. Victoria, this is Jonathan."

She looked up to a handsome, smiling face, perfect teeth except for a slightly protruding incisor tooth and glowing eyes that appeared too anxious. "Our loveliest ladies come from the west country," he beamed. "But tell me, Miss Victoria, why haven't I met you before?"

"Why, sir, I have only recently come to Kensington House."

"Too bad you did not arrive sooner, although I have not been here too long myself. My past should have had you in it. My future certainly shall. Please walk with me in the garden after the play."

"In the dark. That is not possible, sir. We have just met. And please know I am avowed."

"That cannot be! Where is he? I must change your status. Now! The gravity expressed in Jonathan's voice reflected the alarm he felt. To himself he said, "I cannot lose her! I just found her!"

"He is not here. He is calling for me shortly to take me to his home." Victoria's calm response was in sharp contrast to the young man's emotional utterance.

"I shall intercept him. Why, Victoria, I just met you. You cannot go out of my life." He put his hand on her arm and gave it a squeeze to accent his feelings. Suddenly realizing his forwardness he stated softly, "Oh, Victoria. Forgive me. At least sit next to me during the play."

As he spoke a tinkle of bells announced the play was about to begin. Quickly Jonathan took Victoria's hand and although she protested with a shrug, he directed her to a chair and seated himself next to her. The troupe had placed screens about one end of the hall to form a dressing room and reserved a larger area for the stage. One of the group came forward to introduce the play, describing the plot briefly, and told about the historic Castle of Helsingors in Denmark which became Elsinor in Mr. Shakespeare's play. The troupe appeared and each member was introduced in the role to be acted. The setting of the first act was given and the play began.

When Hamlet entered, Jonathan's hand sought Victoria's. She protested silently, but to avoid a scene of her own, capitulated to his efforts. She felt him looking at her instead of the play.

"It is remarkable," Victoria thought, "how the players present illusions by the use of a chair or table, a curtain, or a gesture to accompany the spoken word."

Costumes were simple and properties minimal but skillfully made to be used interchangeably.

During intermission, Victoria's eye was attracted to the gallery by a sudden movement. It appeared to have been caused by a person withdrawing through the door at the rear of the gallery. Hair on the head was grey, and instantly she assumed it was Mrs. Tatham. "Good for her. She, too, has never seen a play."

Guy and James came over to her, Jonathan was introduced, and the brothers scolded her for not sitting with them. Smiling in reply, Jonathan said, "Give a tired, soaked horseman a chance."

"Were you the rider we saw fighting the rain?" Guy asked. "We wondered how you made it. That was too much of a storm for any one to challenge. Must have been important business you were on."

"The storm looked worse than it was."

After the four had discussed the ride, Jonathan turned to speak to Victoria but she had gone. A cursory search about the room revealed nothing. When the next act began, she did not take a chair next to him, next to the brothers, or anywhere. Had he looked up at the gallery he would have seen her.

Relieved of his annoyances, Victoria gave full attention to the players and concentrated on their lines. The death of Hamlet's father prompted her to think of her own father's death, and she wondered if the tales she had heard about his murder could be true. "Hamlet learned the truth from a ghost. I wonder if I shall learn the truth and how it will be presented to me."

As soon as the play ended, Victoria hurried upstairs, but her plan to escape his attentions failed. She no sooner entered her room when a knock was heard. Before she could reply, the door opened. Jonathan walked in, his eyes finding her at the foot of the bed.

"Victoria. Forgive me. I had to see you. Please, let me talk to you."

"You forget, sir. You are a gentleman. You violate the courtesy of your host by coming into this room. Please leave." Her voice was adamant.

"Please. Let me talk with you. I must. I have never seen anyone like you. You put me on fire. Those eyes of yours." He walked as he spoke. "Just let me look at you."

"Stay where you are"

He stood directly before her. She looked up at the face, appearing determined. Shortly his hands came up to take hold of each of her arms. He drew her to him as he looked loving at her. He kissed her gently, then hardened his kiss, pressing into her lips.

She tried to withhold a response, but she discerned herself giving in. She felt him pushing her backward to the bed immediately behind her. In the quiet of the moment, she heard scratching.

Scratching! She! He! Both were in full view of the peek hole! Awareness returned her senses, and she pushed him back, away from her.

As she did so he released her, and she took a step away from the bed and turned, putting her back to the mirror. He reached for her, placing his hand on her shoulders. Expecting him to grab her again, she struck him hard on his chest. The blow was unexpected, and as he stepped backward he pulled on the shoulder of the gown, ripping it so that it fell away, exposing her left breast and back.

The sight of her breast inflamed him and he came to her, eyes directed fiercely at it. This time she pulled her arms across her breasts as if to protect them but stumbled within his arms as they reached around her waist. She dropped her head into his chest to avoid another kiss.

Suddenly he relaxed his hold, his stare directed at the mirror. Quickly he turned her around and looked at her back. "That mark!" He stared for a moment, strode out of the room, slamming the door behind him.

In minutes the sound of hooves on the driveway grabbed her attention. She hurried to the window and looking out, caught sight of a rider on a black horse speeding on the road leading away from Kensington House.

# Chapter Fourteen

Servants, staff and service workers were all discussing Brixton Village Fair with great anticipation and their enthusiasm reached the guests. Any hopes Mrs. Cleeve had of keeping the fair a secret and then offering it as a big surprise to her guests were dashed

"For our ladies from London, this will be their first country fair," Mrs. Cleeve informed Victoria. "Most have been to Bartholomew and Southwark Fairs, but they know that this one in Brixton Village will be different. They also know that all fairs around London have been cancelled for the duration of the plague. That thought alone will make ours very attractive to them. Even our male guests are excited after listening to discussions in the service area, Christopher tells me.

"Since I can't surprise them with the fair, I can ask them to help me with a project. I accepted the vicar's offer to make articles for the church booth, something that could be sold to produce money for restoring the church's Norman tower."

Mrs. Cleeve assembled the women in the long gallery around Victoria and presented the vicar's proposal. She was surprised when they accepted the challenge since they had never been asked to do such a thing. "We need to decide what we can do," she added. As the women talked about possibilities their enthusiasm grew, and they listed several ideas. Of all those presented, they decided on lavender sachets, draw string bags and garlands of herbs tied with ribbons and lace.

Lavender and herbs were available in the garden, Victoria had lace and ribbons for the sachets and materials for bags were on the floor of the sewing area.

It was organized so that some of the women would collect lavender and herbs and make garlands, others would make sachets and the rest would make bags.

Victoria had to teach the use of a needle to all sewers, but their eagerness made them avid learners. She also demonstrated how ribbon could be used to tie herbs together in an attractive manner. Having learned the basic skills, the women went to work, and the long gallery became a factory.

Stories about Southward and Bartholomew Fairs were told by those who had attended in former years, and laughter grew when a mare horse that counted money was described. But there was greater interest as Lady Arlington recalled a visit Queen Catherine made to the fair last year. "She attracted much attention, but she and her ladies in waiting looked rather drab. Even though it was August, her colors were dark, and she appeared to be unimpressed with what see saw. She didn't stay long."

"That is not like the king," a voice interjected. "He loves fairs. He is so jovial. And the ladies in his entourage looked so dashing in their bright colors. The king played some games and laughed with the people as he walked about. He is gaining favor as the people see him participate in their activities."

It was decided that for the three days of the fair, all estate employees would have a holiday, only the most necessary chores being scheduled. It was also decided that on the first day all guests and employees would go as a group to the fair grounds, riding in wagons from Kensington House. On the remaining days, guests and help would go to the fair on their own as they liked.

At nine o'clock of the appointed day, wagons filled with guests and estate personnel. The sun was bright and warm with only a few fleecy clouds spotting a blue sky. A clownish spirit was already moving among the revelers as merry chatter was punctuated by joyous laughter and shouts. To add to this festive mood, someone had placed bows and ribbons on horse trappings. As the parade moved out, singing started, and one after another, folk songs were sung, lasting all the way to the village.

This was a new experience for the Londoners, and they soon became caught up with the spirit of revelry, joining in singing when they knew a country tune and introducing songs known to the city people.

The parade of wagons entered the village in jubilation, their occupants waving arms and cheering in loud voices to announce their arrival. Villagers waved back with shouts of recognition and welcome. They had mounted flags along Plymouth Road, and the entrance to the inn was covered with bunting.

The wagons passed through the village to the fair grounds where drivers found an area designated for them. Nearby was a lot reserved for housing booth operators, sellers and other workers. Some wagons already parked belonged to professional fair participants who had built permanent houselike structures on flat bed wagons and painted their names on the sides of their mobile homes. They, as itinerants, moved from country fairs to market days in towns and cities. Washed clothes had been placed on bushes and hedgerows to dry. Fireplaces had been created by placing stones together, and pots, totally blackened, were sitting on top. Older children were caring for younger ones as they played with dogs.

The large group from Kensington House broke up, individual interests scattering them to various parts of the fair. Their only agreement was that all would meet at the wagons at sundown for the trip home.

Victoria paired with Mrs. Cleeve for a get acquainted tour. While joining in the gay spirit of the occasion, she subconsciously kept alert for anyone who might recognize her or she them. She had done what she could to change her appearance from the fifteen year old the villagers knew three years ago to the young lady of today by wearing braids wound attractively about her head and painting her face.

Although the morning was still young, numbers of people were milling about. Brixton Village fair was a well established tradition, and families throughout the west country planned well in advance for the event. Some stayed the three scheduled days, camping on the grounds. Others stayed part time. For many the fair was the one major event of the year that gave people an opportunity to change routines, meet others, renew friendships, do things they would not do at home, and spend money that should not be spent except that this was a fair and money was needed for a good time.

"I didn't see Mr. Cleeve in any of the wagons," Victoria commented as they entered the fair grounds. "Is he not coming?"

"He had to take care of some business this morning. He will be here this afternoon. He purchased a horse from Lord Covington and wants to show it in some activities. He thinks that will be great sport."

The mention of Lord Covington brought a picture of Edward to mind. Her heart leaped up in pleasure at the thought of her lover, and she imagined him next to her, laughing gaily, enjoying activities, eating a pasty, trying his luck in horse showmanship, walking arm in arm and sneaking kisses throughout the day. "Oh, Edward! When are you coming for me?" she kept asking as thoughts of him burned at her aching heart. At times the wanting of him was almost too much to bear. Now her yearning was at the breaking point. "When?"

"Let's see if our handiwork is selling at the church booth," Mrs. Cleeve suggested. The proposal came at a moment when tears were forming in Victoria's eyes, but she forced a smile in agreement.

The two passed among the crowd and approached the booth, a simple temporary structure with a broad counter. Above was a painted sign announcing "Brixton Village Church." Women were in front of it, and one was buying a draw string bag. A pleased Mrs. Cleeve was smiling. "She likes what we made. Let's see what was made by other women. Perhaps I can find something to buy."

At that moment Victoria saw Mrs. Battey. Quickly she maneuvered herself to stand next to Mrs. Cleeve, selecting an item from the counter to inspect, and lowered her head to avoid recognition by the former housekeeper at Castelamer. A voice called out, "Good day, Mrs. Battey. It has been years. How are you?" greeted Mrs. Maitland. "I haven't seen you since you left Castelamer. I knew you left the big house, and then I heard you moved to Falmouth."

"Ah, Castelamer. I often think about those years with the Framsdens," Mrs. Battey reminisced. "When the new owners came, they wanted a completely new staff, so I went to my brother's. That last year at Castelamer was sad with those two girls."

"You were so upset. I remember. You looked for that one. I don't remember her name."

"That was Patience. I still think that one was so upset seeing her sister die that her brain collapsed and she wandered off. One day someone will find her body. The other was Pen. ... ."

"I like this fancy tatting, Victoria. It is well done. I could use it in my bedroom." Mrs. Cleeve was speaking right at her, breaking into Mrs. Battey's comments." I want to come back and buy some." To the lady behind the counter she added a louder voice, "Please save this for me until this afternoon. I am Mrs. Cleeve."

Victoria could have melted on the spot. There was dead silence from Mrs. Battey and Mrs. Maitland although Victoria could feel their stares. "Turn your back to them, she told herself. "Look down." As she followed her directions, she heard Mrs. Battey's soft voice say," "That's her," in a contemptible tone referring to Mrs. Cleeve.

"Let's do some more looking. I may find something else I like." The pleasure in Mrs. Cleeve's voice was obvious. As they walked along, Victoria considered Mrs. Battey's comments. "So that is what the villagers think. Wandered off. Dead." The knowledge disturbed her, for she realized once more she had caused worry and heartache for some, added work for those who searched for her, and anxieties for those who knew her and still wondered.

The more she thought the more she wished the conversation between the two women had gone on, for they may have spoken of the Framsdens.

Beyond the sales booth a puppet show was being presented in a small portable theater. Children gathered on the ground in front of it, and a large number of adults stood behind them. Puppets were dressed like knights and ladies from the Middle Ages. The story was about a bad knight who stole a lady, and a good knight who was in pursuit on a white charger. The children were grossly involved with their feelings being expressed by hand clapping and shouting whenever the good knight had some success. Victoria and Mrs. Cleeve joined in applauding and contributing to a hat when it was passed around.

The entertainment section of the fair had a variety of interesting booths, each charging admission. A few booths presented samples of the show inside by letting the public on the outside see an intriguing act free. One was a monkey doing stunts on a rope, At another booth, one man held in his arms a goose with four feet and yelled out, "See these amazing wonders. A horse with hoofs like a ram's horns. A rooster with two heads. A goat with two bodies." A trained dog show looked interesting, so the two went inside to a large area enclosed by tall folding screens. In the center was a roped off section forming an area within which the dogs performed. People stood outside ropes to watch the dogs do a variety of stunts, some quite complicated.

A sound of music took their interest. Approaching was a marching group of musicians, four men dressed as buffoons, three hopping about forcing little bells on their multicolored suits and hats to jingle. One man beat on a large drum held in front of him while on a rhythmic note he struck a cymbal or blew on a horn attached to a wire collar. Two other men strummed on stringed instruments as the fourth man danced wildly as he shook a tambourine. At a signal they broke out in a rollicking folk song, loud, joyful music that motivated hand clapping in unison and jigging on the part of some in the audience.

The food section was particularly appealing with its variety of inviting aromas, most specializing in one or two kinds of foods. There was leg of mutton hot pie with crusts baked to a golden brown, meat and kidney pie prepared in small, individual servings, pasties loaded with mutton, potatoes and peas, and of course at this time of the year, strawberries and double cream.

As they walked along, Mrs. Cleeve became aware of two young men following them. "Let's see what they will do. Be nonchalant, but be receptive."

Each man was in his early twenties. They were tall, lean and obviously out for a good time. They laughed noisily at their own wit, whistled, and finally drew close enough so that the women could hear their comments. "You take the short one. I'll take the tall one. How old do you think they are? Yours is a looker. You speak first."

There was a quiet moment. Victoria looked up to see one of the men matching strides and walking along with her. The other was next to Mrs. Cleeve. "Good afternoon," he spoke in greeting.

"Why, hello."

"Hello, Miss," Victoria's man said rather timidly.

"Hello to you," she acknowledged, ready to say goodbye to both of them, not savoring this action too well, but she decided to let Mrs. Cleeve take the lead. It was apparent that not only did her employer enjoy this tete a tete, but she was experienced in it.

"Are you enjoying the fair?" He was bolder than his friend, but experience was lacking.

"Oh, it is a marvelous fair," she responded with a lilt in her voice. She was making an effort to act younger than her age, so it seemed to Victoria. "Are you Cornish men?"

"Indeed we are. From Chadcombe. And you?

"Brixton Village. Will you be here long?"

"Just as long as it takes for us to get well acquainted with the both of you." His courage was mounting.

"What have you seen of the fair?" Victoria's man asked.

"We have been walking through the sales booths and entertainment sections and we had something to eat."

"You haven't seen much." Mrs. Cleeve's man saw an opening. "Let's watch the archers. I have a friend in the competition." He took her arm and nodded to Victoria's man to do the same.

"My name is John. What is yours?"

"It is Liz and this is Vicky."

Mrs. Cleeve looked at Victoria and winked, her smile revealing the good time she was having. Victoria was aghast, but because Mrs. Cleeve was enjoying the lark, she reluctantly participated.

"And my name is Mark."

A short distance along they came to a grassy area where targets had been organized. Archers were lined up along a restraining line taking practice aim at them some seventy-five feet away.

"The second man in the lineup is my friend. He has been practicing at his farm for well on a year. Each man pays to enter the competition then the money is divided among the top four men," John explained. "The winner of the Brixton Village contest is considered to be the best in Cornwall. There were so many this year who wanted to win that six rounds had to be arranged. This is the final one."

On order the men raised their bows slowly upward. Instantly after the second order, there was a staccato of zings as fingers released taut strings and arrows flew freely in a trajectory aimed at the targets. Loud pops were heard as their points tore into the targets. There were several bulls eyes.

Competitors shot three rounds then score keepers took a reading of the targets. After a period of study, the first four leaders were announced amid applause. A single target was then prepared.

"Now the final four will take turns at the one target," John continued explaining. "Best score wins." The audience had grown larger and there were shouts of encouragement. "Ready!" The first man shot. By the time John's friend shot fourth, the center circle was crowded with a forest of arrows. But practice was paying off, for his arrows found their mark to increase the collection at the bulls eye.

Two score keepers approached the target, took careful readings, recorded the findings and totaled scores. They were brought to a judge who announced the winners. John's friend was second best and was given a package with cash in it.

"I am getting tired," Mrs. Cleeve said.

"How about a rest after all this," John proposed, slipping his hand into hers and drawing her through the disbursing crowd, she following willingly. Victoria felt her hand taken by Mark and off she went, reluctantly, not wanting to keep up.

John led them to a grassy area spotted by trees creating inviting shade. He motioned Mrs. Cleeve to sit next to him. "What does he have on his mind?" she thought, recalling unhappy, violent experiences of the past. "If he gets fresh I shall have to be violent, too." Mark watched John and copied his friend's actions. He planted an elbow on the turf and rested his head on the raised hand. This position he discovered gave opportunity to look at Victoria and to reach out to touch her. He began running his fingers across her back then down her side. She glared at Mrs. Cleeve only to see John maneuvering his hand across her leg. She was giggling like a little girl at what he was saying to her. Victoria felt abhorrence. "And she a married woman. It must be the London way, like flirtations at court."

Mark's hand found Victoria's leg and started roaming. She pushed it away but said nothing. Before long his hand was active again, Mark saying nothing, just looking at her, his eyes dancing. Victoria had seen that look before in other eyes. Oh, yes, more than once, and she knew what would follow. She was considering slapping Mark's face if he attempted anything and looked about to avoid his pleading glare. She saw Cleeve. "Oh, Mrs. Cleeve. There is your husband," she warned.

Mrs. Cleeve reacted with a horrified look. Immediately she jumped up, straightened her gown, and spoke to John. Surprise spread over his face, then fear. Instantly he shouted, "Mark, come on. Let's get out of here," jumping up as he spoke. Mark rose at once and joined his friend trotting off and into the crowd.

Victoria got up, pulled her gown into place, then felt Mrs. Cleeve slip her arm inside hers. "Let's catch up to Christopher," she smiled. He was just ahead walking in the crowd. Mrs. Cleeve left her, stepped ahead, and from the rear pushed her arm through his. Surprised countenance changed to recognition when he looked down on her. "Where's Victoria?" he asked at once. At that moment she matched steps with them. "Here," she announced.

"Good. How would you two like to see the horsemanship competition and horse jumping? George is going to work the horse we got from Lord Covington. I want to see how good that expensive piece of horse flesh is."

Mrs. Cleeve did not express an opinion, but Victoria spoke enthusiastically. "That should be interesting. Who trained the horse?"

"Lord Covington's stable people. They are supposed to be good. We shall find out," he clipped, appearing to have some doubts.

Horses entered in horsemanship competition were guided through a series of skills and judged on their ability to do the tasks. One by one they performed such assignments as side step walking, executing a tight circle, prancing to a set rhythm, rising on hind legs to paw the air with front legs, demonstrating a variety of gaits and bowing.

His horse did reasonably well for a first competition, but Cleeve was disappointed. "Well, maybe he will do better in jumping." He did, finishing first. Under skilled guidance by George, he took all jumps, knocking over only one barrier. Cleeve felt great pleasure in the victory for not only was he congratulated by Cornish horsemen whose respect he sought as a newcomer, but he would build some reputation for his stable, a status in the west country.

"That takes care of all the business for me," said Cleeve. "Now your choice. What shall it be?" There was silence. Victoria waited for Mrs. Cleeve to make a suggestion but none came. "How would you like to see Lord Arlington in the shooting competition?" Cleeve proposed.

Mrs. Cleeve gasped. "Not Talbot! Fancy him competing at a country fair. Let's do. What will her ladyship say to that, especially if he loses."

"I doubt if she'll mind. He got so excited over the idea of competing that we had to take him back to the house for his guns and ammunition. He is a big little boy in his enthusiasm."

Victoria noticed Mr. Cleeve nodding in recognition as he saw people he knew, and she thought that in the two years he had been at Kensington House, he was having success in establishing himself. He stopped a moment to shake hands with a man dressed in the manner of a gentleman farmer. "Hello, Geoffrey. Enjoying the fair?"

"Yes, I am, Christopher. Just bought some sheep. How are you?"

"You know Elizabeth. Meet Victoria, Elizabeth's companion."

"Hello, Elizabeth. How do you do, Victoria."

Victoria looked into an interesting face, square in design, lean with high cheek bones well defined, and a chin with corners like a box, a cleft in the middle. Eyes were dark, deeply set below busy, black brows. The complexion was dark, too, due possibly, she thought, to work in the sun. He looked down at her from a six foot frame, well proportioned. "The face looks familiar. I shall have to recall why."

"Join us, Geoffrey. We are off to the shooting competition. One of our guests is entered."

"Why, thank you. I would like to." He stepped next to Victoria and the two walked behind the Cleeves. "Are you from these parts, Victoria?" His voice was deep, warm and had the quality of authority.

"I was born and raised in the west country, but I came to Kensington House only recently. Do you live nearby."

"Not far away. My land has a common boundary with Cleeve's estate. What do you think of the fair?"

Victoria liked Geoffrey's voice, the resonant quality giving it interest. "It is large, so many people, and such interesting activities. But I haven't seen all of it yet."

"May I ask to be your guide after we see the shooting competition?" His question was prompted by more than just a feeling of politeness. He was experiencing a growing interest in the girl next to him.

"That is very generous of you, Geoffrey. I accept."

A crowd gathered in back of a restraining line along the shooting range. Competition was already well underway, and Cleeve learned from Lord Arlington that he had his first round of firing. "You have some excellent shots in Cornwall," he granted. "I barely made it into the finals, and I am a pretty good shot myself."

"Remember, Talbot, these west country men shoot for food, not just for sport. Hunting means meat on their tables. They have to be accurate. You are good, too, Talbot. Let them know it."

"I have to uphold the honor of London. I can't have country people beat me," he laughed.

Lord Arlington was better in the finals. He took more time aiming and put his three shots within the bulls eye. Each competitor did the same, making judging very difficult. After measuring carefully and deliberately, it was announced that Lord Arlington placed second, a man from Terice beating him by only a fraction.

Applause rewarded the winners, and Lord Arlington raised his winnings over his head and amid a broad smile, invited everyone to an ale. It was obvious he was having a fine time.

"Now, Victoria, what shall it be?" Geoffrey had not forgotten his promised role as a guide, for he wanted to get to know Victoria better. He held out an angled arm in invitation, and she slipped hers inside. It was a good feeling. "I appreciate the attention of a gentleman, properly introduced, and one who doesn't immediately want to begin pawing at me," she mused.

"Have you seen the animals?"

"No, I haven't. I would like to see them."

Geoffrey led the way in and out of surging people. Victoria at one time saw John and Mark attempting to engage two girls in conversation. As she passed, Mark looked up, smiled first in recognition, then looked bewildered as he realized she was well entwined on the arm of a man. Across his face was written his thinking, "My competition! How comes he succeeds?" She nodded a greeting then looked at Geoffrey.

"Have you always lived near Brixton Village?"

"Yes and no. I was born in my present home, but seven years ago I was sent to an uncle. It was thought I could learn to be a better farmer by taking instruction from him. I returned to my home about two years ago. My parents gave me their farm and went to Falmouth to live."

"I was living in Exeter. I met Mrs. Cleeve there and she asked me to be her companion. You have known Mr. Cleeve long, then."

"No. We met one day while he and I were riding. I like him. He is interested enough to become a good farmer. He has asked me for my opinion, and I have made some suggestions. It is unusual for a Londoner to come here and want to be a practicing farmer. Most men of means are the absent type, only coming here for short periods of time to get away from the city. The reason I asked where you lived before coming here is that your face reminds me of twins, girls who lived at Castelamer with the Framsdens. It is the fair that makes me think so, for before they went, the Framsdens put the two girls in my care for a day at the fair."

Victoria almost said, "Oh yes, I remember!" but she caught herself and thought, "It is true. I must have been nine or ten then, and the Framsdens had to go to Plymouth on business. This big boy took us to the fair." Aloud she said, "I hope we can see some baby animals."

"We might just arrange that. Let's look." As he guided her about the animal area, he felt himself warming to this young lady. "She is sweet, gentle, very appealing. I like her company. It is nice to have an attractive girl on my arm. Those eyes! They are turning me inside out. She has a love of animals, something very necessary in a farmer's wife." The idea of a wife caught him unaware. He had not been consciously seeking someone to marry, but the thought of one made him realize he was in need of a companion and that Victoria was a possibility. "I shall pursue this consideration," he promised himself. "Look! What do you think of this, Victoria? Brand new."

Below them on the ground was a huge, fat brown sow stretched out on her side, exposing her nipples to twelve little ones, all hungry, all squirming to feed. Geoffry reached down, picked up one and handed it to her. "Oh, it's sweet," she murmured, snuggling the tiny bundle while it squealed in protest. She put her finger in its mouth and he sucked on it, but only for a moment. "He is such a dear. Ah, put him back. He must be hungry."

There were other little ones mingled among adults, lambs, calves, and Victoria had to stop to pet or pick up a few including a little kid that liked her attention. "I think if 1 had a farm I would find a way to keep all babies from growing up just so I could love them. But then that is not practical, is it?"

"No, Victoria, it is not. I think you need a pet. How would you like a baby something? What shall it be? A little kid?"

"Oh, yes, but how shall I keep it?"

"An idea. When I have some kids, you may make a choice, we shall call it Vicky, and it is yours. You may leave it on my farm, but it will require your visits and some loving." Geoffrey thought the idea would bring her to his farm and a further opportunity to get acquainted.

"Accepted!"

"Another idea. How would you like something to eat?"

"I would like strawberries and double cream."

"Strawberries and double cream it shall be." He spoke enthusiastically and the deep voice was tinged with pleasure, yet to Victoria it had a touch of command. "Our strawberries are the best, and with double cream they are God's gift to Cornwall." Geoffrey's smile revealed his happy feeling, and he took her hand to guide her among people swarming about the food booths.

"How different his hand is compared with Mark's. Geoffrey's is so firm and confident, the roughness revealing the hand's hard labor, the clasp telling me of his interest. It does feel good in mine," she admitted to herself. "This is how I shall feel with Edward next to me. When he comes for me we shall walk like this, hand in hand, an expression of our love."

"Two strawberries with double cream," he ordered. They found a place on the grass to sit, and Victoria expressed her appreciation. "Do you grow strawberries on your farm?"

"Yes, we do. But somehow these seem better perhaps because I am eating them with you," he said looking directly at her. "I enjoy your company, Victoria. I hope you will let me call on you at Kensington House."

Victoria hesitated answering because she was avowed to Edward, and she did not want to violate her pledge by agreeing to see another man. After a moment she responded. "It is difficult to say because of the Cleeve's guests and my responsibility to Mrs. Cleeve as her companion. Perhaps at a time when I am not needed, and I can let you know."

"That is alright. I understand. I shall be patient." He smiled, giving her the feeling he knew he would call on her.

They chatted for a while then both noticed the sun sinking. "I must return to the wagons. Everyone agreed to meet at sunset to return home," she explained.

"I must not tarry either. A farmer lives by the sun, and there are a few chores to do this evening. Thank you for a lovely afternoon." He put his hand on hers for a moment then he helped her to her feet.

"It is I who thanks you. I appreciate your skill as a guide, and you must not forget my unborn pet."

They walked along, he not letting go of her hand, and she not wanting him to. At the wagons he stopped to speak to a few people then took his leave. She watched him go and felt a strange longing. "Stop that, Victoria. You have Edward."

The ride home was far less boisterous, for everyone had a busy day and fatigue was evident. There was a comparison of experiences, some showing what they had purchased, and then Victoria noticed that Mr. Cleeve was not present. She wondered why. A feeling of loneliness fell over her as she thought about Mrs. Cleeve and the need she must have for her husband at this moment. "Going home without the man who is one's own to touch, to embrace, to share love in the fading light of day is a lost time." She thought of Edward.

Then the face of Geoffrey appeared in her thinking. "He is on his way home. He has no one either, no one to call his own." Almost immediately she felt a tug in his direction. "Strange," she thought, "why him? It is Edward I should be thinking of. But, Geoffrey was so sweet to me today."

As she prepared for bed she thought again of Geoffrey. Little did she know that this man who had just entered her life would remain for a while.

# Chapter Fifteen

Continuously reminding Victoria of her promise to ride with them, Guy and James finally inveigled a definite commitment for a date. She did not want to go, but she decided it would be easier to agree to a date, get it over with, and not be harangued by their nagging.

The morning designated proved to be overcast, damp and threatening. She dressed warmly in a woolen skirt, heavy jacket, and arranged a colorful scarf around her neck. The boys were waiting for her at the stables and both greeted her warmly. The master of horse had selected a beautiful black stallion, finely groomed, with metal shinning on the harness. As he led the horse out of his stall to her, Victoria felt a resurgence of interest in the sport. "We call him Socrates, Miss," the master informed her. "He is gentle, but he likes to take the rein. Just let him know you are in command. He'll respond to your commands."

Victoria patted Socrates' warm, sleek neck, saying his name and talking to him lovingly. He moved his head quietly as if he enjoyed the attention. It was the odor mainly that evoked the past. When a child, Victoria helped feed horses, wash them and rake stalls. Later she was allowed to exercise them and then she took riding lessons. Soon she was on her own, running horses about the countryside.

A call of "Let's go, Victoria!" from Guy broke her reverie. The three took a lane leading to the Forest of Leigh. It was hardly a forest in the pure sense. Perhaps in the long, long past trees were taller, grew more densely and covered a greater area, but the name did not matter. After the rain, odors were of spice and musk, and the floor oozed a bit as Socrates trod on the wet cushion of leaves formed by tree droppings during the passing of years. The sun penetrated lightly, creating muted shadows. She let the boys choose the way, controlling herself enough to remember that she must in no way give them a clue that she was on familiar territory. They were no strangers here either, for they had been riding at every opportunity.

A fresh salt breeze wafting her face was refreshing, wiping away thoughts of an antagonist, the annoying scratching, and the charade of cover up she was having to play. She felt herself alone, for as the lane curled among the trees, the boys were often out of sight. "It is just wonderful to be alive!" she laughed aloud.

She followed the boys as they entered meadows surrounding some ruins. She reined, dismounted and joined them where they stood on a pile of grey rocks, some of which long ago had been squared and polished.

"This is all that is left of Eyton St. Mary's Abbey we are told," James volunteered. "Monks of the Cistercian Order built the abbey and had a large community until Henry Eighth dissolved it. He took the property as crown land, then later a portion of it was given to the Castelamer family by Queen Elizabeth for devoted service to the crown in the struggle against Spain."

"The ruins are beautiful!" Victoria exclaimed, covering the fact that she knew them well.

"Guy can tell all about this abbey. He asked some farmer who was here one day and got a complete story.

"You are sitting on a column that supported the nave ceiling," Guy began, acting very much the tutor. "The transept stood there with the chancel and altar beyond. If you will follow me, I shall point out the other parts of the abbey."

With that, James broke into laughter. "Come off it, Guy. Victoria does not want to hear all that. Let's just sit here and talk. I want to make plans for taking Victoria to London."

"Of course. Let's go to London, Victoria. You will love it." Guy was exuberant. "If you enjoyed the play in the great hall, wait until you see plays in the theaters of London. The orange girls are cheeky, and the actresses! Mmmmmmm!"

"We have many parties. We'll take you to the best, only the best." James was getting enthusiastic. "You will meet Edward. He is a gay blade, quiet until he gets going. The women love him and he does make out. He's jolly good fun."

"But he is not for Victoria. She is ours."

"Of course," James agreed. "By the bys, Victoria, remember the rider who came in on the storm? We had a long talk with him in the stables. He gets to London all the time. He gets to places we have not even heard of."

"Now, James. Those are not for Victoria."

Victoria had not seen or heard of Jonathan since he stamped out of her room. "I still cannot understand why he left me so suddenly," she mused. "Fortunate for me. I truly expected a fight on my hands."

"Will you go with us, Victoria?" she heard James say, stopping reverie.

"We'll see." As she spoke the first drops of rain fell on them. "Best be getting the horses back," she suggested. "I must work, you know."

The ride over, she went to the long gallery and started sewing on the last gown ordered. While she worked, women gathered around her as they always did on inclement days. Mrs. Cleeve joined the group and very shortly heard her say, "Have you heard the latest about Edward?"

175

"You mean Edward, the notorious grandson of Lord Covington?" someone asked.

Victoria heard Edward's name and instantly stopped work. Her first thought was that he was injured.

"What girl is in trouble now?" another asked

"You shall know," Mrs. Cleeve continued. "The rider whom you saw approach the house on that awful stormy day had just arrived from Lord Covington's office. He had all the news. The old man is greatly agitated. Edward has asked permission to marry. The girl is of the working class."

Victoria blanched.

"Well, the girl is pregnant and her father is furious. The townspeople are with the girl's father, even to the point of threatening Edward's life. Edward is fearful they are serious. Lord Covington conceded so Edward is to become a husband and a father."

Victoria sat stunned. The accusations continued.

"It is time his escapades caught up with him," she heard someone comment.

"His approach is always the same. He appears gentle, convinces the innocent girl she is his first love, promises marriage, then after she capitulates, he drops her. His reputation is all over London."

"That must be how he was exploiting his unknowing countryside."

"He only does what all the other gay blades do."

"Those of us who know should tell all the truth. Edward takes after his grandfather."

The rest was lost. Victoria slipped her needle into a cloth, got up unobtrusively, went to her room, closed the door, strolled to the window and became involved with her thoughts. "My love, my true love. Edward. You could not have done what they say you did. How beautiful you were, so gentle, so loving. Your touch was so tender. I have imagined the beauty of our lives together, complete devotion, you for me, I for you. Oneness. Enduring.

"I cannot believe you were not sincere. But I should have read the clues, comments Mr. Cleeve made and those of the boys. No word from you. I waited in vain. You never intended to come for me. So you talked with maidens, convinced them of your love, that it was your first. That is what you said to me. Your gentleness deceived me. You took me completely. I was yours and you made me believe it. Victoria, you were a fool. What was that vow in the cathedral? You broke it and now you are paying for it.

"Now I must think of leaving Kensington House. I had intended to stay only until Edward called for me anyway. I certainly cannot stay beyond the time when the guests leave.

"It is not my intention to remain unmarried. I do not see many gentlemen bachelors vying for my hand, however. I need to be where I can be seen by eligible men so I can make a selection. I should go to London. London certainly has a quantity of eligible bachelors."

Her considerations were interrupted by a knock on the door. Victoria opened it to find Mrs. Cleeve. "My, dear. You looked pale when you left us in the long gallery. Are you alright?"

"Please come in. I am fine. I felt a little weak and thought I should rest a moment. Whatever it was, it is passed."

"Oh, that is good. I want to talk about an idea. We have reports from London that the plague worsens. It is said thousands more died last night, and our guests are reluctant to return. Of course that means they will stay for a time. Meantime we will continue entertaining. It was suggested we have a masked ball. If we schedule a ball, the guests will need costumes. That means you will be asked to help with ideas and sewing. Do you feel up to that?"

"You know I shall help in any way possible. It depends on the date. I am almost finished with orders for gowns and cloaks. I can help providing the costumes are not too elaborate."

"Let's put a limit on costumes. Suppose a person must use a garment of his own for the basic dress and that garment only can be decorated. We can give prizes to those who best follow this requirement."

"That will be easier."

"We can set the date for a fortnight from now."

"There is one problem," Victoria stated thoughtfully. "Each person will want his or her costume to be a secret. If I sew in the long gallery, everyone will see what is being made. Suppose I work in the schoolroom."

"Good idea. I can schedule those who want help so they can work with you alone. Shall we do it?"

"Of course." Victoria agreed knowing that keeping busy is best for healing broken hearts.

"Now, dear, our sky has cleared. Perhaps a horseback ride would be good for you, and no more work today. Dress warmly. The air will be cool after the rain."

The stable master gave her Socrates again, and she allowed him free rein to follow a path to the Dale of Strothem, a lovely glen depressed between gently rising cliffs and drained by the Stream of Philruan. The ruins of Eyton St. Mary's were at the end of the dale. A flock of sheep roamed the grassy grounds, their heads moving along the ground like mowers.

Victoria secured Socrates then walked through the sheep into what was once the nave, column ruins giving it outline. She passed the crossing of the transept and entered the choir where three shafts of fluted granite columns were joined by two arches designed in the gothic style of the Middle Ages. Immediately adjacent were remains of a column rising to a considerable height. Ivy covered much of it.

She chose a smooth granite stone at the base of the column on which to rest and contemplate. She was aware of movement but thought a sheep had wandered nearby unaware of her presence, and she gave it no attention. "I need to go to London. I have saved money. I have Mrs. Hardy's salary, Mrs. Cleeve paid me and all the gowns are paid for. That could be a start on a dress shop."

Something black caught her eye, but it moved from sight instantly. She stood and looked into the black eyes of a big, brownish black face.

Terror seized her, and she almost fell backward. Her awkward position interfered with a first impulse to get away. She fumbled to get into a position to turn and jump, but her hands could not locate anything she could grip. Her head bobbed about from side to side looking for a quick way down. In their intense search, her eyes again came on a level with the face. It had not moved, the eyes still intent on her.

"It is a wolf!" The stories she had heard about wolves filled her with fright. She heard a whimper, like a hurt cry. It came again. There were no barred teeth. No fangs.

She stared, too, and found enough courage to ask timidly, "What is the matter?" A cry came from a slightly opened mouth.

The animal backed away slightly. Victoria with less fear turned her head to find a way to get off the column. She started to make a move when her attention was caught by the animal. It was on the ground, its eyes directed at her.

"I cannot stay here," she decided. She fumbled her way off the column, almost falling in the process. After one step she heard a growl and stopped. Now the whimper again and a loud cry, pleading.

Victoria stepped backward and sat down on a tier of the column. The animal sat down, too, then stretched on its stomach. Slowly he began crawling to her, whimpering as he approached.

Fearing he might leap at her, she reached for a rock thinking that if he did attack, she would try to strike him on the head.

Now almost to her feet, the animal dropped its head and cried pitifully. Her fingers wandered down the back of his head to the neck where she felt leather. There was no space between the collar and the neck. The collar was slowly choking the life out of the animal.

"Perhaps it is a dog gone wild. Maybe it was mistreated and ran away." A feeling of sympathy for the animal relieved her caution.

Slowly she stood and knelt beside the stretched out figure that had not moved. She carefully reached under his neck feeling for the clasp, then slowly moved the collar around his neck until it appeared. She noticed blood on her fingers. Quickly she released the clasp and let the collar fall free.

The animal stayed as it was. Only his eyes were moving. She patted his head. He rose first to a sitting position, licked her hand in gratitude, then stood, looking at her. He gave himself a mighty shake as if feeling freedom from his shackle. Quickly he turned and trotted off.

Victoria watched him go then she walked down the abbey nave. "Strange, isn't it." she pondered. "I came here distraught, feeling my world had been shattered. Then I help a fellow being and my world is solid again."

Socrates awaited his mount. "It would be the abbey that gave me reassurance. It must have been so for the pilgrims who came here to revere a relic." She looked down the nave in deep thought.

"Forgive me, Victoria, for intruding. You were in such deep thought, I could not disturb you. I regret the interruption."

"Hello, Geoffrey. You did not disturb me. I came to the abbey to rest and had the strangest experience. A huge animal, black and wild, came to me for help. A collar was choking him, and he asked me to remove it. I did."

"Do you mean to say you put your hands on that animal! That is a wild beast. Maybe at one time it was a dog, but this part of Cornwall is after him. Shoot on sight. Farmers have lost lambs, kids, chickens. He is like a wolf. There has been no report of an attack on a human, but that could happen. You took an awful chance."

"The poor creature needed help. I did not ask his background before giving it. I dare say some man created what you say is a wild beast. That man is the one to be shot."

"This is Victoria. All caring. All loving. Were I that animal. May I join you for a ride?" His voice changed from alarm to softness, and the deep quality that fascinated her again had its effect.

"That would be nice," she agreed, genuinely pleased with his company. "Where shall it be?"

"Your choice," he offered, just happy she accepted.

"I shall follow you, but do not make it too far."

"No, not follow. Ride next to me. That is where you should be. Let's cross the fields. All the farmers were greatly worried about the storm, for some of the grain crop is yet to be cut, but there was relative little destruction. A loss of even part of a crop would have caused hardship this winter."

"You are a farmer always, and I would judge a good one," she complimented.

"I don't know about that, but I do love the land and continue to be fascinated by what we can do with it. As for always, no, not always. I do have other interests, such as my interest in knowing about your interests. What are they, Victoria?" He had wanted to say she was his interest, but at the moment of expression, he modified his statement.

She would like to have said that he was a new interest but cautioned herself that such a statement would be too bold. Instead she replied, "Most important is my sewing. It is my livelihood, and I have intentions of opening a shop of my own."

"That would take you away from Kensington House." Concern was evident in the voice.

"Yes, I am thinking about a shop in London."

Her declaration created instant anxiety. "How," he thought, "can I keep her here. I must take action, but I must not be too bold." After a moment, he said aloud, "That is a bit in the future, isn't it."

"Yes, a little. I cannot leave until the Cleeve's guests go their ways. With the plague still rampant, their leaving is not immediate."

Geoffrey relaxed slightly. "A little lead time is all I need," he considered. "Court her with dignity, but don't tarry." Then he said to her, "There is some time for me to enjoy your company. Can you give me a time for calling on you?"

"I have not forgotten my promise to you, Geoffrey."

"You will let me know when your time will be mine."

She caught a pleading in the deep voice and answered, "I wont break my promise, Geoffrey."

He guided her back to Kensington House and helped her dismount at the stables. He held her hand and spoke gently, letting the quality of his voice carry the sincerity of his words. "Thank you, Victoria. I enjoy your company each time I am with you. I trust our next meeting will be soon."

He mounted his horse and departed. Victoria watched him go, allowing herself the pleasure of savoring the joy of the past two hours. She turned to face Cleeve.

"Good afternoon," she smiled.

"You seem happy. It must have been an enjoyable ride."

She noted a speck of jealousy in the comment, but she answered elatedly. "Riding is always enjoyable. Socrates is an excellent horse."

"Your next ride is with me. I seek the privilege of the host." It was a voice of command.

"At your pleasure," she replied and departed.

Her thoughts as she sewed were deliberate and considered, and they produced a decision. "To be pursued by a married man is dangerous."

# Chapter Sixteen

Mrs. Cleeve's announcement of a masked ball provoked much excitement. Even the male guests involved themselves in the discussion, and all exchanged ideas about costumes. Victoria arranged the schoolroom to display odds and ends of materials from which she had made gowns and cloaks. Ribbons, laces, strings and bows were organized on a second table. Screens were set up to provide a dressing area. Two schedules were formalized that allowed each guest to meet with Victoria, first to discuss a costume then to return for a fitting. All who wanted help would meet immediately to evaluate ideas and make material selections. She then would prepare a list of needs which would form the basis for a shopping trip to Plymouth.

By the time the first meeting was concluded, the need list was lengthy. "Now, dear," Mrs. Cleeve advised, "I'll arrange for the coach, and you go to town to shop. Stay over if you like. A one day trip is too tiring. Stay at the private inn where we stayed. The keeper and his wife know me. This has enough money in it to pay for all your needs," she added, handing her a black leather money folder. "Now enjoy the trip."

The coach was ready early the next morning giving Victoria time to shop at ease. After shopping she decided to visit dress shops with the intent of getting ideas for establishing one of her own. The notion that she might open a dress shop in Plymouth or London was growing the more she considered it, and discussions with shopkeepers would help her reach a decision.

She first made arrangements at the private inn. "All of our accommodations are taken," she was told by the innkeeper, "but because you are with the Cleeves, I can put in with one of our lady guests. She doesn't mind, and she is out much of the time anyhow."

Victoria's bag was taken to the room. She put her personal things on a table and hung her few clothes in an armoire before leaving. Since her shopping needs were found quickly, she began visits to dress shops. There were not many, and two women were willing to talk to her about their businesses, particularly one who wanted to sell her shop. All were of single ownership, all were able to make a reasonable living, and all made gowns to order. For the most part, fabrics were purchased from a local dealer. All owners sewed as well as managed, some hired one or two seamstresses, and all but one owner lived on the premises. Customers were generally from Plymouth and the surrounding area. Each shop had a regular clientele.

She evaluated what she had learned. "I could be successful here by living at the shop sewing by myself, at least at the beginning. I know I can match the work being done in the shops I visited. The fabrics they use are not the finest so they can keep their prices down. If I used expensive materials such as Mr. Cleeve deals in, I could not survive."

In the late afternoon, Victoria entered a coffee shop. She ordered coffee and wild blackberries with clotted cream. As she ate she noticed a woman she recognized at once as the person Mrs. Cleeve thought resembled herself. There was opportunity this time to look at her and yet be unobtrusive. Although the woman appeared to be older, there was a striking resemblance. "The facial features are similar to mine, and as she smiles, I see the same irregular incisor tooth as mine. I wonder if she could be a relative, perhaps a cousin.

The woman rose with her escort. "She is of my height and figure. I should like to speak to her, but how can I without being too obvious? Well, it is just a passing thought."

At the inn she ordered hot water, bathed, then went downstairs with the intention of having supper. She was just speaking with the innkeeper when a familiar voice spoke, "Why, good evening, Victoria. I was hoping to see you. Elizabeth said you were in Plymouth so I rode over to take care of some business. Please join me for supper."

Surprised by the intrusion and angered by the fact Cleeve caught her off guard, she could not think of an excuse to say no. He took her by the arm saying, "I have just the place where we can sit, talk, and enjoy a good meal. Come." Putting his hand on her elbow, he steered her away from the innkeeper, out the door, and headed in the direction of the docks.

"It is such a nice evening, and I never like to eat alone. You are the best company a man could wish for." He opened a door for her, and as soon as she was inside she saw the innkeeper of the Captain's Helm Inn, still tall and portly, and still in his long white apron.

Victoria felt fearful. "He will try to take me as he tried before. He has planned this purposely. He had no business in Plymouth except the business he has planned for me."

"I have reserved a table for us." He continued to guide her through the busy room, passing in front of the inglenook fireplace with a beef joint turning on the spit, then stopped her before an alcove. "You sit there, Victoria."

"This is the same room where I sat that night when he kissed me so roughly. I wonder if he remembers that night or if every girl in Plymouth has been brought to this alcove to be fed, kissed, then bedded in his reserved bedroom. He would not remember three years ago. I would have been just another on a long list. What difference does one girl make in such a line?"

"I must have ale first. Will you join me?" His hands were on the table and they were beginning to travel toward her. Quickly she placed her hands on her lap. "No thank you."

He gave his order. Ale was brought. She recalled that he started the same way last time. "A slice of the joint would be tasty. May we eat now?" she requested.

"Of course. Whatever you like. But I do enjoy ale first. Do you mind? Did I hear you say, 'Mr. Cleeve?' Come now, Victoria. I want to hear you say, 'Chris' whenever we meet and whenever we converse. Say it." The voice was different from earlier in the evening. It now had the quality of command in every word. His face, too, showed an expression of authority.

"Chris," she mumbled.

The scar looked brighter, more defined. "Is it the ale that incites it or is it his anticipation of me?" she wondered.

After two more tankards of ale, supper was brought. As she ate, he looked at her, longing building up to the point where he was having difficulty eating. Desire led him to anticipate the time after supper. He thought, "Victoria, you do not know what you do to me. Those eyes of yours alone are enough to drive me mad. I want my kisses on your lips, on you. I want to carry you to our bed where I will give you the greatest joy a man can give a woman. I want to ravish you. I love you. It is you who takes my heart. I shall tell you all tonight, and you will wait until I am free to marry. But I cannot wait. I lust. Victoria. My desire is....."

"Hello, Mr. Cleeve. Hello, Victoria." The voice shocked Cleeve from his silent confession. He turned quickly to find Guy and James. "Damn!" he explicated to himself.

Victoria greeted the two young men happily, seeing in them an escape route. "Hello, Guy, James. Have you had supper?"

Courtesy forced Cleeve to offer, "Have some ale. Waiter!" He was glum.

Victoria ate and conversed with the boys as they drank, but Cleeve picked at his food, disgusted, completely irritated at the intrusion. "Bloody hell!" He summarized his thoughts to himself.

The young men talked about their visit to Plymouth and giggled about their "bit of diversion."

"We are staying at the inn where you have your room, Victoria. Since Mr. Cleeve is staying here, we can escort you there."

Cleeve's bubble burst completely at that, and Victoria saw his face become livid, his scar reddening. She guessed his thinking and smiled inwardly. "Thwarted and I am saved by Guy and James."

After supper, Victoria was returned to her inn. Forgetting that she was sharing a room, she was startled to find a lady in the act of dressing. "Excuse me," she said automatically.

"It is alright. The innkeeper told me you would be here. Make yourself comfortable."

Light from a few candles was sufficient for Victoria to identify the lady as the person in the coffee shop. She removed her own dress and put on a robe.

"May I ask you to help me fasten the gown?"

"What a beautiful gown!" Victoria exclaimed as she responded. It was obvious to her that the gown was well made and as she put her fingers on it, she could feel the material was of the finest quality. She stood behind the lady, and as she adjusted the gown to bring the clasps together, she saw a birthmark on the left shoulder, of bluish red color, and shaped like a bow.

"When I go to Paris, I spend time in the shops. I have bought enough gowns to open a sales room. Some I have worn only once."

"This gown is beautifully made. The stitching is done so expertly."

"Do you sew?"

"Yes, I do. I make my living sewing."

"A few gowns are here. If you like, take them out and look at them."

"Oh, thank you. I would like that."

"And rest well. I wont be back. I am out for the night."

"You will be the loveliest lady at the party."

"No, dear. It is not that kind of a party. I must hurry. A coach is to call for me."


Once home, Victoria organized all her purchases. As she prepared to leave the schoolroom, Mrs. Cleeve entered. "How did you get along, dear?"

"Very well. All of our needs were purchased. Let me show you."

She reviewed all the purchases and complimented Victoria on the organization which was by the name of the person who required them. "Has everyone been scheduled?"

"All but Mr. Cleeve."

"He is on business in Plymouth. He knows that if he needs your help he is to see you. You will have to adjust your schedule to accommodate him."

Victoria went to her room, and as soon as she closed the door, she heard a knock. Mrs. Tatham entered, closed the door and pushed the bolt in place. "The lights were used last night. I know you were gone so I just watched. I saw no one, but the night was clear. The lights went on and off the same way as when you saw them."

"I should have been here," Victoria commented to herself. "Mr. Cleeve is the owner. If he is involved with the lights he would have been here. The lights may be used only on nights he is not here. Maybe he doesn't know what is going on. Perhaps I should tell him."

"Victoria," Mrs. Tatham continued, "later I went out of the house by the secret passage and through the south garden, keeping in the shadows. It was a dark night and I had on dark clothes. I stayed south of the lights so I could look over the palisades. A skiff was in the shallow water at the opening between the rocks. Two men were unloading boxes from the skiff and carrying them to the beach. I stayed long enough to see that much and came right back."

"Were you seen?"

"I don't think so."

"I need to get to the beach for a walk and see if I can detect anything."

"We need a signal. I don't want to keep coming down when I want to see you. Suppose I hit my floor like this, bump, bump and bump, three times."

"That is fine. And if I need you, I shall pound on the wall. How is this?" She hit the wall, strike, strike, pause, strike.

"Fine. Now I need to show you how to open the panel to my stairs from the inside. Come."

"Before we go, Mrs. Tatham, may I ask you to look at my left shoulder."

"Of course."

Victoria released a catch and exposed her left shoulder. "What do you see?"

"Why that is your birthmark. You have had it since you were born. Both you and Penelope have it. They are almost identical. Your mother and I would talk about them when we bathed you. You were like two peas in a pod."

"Tell me what it looks like."

"Well, it is small, a bluish red color, and we used to say a little higher and a bow would have placed it in your hair."

"Hold this mirror so I can see it in the wall mirror."

Mrs. Tatham held the mirror and Victoria maneuvered to place a reflection of her shoulder in the mirror. Moving closer she could see the mark. "I never thought of looking at my back in a mirror. Did Jonathan have the same mark?"

"I don't know."

Victoria covered her shoulder with her dress. "It is the same mark I saw on that lady," she recalled to herself.

"We must hurry."

The wall panel opened and they both went through the priest's hole. The panel leading to the tower room opened. "Get inside," Mrs. Tatham ordered. Victoria crawled through. The panel closed behind her.

Darkness. Thick. Black.

Victoria waited. Nothing. Trying to be calm, she took a deep breath. She waited. "Where is she?"

A noise. "What is it?" She put her ear to the panel. A step. A dragging sound. A step. A dragging sound. A step. Getting louder. A step. A dragging sound. Now quiet. The scratching noise! "The priest's hole. My panel is open! Where is Mrs. Tatham?"

Victoria tried to be quiet, but she had to admit she was trapped. "She trapped me!" Frightened, she began pressing about to open the panel. "Calm," she encouraged herself. "There is a way out." Using her finger tips, she tried again. Additional effort made no difference.

"This proves it to me. It is Mrs. Tatham. She is the one. She duped me. I should have known."

Victoria waited in the small space not sure what she was waiting for. "Death?" What else. Who would know where I am. Mrs. Cleeve will come to my room. They will search. Nowhere to be found. Then what. Nothing. I am trapped in my own tomb."

She became alert to a noise above. The panel opened. "Victoria, I am so sorry. I was caught. I may know who is after you. It is a man. Just as you went through the opening, I heard someone climbing the passage stairs. I closed the panel to hide you then I went through the opening to your room. After I closed it, I hurried to the door. The bolt stuck. I couldn't get it to open. Steps in the passage had a dragging sound. When I turned around I saw the armoire was open. I stepped inside among the clothes. The door didn't close perfectly. A slit of light came through. I looked through the slit. I could barely see the priest's hole. A man came through it. As he rose he turned to the wall. I could not see his face. He moved out of sight, but I heard the bolt slide then the door opened. I waited for some time. I went through the long gallery to get to you."

As she listened, Victoria recalled that the bolt at times does stick. Yes, the armoire door does not close tightly. Yes, I heard the step and drag. And I heard who ever it was go through the priest's hole. Aloud she asked, "How tall was he."

"I could not tell. As he was standing up, he moved out of sight."

"Are you sure it was a man?"

"He was dressed like one."

"Please, Mrs. Tatham, show me how to open this panel"

The panel was opened and closed from the inside by pushing a foot against the rise of the second step. Victoria tried it to practice.

"The last panel you need to learn is just at the top of these stairs and near my door, then you know all the secrets I know!' The teacher taught the learner.

"It is remarkable what was done by the builders of these Tudor wings," commented Victoria. "I wonder if they used the passage for other than protecting priests."

"They must have, but I have not heard stories as to what. Now, child, you must go. Remember our signals."

Victoria went through the opening, down the stairs, through to bottom panel, then through the priest's hole to her room. She concentrated on remembering all the touch places hoping she would never have to use them in an emergency.

She also pondered the meaning of what she had learned these past two days. "I want to know my relationship to that lady in Plymouth. Mr. Cleeve seems to be getting more determined to be with me, and that makes me think there is something wrong with his marriage. And what Mrs. Tatham tells me about a man in my room makes me wonder who he is and what he has on his mind."

In time Victoria would learn the answers.

# Chapter Seventeen

It was a jolly time at Kensington House the next few days. There was much levity among the guests as they prepared for the masked ball, each person trying to learn how the other was dressing, telling misleading facts about costumes, guessing as to what was being made, and Victoria was the center of it all.

She was quizzed constantly and had to tell fanciful stories so as not to give away any dress secrets. Her work was progressing, and most of the guests kept their appointment schedules making the undertaking easier.

Shortly after the trip to Plymouth, Mr. Cleeve entered the schoolroom and asked if he could have a costume made. "You are working too hard again, my dear, and you give me no time for the pleasure of your riding company. Socrates tells me he misses you."

"Tell Socrates I shall meet him when preparations for the costume ball are completed."

"It seems there is always something to take you away from me, Victoria." His face had lost his carefree tone, becoming more serious. "I wanted our company at the inn, but Guy and James became more important to you. That did not please me." His expression was haughty as she looked at him.

She admitted to a strange emotional attraction to his closeness, noticing it as soon as he approached. The scar she no longer noticed, the handsome features of his face relegating the blemish to insignificance. His manly physique attracted her, and she struggled to remember that he was a married man. "I don't understand myself," she considered silently. "What is wrong with me? At the inn I did not want him to touch me. I did not even want his company. Now he excites me. I am fearful that if he does touch me I may not be able to control my emotions."

She faced him and spoke, "Now, Mr. Cleeve, how will you dress for the ball?"

"It is 'Chris.' Remember."

"Chris."

"Why must I remind you? Why is it so difficult for you to remember?" His tone was almost threatening.

"I cannot assume the freedom of calling you by an intimate name. I am a companion to your wife, and you are my employer." The tone of her voice took on the quality he had used.

"We are two people, two human beings, and we can be more friendly than as an employer and a girl on the household staff."

"Of course." She thought it better to end the conflict, but she could not submit to his wish. "Mrs. Cleeve said you would be dropping in. Do you have any ideas of what you would like to be?"

He looked at her intently, seriously. "You must know what I would like to be, but you wont let me."

His reply stunned her. "Careful," she warned herself. Trying to ignore his inference, she gave his comment a twist. "Not only will I let you, but tell me your wishes and I shall try to create your fantasy."

"Very well," he smiled. "How does a lover dress?"

"Let me think." She spoke to him in a light mood, almost cheerfully, to give herself an opportunity to consider a reply. "Oh, you want to be Cupid."

"Come now, Victoria. You are being coy. You evade me. Every man who sees you, married or not, desires you. I will play the game, too. When will you stop eluding me? You can't keep this up always."

His effort was becoming upsetting to her. "Here you are a married man," she wanted to tell him. "I am your wife's companion. She is very kind to me, and you violate the hospitality of your home." She had to admit that were he not married, she would accept him. "My respect for her is too great for you to overcome," she said aloud with darts flashing in her eyes to emphasize her statement. "For her sake and mine, I ask you to conduct your business."

"Very well for now. Prepare me for the ball."

"Is it to be Cupid?"

"Make me Cupid. But beware of what you fashion. You shall love what you create as Pygmalion did."

Ignoring the comment, Victoria thought immediately of how to design a cupid costume, a simple one with two wings protruding from the shoulders and the suggestion of a bow and arrows. The basic dress would be tights. Not trusting herself to touch him or demonstrate her ideas, she thought it better to tell him.

"As you want. But you must fit me as you are doing the others. Be on guard." With that he left the room.

Victoria sat down and gave a sigh of relief. "He can be troublesome. But he shall not break my barrier. He grows more brazen, but he will find me impossible to get."

Throughout the morning, guests arrived on schedule and Victoria enjoyed bantering with them. They found her imaginative and creative, making suggestions to enhance their costumes. She worked diligently to please them and they believed her to be greatly successful.

By afternoon she wearied of her concentrated efforts and since the schedule was complete, she decided to take a walk to the abbey. Since her meeting with the dog, she had returned to the site as time and weather permitted for she enjoyed the quietness of the place and an atmosphere that contributed to constructive reflection. Each time she brought something for the dog to eat, a collection of bones and meat provided by cook. This time was no exception. She stopped by the kitchen and was given a package.

She arrived in sunshine and welcomed the isolation among familiar, quieting surroundings and wandered aimlessly. She deposited the bones at the base of the column where she had removed the dog's collar, then stepped up a short incline to the top of a little rise where she sat in the sun. It was refreshing to feel the warmth. At such times problems seemed to be borne away.

Her reverie was broken by the sight of the wild animal. She watched him look around the column ruins, then up at her, and down to the bones. Hesitantly he stepped up to them and whiffed. He looked up again at her and wagged his tail.

"The wound from the collar seems to give him no problem. Perhaps it is healing, although I would like to take a look at his neck to make sure. At least his general appearance is better. The food I have been bringing him undoubtedly is better than what he gets hunting." Quickly he snatched one bone and with his tail between his leg he trotted off. "Poor wild thing," she uttered to herself.

She lay back on the grass and felt comfortably warm. She closed her eyes and let her mind wander to the dress shop before she slept. When she awakened, she was aware of something beside her. She lay quietly then slowly turned her head and looked up to see the dog sitting beside her, his eyes alert, looking straight ahead. Her first reaction was one of joy, for she thought at last she had convinced him of her friendship and he had come to her of his own free will. She started to reach up to touch his throat, thinking of checking the wound, when she realized his intense stare had not altered since she noticed him next to her. She raised up to see what took his interest. A man was sitting on a horse not more than ten feet away.

"Good afternoon, Victoria," he greeted her. "You can rest secure with a protector like that animal. I am not anxious to come closer."

"Good afternoon, Geoffrey," she smiled. "Forgive me for not recognizing you immediately. I must have been asleep." Then referring to the dog, she added, "A friend is always a protector. He is a handsome beast despite the show of ribs. I awakened to find him next to me and was beginning to feel elated because I thought he came to me out of friendship. Then I find him looking at you."

"That is more than friendship. It is devotion in its purest form. He is protecting you. Do I conclude that all living things have a love for you?" The deep voice was used to convey more than the meaning usually given to those words.

"Would that all living things had love for one another. I would like to see if his neck wound is healing, but I am hesitant to touch him. I am not sure of his reaction."

"I would guess you could touch him. Go ahead, check the wound. As long as he is watching me so intently, I am sure you are safe."

She carefully moved her position to look at the dog's neck. Instead of being raw as it was the day she removed the collar, it was a pink skin devoid of hair. "Oh, Geoffrey. It is healing!" Her joy brought a laugh from him.

"Would you care so much for me if I were wounded?"

"You tease me. Here is a poor animal that could not help himself. Wouldn't it have been a shame if some farmer shot him. Have you heard any more tales of a wild dog killing farm animals?"

"No, actually, I haven't. I suppose you told that beast to stop taking a farmer's animals."

"No, but I do bring him food hoping to satisfy his hunger so that he wont have to hunt."

As she spoke, Victoria found herself admiring the handsome Cornish farmer seated on his horse in such a commanding position as if he owned all he surveyed. "He is a fine specimen of a man," she thought. "He seems a true gentleman."

"Do you think he would let me off this horse to sit with you?"

"Perhaps. Let me ask." Victoria mumbled something to the dog, but the animal did not take his eyes off Geoffrey. "He says fine, but walk slowly."

Geoffrey dismounted and walked gingerly up the incline. She noticed a tenseness develop in the animal, so she spoke to him as the man approached. Her gentle words were meant to reassure him that the stranger was a friend, and she patted his head to emphasize her point.

With intent, the dog followed the man's every move, concern expressed in his eyes and a tenseness of his body, but for a concentrated stare, he gave no trouble. "Don't leave me alone with him, please," he said as he sat next to her. "I would not have a chance." When he was seated, he added, "Do you mesmerize all males in the same manner? Like your friend the dog, I, too, could sit beside you and guard you. Have you been busy?"

"Everyone has been busy preparing for the costume ball. Will you be coming?"

"Yes. I am invited, but I dare not tell you my costume. I am looking forward to the party. May I have a dance?"

"Certainly. I notice the word is singular. Is it only one you want?"

Without hesitation he quipped, "I could send the others away, and we could have the ball to ourselves. The Cleeves may not be very happy with that idea, however."

"Do you come to the abbey often?" She was finding she enjoyed his company and wanted to make conversation, perhaps to have him linger a little longer.

"As often as I can. There is a reverence here."

The deep voice was mellow. Victoria thought, "He loves this place, too."

"Even a farmer must escape his cares." she heard him add.

"Is your farm a problem?"

"No. My problems are those all man have, the need for someone to love and be loved in return."

She was aware he was looking at her, but she did not reply at once. She was considering his statement. Then she spoke quietly, "I have heard it said that when love comes to two persons, they know it without the telling or the asking. Do you think it is so?"

"I am not sure. I do think though that asking and telling makes the love deeper."

The two sat, neither moving, neither speaking, each letting the silence communicate their thoughts.

Geoffrey was the first to speak. "Please do me the honor of letting me escort you back to Kensington House."

"Very well."

The dog remained alert as Victoria stepped down the slope aided by Geoffrey. He helped her mount his horse, he taking a place in front of her. A quiet order was given and the horse trotted off, down the nave and away from the abbey. She looked back to see the dog follow at first, then cut off to disappear in the brush beyond the nave.

Victoria's arms were about Geoffrey's waist. She could feel his strong lean frame as he rode erect, her body against his back, every muscle attuned to the rhythm of the horse's step. She felt his hand close over her entwined fingers. She did not protest. She luxuriated in the wonderful feeling of security, and she was not anxious to have the ride end as of course it had to.

"Thank you for your protective ride, Geoffrey. You were most considerate. I shall look forward to seeing you at the masked ball." There was more enthusiasm in her voice than she knew.

"The pleasure of your company shall remain with me." His smile was warm.

"Please let me know when we can ride together."

She watched him ride away then she returned to the schoolroom. She felt exuberant as she recalled her unexpected meeting with Geoffrey, reliving every minute of it. "I like him," she admitted to herself. "He is courteous, thoughtful, and I like the feel of him. It was good to have my arms around a man like him."

The door opened and Mrs. Cleeve entered. "Good afternoon." Victoria greeted her warmly. "Look how one idea is developing," she invited, holding up an elf costume.

"How sweet," came a giggle.

"Mrs. Cleeve, have you heard any more about Lord Covington's grandson? I recall your announcement of his marriage."

"Oh, Edward. That wild one. Yes, Jonathan returned yesterday and brought the news that Edward married the girl in a small wedding. It wont last long, of course. No one can tie Edward down.

"I am glad Jonathan is back. He is such a fine young man. I want you to know him. Christopher thinks he is very dependable and will be a wonderful business man. In fact, I think we shall have a little supper of our own tonight so you can get acquainted with him. Say seven. We shall have it in the breakfast room to be more cozy."

Victoria wanted to protest, but at that moment she could not think of a reason why she should not attend. After that bedroom episode the night of the play she had not seen Jonathan, and she had no special interest in meeting him again.

A little after seven, Victoria made an appearance in the breakfast room dressed in a conservative grey satin gown with spangles of white lace at the collar and sleeves. She was greeted first by Mrs. Cleeve and then by the two men. Mr. Cleeve winked at her as he spoke, and Jonathan gave no indication of their meetings other than the one at the play when he said, "Sitting with you at the play was a remembered pleasure."

Conversation turned to the plague since Jonathan's business assignment had taken him to London. "It is reported that some 70,000 people have died in London alone and additional lives have been taken in the shires about the city. Carts are still carrying away the dead. Few people are about. Streets are mainly deserted, a strange sight for that busy place. Too bad the source of the disease hasn't been identified."

"It is filth. I am sure of it. Something will have to be done to clean up the rot," Cleeve commented. "All kinds of disease must run rampant where people throw their excrement out of windows, where rats feed on garbage that is allowed to collect where people walk, and animal droppings are everywhere."

"Maybe Parliament will discuss the problem. I am sure Lord Arlington would appreciate your thoughts, Christopher."

"I know our guests are still concerned about the plague. They talk about going home but are afraid," Victoria reported.

"I believe some will return to London before long. One gets homesick," Mrs. Cleeve predicted.

"All have enjoyed their stay and all are very grateful to you for providing comfort at such a time," said Victoria.

"I am sure they are," Cleeve agreed. "And we appreciate all the help you give us. I would like to show you how much, Victoria," a glimmer in his eyes.

She wondered if Mrs. Cleeve caught the meaning. "Just being at Kensington House is reward enough."

The gathering ended after supper. Jonathan came to her and said, "Please, Victoria, I would like to take you to Plymouth to meet someone. Trust me. I shall return you safely home."

"I shall consider your request." With that she went to her room.

"Imagine the gall! After his violence in this room, he is now asking me to Plymouth! So he will bring me back safely. But what does he intend to do between the going and the coming?"

Scratching! She caught the sound shortly after entering the room, and she listened. Yes, there it is! Being as unobtrusive as possible, she slipped out the door, ran up the stairs and knocked on Mrs. Tatham's door. As soon as it opened, she hurried across the room to the panel at the stairway, opened it, crawled through it, and lightly stepped down the stairs using a glow from the room to show her the way. Carefully she opened the peek hole Mrs. Tatham had shown her. Candlelight in the passage way outlined a figure, a man bent over looking into her room. Hanging from the neck on a chain was something, perhaps a medallion, rubbing against the wall. She watched the dangling object move against the wood each time the person moved, and each time it created a scratching sound.

"Little does he know he warns me every time he peeks."

She concentrated on identifying the figure, but it was impossible to make out the face. Because he was learning over the hole, it was impossible to determine how tall he was.

"This is ridiculous," she smiled. "I am watching him as he thinks he is watching me."

Suddenly the candle he was using went out, plunging the passage into total darkness. She heard the step, drag, step, drag sounds she associated with her antagonist. He was entering her room.

Quietly she returned to Mrs. Tatham's room. "I saw him, but I could not tell who he is, or could I tell anything about his figure. I wonder about the step, drag, step, drag sounds. Do you think it could be a man who limps?"

"I could not tell if he was limping when I saw him in your room. Since I returned to Castelamer, I have not seen a man with a limp. I did see that man in the garden with Mr. Cleeve who drags his foot. Remember, it was the day the wind was blowing. The day Mr. Cleeve met you on the brink."

"I recall that very well. You told me about him. If this is the same man, then Mr. Cleeve knows him. That man knows this house, too. Strange he isn't seen about."

"Now you know for sure someone is interested in you. When we know why, you will know who it is."

"Who is it?" The question nagged Victoria as she returned to her room and prepared for bed. "Why does he threaten? Or, maybe it is a man who wants me, wants me as a woman.

"There is that object at the end of this chain. I must watch for that, but many men wear chains with dangling objects. Tonight I recall Mr. Cleeve wearing a medallion on a chain, and Jonathan, did he wear one? Why, yes he did!"

The next morning, Victoria made a point of speaking to Mrs. Cleeve. "After supper last night, Jonathan asked if I would accompany him to Plymouth to meet a friend."

"He told me of his intention to speak to you. There is a person in Plymouth he is anxious for you to meet. He did not say who it is."

"Do you think I should go with him?"

"Of course, my dear. There is no hurry about it, I don't think. Jonathan tells me he will be here until after our masked ball, and if you can not take the time before, you may go after. There should be no sewing demands on your time after the ball."

"I am just concerned about taking a trip like that with a man who is a stranger."

"That is being wise. But Jonathan is an honorable man. Christopher thinks highly of him. I myself will be responsible for his integrity, and should there be any problem violating my trust, Jonathan will no longer be employed by my husband, you can depend on that."

Victoria considered her reply to him.

# Chapter Eighteen

Her diligent efforts helped Victoria complete costume assignments well before the party date except for the cupid design for Cleeve. It was the only one hanging on the wall, and it was finished but for the addition of wings, bows and arrows.

She made a decision. "I will not remind him to come here. He must come to me. Meantime, I am going to explore to see what I can find out." She had been thinking of the beach, and since the sun was shining, she decided to ask cook for a pasty to eat on the rocks and to spend most of the time along the surf.

She walked to Hythe Haven, skirted the western shore under Bodacombe Bluff, then turned at the base of the cliff to come onto the beach below the south garden.

"I must follow my plan. Should anyone come along to question me, I shall appear to be on a casual outing, just eating a pasty on the rocks and enjoying the beach. If apprehended, I shall be nonchalant. But I shall be looking for something suspicious."

Victoria walked slowly on the beach. If someone was watching he would have seen a girl leisurely taking a stroll, looking out to sea, picking up shells, climbing on rocks and running away from chasing waves. She chose a boulder, sat down, watched the sea rolling in, but especially she searched for something suspicious.

Something caught her eye. She placed her pasty on a rock and walked to a point at the base of the palisades. She tossed some stones, but nothing developed for her efforts.

She returned to the boulder, picked up the pasty and began to nibble. The large delicious pancake was wrapped to enclose a cubed potato, minced onions, a chopped vegetable and generous pieces of mutton. Her eyes continued to roam around the palisades and along the base where so many boulders and rocks were collected in piles. As her eyes reached the top of the cliff, she thought she observed a person looking over the brink. She looked away quickly so as not to indicate her purpose in being there, but slowly she brought her head up a bit then let her eyes roll upward.

A head came into focus. "It is Mrs. Tatham. That grey hair blowing in the wind is unmistakable. Perhaps she saw me go through the garden and use the path to Hythe Haven. She may know I am looking for something suspicious and wants to protect me. I should have told her I was coming here, but now she knows."

Looking at the rim of the cliff made her think of that day three years ago when Mr. Wyatt became aggressive and fell over the brink. She cautioned herself as to her purpose and passed over her thoughts about Wyatt. Discouraged at finding nothing suspicious, she gave up her sleuthing and returned to strolling along the beach, picking up shells to study them, throwing rocks at incoming waves and kicking pebbles. She became interested in a buildup of rocks and boulders at one spot along the base of the cliff. She climbed to the top of the mound, gaining considerable height above the sand. She sat down on one of the rocks at the top, faced the sea and enjoyed the view. Her eyes found a large rock on the surf, and she challenged herself to hit it. She slung a rock at the target. "What a miss that was," she guffawed aloud. "Try again." She reached back of her and felt for another rock, brought it forward, juggled it in her hand as she determined her aim, then threw it. "Mmmmm. Closer. Looking about she selected the best rock for the job, picked it up, then noticed something strange. "There is no wall of dirt there. Has the sea made a little cave? That is different."

What she saw appeared to be a small cavern. Removing rocks that had built up near the entrance, she created a small opening. On hands and knees she looked inside. There was enough light to reveal a large area. She removed more rocks, making the opening large enough to crawl through. She found a chamber, perhaps six feet high and about six feet wide. She faced the rear. The light was not good, but there appeared to be a larger cave beyond. She started in that direction when she heard noises at the entry.

Someone was entering the opening she had created. As the figure stood up, she could see it was a man. He came toward her. "Why, Victoria, what are you doing here?"

She moved so that the figure turned to face her and in doing so picked up some light. "I thought I recognized your voice, Jonathan, but I was not sure. I should ask you the same question."

"Come. I shall take you home." He ignored her question completely.

She considered challenging him but thought it was wiser not to. She could come at another time now that she knew how to enter the cave.

Jonathan helped her through the opening then he passed through it. He replaced the rocks to cover the opening. The sun was still high as they walked along the beach, turned the corner and headed for Hythe Haven. "What were you doing in the cave?"

"Why, I was an explorer making a discovery and you thwarted my efforts," she laughed.

"It is best the exploration stop." He was serious and direct.

"What is in the cave you don't want me to see?" She stopped, putting a hand on his arm to restrain him.

He faced her. "It is a friendly warning. Stay out of it. By the way, you haven't given me an answer to my request to accompany me to Plymouth."

"I am still considering it. You shall have an answer after the party." Her voice was steady.

There was no further conversation until they reached the house. "Remember, Victoria, stay out of the cave." His voice was filled with authority.

She went immediately to Mrs. Tatham's room. As soon as she entered, she asked, "Were you watching me from the brink?"

"Why, I haven't left my room. I have been here all day." Her surprised tone told Victoria that she could be telling the truth. "I saw you looking over the brink. Your hair was easily identified."

"You saw someone else. I have been here all day, and that is the truth."

"I saw only the head of the person looking at me. Wind was blowing grey hair just like yours." Her tone softened.

"The person you need to ask is the person who has grey hair like mine. I was not there."

"I am sorry, Mrs. Tatham. I do believe you. I am trying so hard to learn what is going on. It could be the person we are looking for has grey hair similar to yours."

"Mmmmmm. That's interesting." Victoria noticed Mrs. Tatham's face brighten a moment as she spoke then change to serious contemplation. "It could be the man I saw in your room. He has grey hair but not so much as I have."

"Wind was blowing. It was strong enough to make his hair bushy." Victoria thought for a moment, giving her face, too, an attitude of contemplation. "We have a partial description of the man we are looking for. He is not tall, although we have not seen him standing straight up. He has grey hair, possibly bushy, and he may walk with a limp, probably dragging his foot. He undoubtedly wears a medallion."

Victoria left the old lady and went to her room. As she entered she found Pall cleaning. "I wont disturb your work, Pall. I am going to the schoolroom. When you finish here, please come to help me."

She was placing the schoolroom in order when the door opened. Mr. Cleeve entered.

"Hello, Victoria. I have come for my final fitting."

"You are the last to do so." Taking down his cupid costume, she handed it to him with the direction, "Change into your costume behind the screen. That is our dressing room"

"Thank you, Victoria. It is 'Chris,' remember. I am looking forward to this fitting." He went behind the screen and came out in tights. She looked at him, noticing his fine muscular physique, fully outlined in his costume. Now displayed were broad shoulders tapering through a well defined torso to a thin waist, arms that showed strong biceps, narrow hips and muscled legs.

"Please, Chris, and you noticed I use your requested name, step nearer the light so I can arrange these wings. She put her hand on his back to touch a ripple of his hardened muscles. Immediately she felt a reaction in her own body accompanied by an urge to touch more of him. She stepped back to relieve the urge and regain her composure.

"Please stand steady. I must mark the place where the wings will be tacked to your garment." Quickly she made a mark. Again she touched the firm flesh under the cloth. She felt a renewal of a compulsion to throw her arms around his neck and to caress him warmly. Unsteadily she marked a place for a second wing. She was completely unprepared for his quick turn. He was facing her and smiling.

211

"You want me, Victoria, don't you. I felt a tingle in your fingers when you touched me. You had to step back to relieve your nervousness. You have been waiting for me to come, haven't you? You suggested Cupid so you could see me in tights. You wanted to see me as close to being nude as you could. Come, Victoria. Touch me. Feel this body that longingly waits for you. Put your hand here. Put it here, Victoria." His voice was commanding.

She stood mesmerized. She felt herself giving in to his demands. She started to raise her hand. He stepped forward so that his wrist touched her fingers.

"Now your other hand. That is right. Come to me. Put your hands on me." With eyes staring directly at her, he shifted his body slightly, fitting himself within the reach of her hand. "Now put your arms around me. That is right. Squeeze me, Victoria. Squeeze me. Tightly. Look up at me." There was a smile on his face reflecting his feeling of control over her and his anticipation of the coming tryst.

She followed his directions, not wanting to, but unable to reject his commands. As she raised her face to his, he murmured, "Your eyes are lovely. They captivate me." He bent down and kissed her gently. His arms went around her and drew her to him. His kiss became harder and his tongue probed.

His action recalled to Victoria that night in the inn three years ago when Cleeve frightened her. His violent ardor now broke his spell over her. A picture of Edward appeared in her imagination. "He kissed me, too. He played with me. He broke his promise. Stop, Victoria!"

She released her arms then tried to push away from him, trying to free herself from his hold. "No, Victoria. It is not ended. Stay close to me."

"No!" she shouted. "Get out."

"Shout if you like," he challenged. "No one will hear you. Everyone is out. Shouting pleases me. I like to struggle. You become more fascinating. Sweet Victoria."

She watched his eyes take on more fierceness. There was no mistaking his purpose. The scar took on a purple tinge. She tried to build a resistance. He grabbed her. She felt his strong fingers dig into her shoulders and pull her to him. His left arm slipped to her waist while his right hand lifted her chin until she looked directly into his eyes. He kissed her again, fiercely, refusing to release her.

She felt her dress being pulled off her left shoulder. She raised her left hand and struck him in the face. He ended his kiss and laughed at her. "Ah, Victoria. Let yourself come to me. You are going to find happiness. Here. Now. Enjoy my love. I want you, Victoria."

The laugh changed to a smile, then a scowl. "You are going to be mine. Here. Now!"

She struggled, stepping backward in fear, rearranging her dress as she did so. The door opened at that moment and she backed into Pall who was about to enter. "Excuse me, Miss Victoria. I was just--- -"

"Come with me, Pall," Victoria directed as she turned to intercept Pall's entry. She slipped an arm through Pall's and steered the maid into the hall, closed the schoolroom door, and as the two walked together, she said, "We can clean the long gallery."

Victoria's first concern was for Pall. "She must not for a second suspect anything was amiss. A mere hint that something was going on in the schoolroom would provoke Pall into making statements to other staff, and soon there would be a scandal. That would be difficult for both Mr. and Mrs. Cleeve and for me. It must not happen."

Left behind was Cleeve, unseen by Pall, angered by Victoria. "Damn that woman!" His ire was evident in the scowl, the expletive and the manner in which he spit out the words.

As soon as she could, Victoria left Pall in the long gallery and returned to her room, completely exhausted. The ordeal had made her weak. She fell across the foot of the bed. After a reasonable wait she arose and went to the schoolroom to clean up. The cupid costume was thrown over a screen. She sewed the wings at the places marked and placed the bow and arrows on a chair. Picking up her sewing kit, she left the room,

As she passed the study door, she heard a loud, heated discussion. She hesitated in the hallway and caught such words as boats, bales and cave, but she could not hear all of it. One voice was Cleeve's. The other voice was unidentifiable.

Daring not to listen longer, she went to her room. "Curiosity. Be careful. But those words hold answers to my questions." She formulated a plan and quickly put it into effect.

Quietly she bolted her door, opened the priest's hole, lit a candle and entered the passage. Silently she went down the passage to the stairs where the study and passage had a common wall. Ear to the wall, she listened. The men were still in discussion, but it was the unidentifiable voice doing most of the talking.

"You have to take care of the situation," the man was saying. "Too much is known already. A word in the right place will bring destruction to both of us, but to you first. You haven't much time. All of our work depends on complete secrecy.

"Equally critical is the property. You know how I go it, and you know what happened to the former owner. The same could happen to you. Both of us are vulnerable. I warn you, if you want to stay, get rid of this menace, permanently. But I want a go first." There was a pause, then the voice again. "I must go. But a final word. I want to see results."

Quickly Victoria returned to her room. "That voice. I have not heard that voice. It is not the voice of any of the guests. It definitely is a man's voice, but it has a rasp in it. It belongs to a man who does not come here often or I would have heard it.

"Whoever it is, he has power over Mr. Cleeve. What is the threat that will bring him destruction? And what is their work that requires so much secrecy? From the hallway I heard the words 'boat,' 'bales,' 'cave.' Could that be what is so secret?

"There is Jonathan. He was greatly agitated because he found me in the cave. He works for Mr. Cleeve. It ties together. Cave, bales, boat, secrecy. I came on the secret of the cave and they know it. There must be more to the cave than I saw. I must get back there.

"He spoke about property. What property is that? Kensington House? From what he said, it is his, not Cleeve's. That is a surprise. What is the arrangement they have?

"And the Framsdens. He said, 'You know what happened to the former owners.' Could that be a reference to the Framsdens? If he means the property of Kensington House, it would be the Framsdens. I wonder if the man who was talking knows what happened to the Framsdens?

"He threatened Cleeve. What control does the man have over Cleeve?

"What is the menace that threatens the property? It must be serious. It is either the menace that goes or that Cleeve goes. And what does he have in mind if he wants a go at the menace first?"

A knock on the door disturbed her thinking. It was a knock, knock, pause, knock. It was repeated. Victoria recognized Mrs. Tatham's code. She unbolted the door and the old lady entered. "I have been watching for an opportunity to get to the study. Today Mrs. Cleeve was in Brixton Village, Mr. Cleeve was with you, guests were out, so I took a chance. I went to the study and searched, but in the short time I was there, I found nothing."

Victoria thought, "I have an answer to one of my questions." Then she said, "Mrs. Tatham, you must be careful. They are after you. I heard a voice I could not identify say to Mr. Cleeve, 'I warn you. Get rid of this menace.' They must know something about you. Can't you leave Kensington House?"

Mrs. Tatham considered Victoria's remarks then replied confidently. "Only part of my job is done. I have more to do. Then I can leave here. I must return to my room." She slipped out the door and was gone.

Victoria felt better for having alerted Mrs. Tatham to her danger. "Since they consider her a menace, I must help her. But how?" She was considering possibilities when the scratching sound began. Mentally she pictured a stooped figure, grey haired, a medallion hanging from the neck, looking through the peek hole. Nonchalantly she blew out the candle before undressing. Very shortly the scratching stopped.

Quietly she pulled the side table in front of the sliding panel and went to bed.

# Chapter Nineteen

ictoria lay in bed reviewing all the events that had occurred during the preceding day. A dull light came through the window. Rain was falling. "That is what I shall do," she declared emphatically. "It is a perfect day for it. They wont think anyone will be about searching on a rainy day. They will be keeping a watch on Mrs. Tatham anyhow." She bounded out of bed with enthusiasm, exhilarated by thoughts of her planning.

From the armoire she chose a dark green woolen dress, the darkest she had and one that would blend with the dull day. She dressed quickly, slipped out the door, and went up to Mrs. Tatham's room. She awakened the old lady with a light tap on the door, using the code. "I am going to the beach," she was informed. "You might keep a watch on the gardens. See who is about. But stay in your room, and do not admit anyone except Pall. I shall tell you what I learn when I return."

Leaving immediately, Victoria hurried from the house, went to Hythe Haven and on to the camouflaged cave. She removed the top rocks, lowered herself to the cavern entrance, then returned the rocks to their places. She moved into the cave as far as she could in natural light, but when darkness made progress difficult, she took a candle out of her pocket and lit it. As she moved deeper she found the cave broadened and was higher. Many footprints were in evidence. She soon discovered a quantity of bales, mainly of one size, and all coded, several letters and numerals appearing in combinations.

She moved a bit farther into the cave and found a tunnel rising rather steeply from the natural ending. It was evident the tunnel was man made, pick and ax marks appearing on the walls. It was obvious, too, that it was made large enough to permit men to carry boxes from the cave.

Carefully she climbed upward. She noticed more footprints in the dirt that gave evidence to activity that must have taken place recently. The tunnel ended abruptly at a heavy wooden door. Victoria put her ear to the door and listened.

At first she heard nothing, then a voice, sounding as if it were far away, was producing words. "Lord Covington is asking for his order of French wines. In fact he is demanding it. We shall have to move those boxes in the cave up here then load the wagon tonight."

"That sounds like the voice I heard in the study," Victoria thought.

"The material should go to London as well." She heard a second voice. It was Cleeve's voice without question. "But our drivers wont enter the plague area. We are losing money all the while the bales sit in the cave."

"I'll get the materials to London. Raise the pay a bit, and a couple of drivers will agree to go. Money makes men act."

"That is Jonathan's voice!" she said to herself.

"Money does strange things, indeed." It was Cleeve's voice again. "I never thought I would be running contraband, but the profit is excellent. I have made enough, however. I would like to get out of it. Jonathan can take over."

"Not yet you wont. We have much more money to make, much more. I want to buy several surrounding estates and then buy at least a baronet from the crown. Kensington House is going to be the show place of the west country."

"That is the voice I heard in the study last night! I am sure of it. He is the person in charge," Victoria reasoned.

"The sheriff gets his cut, but the crown constable knows nothing of our business," the man continued. "And he had better not know. This is a lucrative business, well organized, and no snags. Except! Have you decided what to do with our menace?"

"Yes. But you want a go at it first." Cleeve answered.

"What do they want to do with Mrs. Tatham?" she wondered.

"I do indeed. I shall get even and then you can have the rest." It was a modified voice, filled with spite and hate. "Let's get organized for tonight. The bales can be moved up here today, perhaps now, and tonight the wagons can be loaded and on the road no matter the weather."

"We haven't our full crew now," Jonathan reminded him. "Not just anybody, you understand, can be asked to move those bales. We have two loyal men and only they can be considered dependable. It is as you say, if the word gets to the constable, we are finished."

Victoria searched about the door to find an opening of some kind so she could peer into the room. She found a slight space between the door and the door jamb. Looking through it she could not find one of the three men, but she could make out faintly what appeared to be a storage room. Several bales were piled within the sweep of her eye and each one had markings similar to those in the cave.

"I'll get the wagons ready for Lord Covington's purchase," Jonathan volunteered. "How much will be made on him?"

The leader responded, "Enough pounds to fill one of the boxes he is getting."

All laughed.

Victoria heard footsteps. She froze. Quickly controlling her wits, she ran down the tunnel, stumbling at times in the loose dirt. As rapidly as possible she opened the cave entrance, climbed through, then replaced the camouflage. Rain had stopped. Walking with speed but not running, she passed Hythe Haven and came into the garden.

"Oh, Victoria. Come walk with me. How nice of you to come along." It was Lady Arlington. Victoria had not seen her in the haste to get to the stables.

"How untimely," she thought, but she smiled and spoke a greeting. She had other thoughts on her mind but could not refuse the invitation.

"It is a lovely morning after the rain. I do wish everyone in London could be away from the plague and in a place like this. Poor London. I want to return, but Lord Arlington must be in Oxford when Parliament sits."

Calling on her reserve of courage, Victoria asked, "Lady Arlington, were you serious about offering to help me with clients if I opened a dress shop in London?"

"Of course. We are very pleased with your fine work. We think you will be highly successful. When you are open, let me know, and I shall indeed help you."

"Do you have any idea how much money would be necessary to open a nice shop and in what part of London?"

"No, dear. But speak to Lord Arlington. He is so knowledgeable about money. He can tell you all about it, all of the business end."

A light conversation ensued as the two walked about the garden together then separated at the house. "Just my luck," Victoria sighed. "I wanted to see if Jonathan appeared near the stables. I have an idea that room I saw through the slit has an opening into the service area, probably near the wagon storage shed. I think I would have seen

Jonathan there if I had not been stopped. Now I have missed him. Oh, well, I have Lady Arlington's promise of support. That is worth something. I shall go to the stables anyhow."

She walked nonchalantly, trying to give the impression of taking a casual outing. She entered the stables and spoke to the master. No, she did not want to go riding. She murmured gently to some horses and patted Socrates' head. She moved farther along to a section where she saw a wagon and two horses. Three men were talking nearby. She lingered, trying to make out the discussion, but one man she did identify, Jonathan.

Wanting to stay and observe their actions, she went to the opposite wall and pretended to inspect harnesses and hangings, glancing frequently in Jonathan's direction.

She did not watch closely enough. The last glance found a vacant spot where the men had been standing. Slowly she wandered toward the site and approached some hangings on the wall in back of a wagon where the men had been. She touched her hand to the edge of the hangings and pulled upward. Nothing unusual. Wait. No. Nothing. She heard a noise. Quickly she turned and strode to the end of the shed, pausing at the exit. Out of the corner of her eye she saw the men reappear. One must have seen her for she heard, "What are you doing here?"

She lifted her skirt and ran as fast as she could. The south garden was just ahead. She darted in and out of the hedges to escape the chase. The passage! She crawled through the hedge next to the house, found the secret panel, touched in the proper place and crawled through the opening. Quickly she closed it. She hurried up the stairs, feeling her way in the darkness, and entered her room. Instantly she rushed to change clothes, brushed her hair, combed it, made some plaits, and formed a bun. She applied some paint to her face, took a deep breath and waited.

Soon a knock. She opened the door to face Jonathan and a young man she did not know. "Excuse me, Victoria," she heard Jonathan say as she kept her eyes on the stranger. She saw him shake his head.

"I, mmmmmm, did I ask if you had decided on the trip to Plymouth?"Jonathan asked.

Seeing his nervousness, she calmly replied, "Why, yes, you did."

"Thank you." The two turned and went down the hall. She closed the door except for a slit. She heard the young man say, "That is not the one. The girl I saw had on grey clothes and her hair was different."

Victoria took a deep breath and leaned against the door. "What if I had been recognized!"

She now had time to think about the shed. "Those men came out of an opening behind that hanging. They had to. There must be a door that slides open. Ah, maybe a large panel wide enough to push a wagon through. That is it. A wagon is rolled in, loaded and then rolled out. Then the goods are delivered."

Satisfied with her deductions, she went to Mrs. Tatham's room. "You are safe!" the old lady beamed. I watched you running in the garden. Two men were chasing you. You disappeared from sight and they did not know where to look. They searched everywhere in the garden.

"I took the secret passage entry. I am so grateful you told me about it."

"What did you learn in your search?"

Victoria reported on her findings in the cave and about the conversation she overheard. "I do believe boxes and bales arrive by boat in secrecy, perhaps with the help of lights we saw. I recognized the voices of Mr. Cleeve and Jonathan, but I could not identify the voice of the third man. He sounded like the man I heard talking to Mr.

Cleeve in the study. Whoever it is, he is the head of the business, and Mr. Cleeve must work for him. He gives the orders.

"They were talking about their business of running contraband. They have French wines and spirits and materials ready to deliver. The sheriff knows all about the business, for he gets a payment to keep quiet. But the crown constable does not know."

"Ah! That is the information I need!" Mrs. Tatham exclaimed with a determined look on her face. "Now I know what to do. I came to Kensington House for two reasons. One is to find the paper that tells me about property ownership. The other is to get even with that man, the one you say is in charge. I know who it is, but since the time the Framsdens left, I have not seen him. Not until yesterday.

"After you told me to be careful, I wanted to know who was after me. I listened at the study wall from inside the passage and heard those voices, Mr. Cleeve and his. I wanted to get a good look at him so I hid in the linen closet. When the study door opened, I opened the linen closet door slightly and looked through the slit. I did not see his face since he turned to his left and went down the hall. He walks with a drag to his foot, is bent over a bit and has grey hair.

"I am sure he is the one who controls Kensington House and all that goes on here. He is the one who must have controlled Castelamer when the Framsdens were here."

"Mrs. Tatham, you must be careful. He spoke about you again today in the storage room. I heard him say to Mr. Cleeve that he had to get rid of the menace."

"Well, I'll be ready. Contraband business is dangerous and only men who get into it are themselves dangerous. If there is a threat to their money, they remove the threat. They have done it before. I must be a threat to them. They must think I know too much."

"There is money in the business, a lot of it," Victoria agreed. "I heard them speak about a bale of profit when the wines and spirits are sold."

"Those men will protect their profit at any cost, even to removing me. But I'll beat them to it."

"What do you plan to do?"

"What is necessary, and it will be soon. I shall be gone for a few days. When I come back they can do whatever they want with me. I shall have my revenge."

"Revenge?"

"I should tell you my story. It is no secret. The village people know it, or at least some of them. I married a Tatham. He was no relation to your father. He worked at Castelamer, and I worked for your parents. One day he came home greatly upset. He said he had been accused of something he did not do. It had to do with his work. He never told me what he did except that he had several jobs. Driving a wagon, loading and unloading bales. Sometimes he would be gone for days. He would only tell me when he thought he would be back. One day when he came home, he said he was sure someone would get him. He would not tell me who that someone was except that the owner was mad enough to kill.

"I said I did not think Mr. Framsden would do a thing like that. He said Mr. Framsden was not the owner, only a chessman to move around.

"The next day my husband was found dead. A few days later another man was found dead. He, too, had worked at Castelamer. Nothing was ever said to me. If I had not been working for your sainted mother, I would have had no home, nothing."

"I am so pleased she was good to you, Mrs. Tatham." Victoria gave the old one a big hug.

"She was an angel. I should let the dead past bury its dead, but as the years went along, I grew bitter. I felt more and more the need to take revenge, to get even for my husband's death. I decided to come to Kensington House. I did not know what I would find or what I would do. Fortunately Mr. Cleeve felt sorry for me. If he hadn't I don't know how I would have done my work. Best of all I was given the south tower room. It was that room that gave me an opening I needed. 'Just keep your eyes and ears open,' I said to myself.

"Oh, I knew about the secret passage. Your mother told me about the priest's room, so in the middle of the night, many nights, I would go to the room you are in, and like you, looked until I found the panel. Then I spent a lot of time in the passage until I discovered the stairs to the tower room. Then I found the exit panel to the south garden.

"I listened to discussions in the study, but never did I hear names mentioned. Like you I could never identify the voice of the man who has discussions with Mr. Cleeve. So many times I went to the linen room to look for him leaving the study by the hallway. But either I missed him or he left by another way. There may be a secret exit of some kind from the study. If there is, it is not to the passage. I have searched for it and have found nothing.

"I am sure the man you heard in the study and the storage room and the man I saw leaving the study is the same person. I am sure, too, that he is the man in charge of the business. The way he spoke to Mr. Cleeve and the orders he gave, why he would have to be in charge.

"Remember I told you someone is after you? I told you that because I heard him say in the study, 'I will get that girl. I must have that girl. I want to treat her to ecstasy and then....., but he doesn't finish. It is a threat, I know, and he has said it often. It is the way he says it that I know he means harm. He has never said your name, but what other girl is here?"

Victoria appeared to be surprised, then a scowl reflected her concern. "Girl could mean woman, not necessarily a young woman. He is either after you or me. Why do you think he is the man who was in charge when your husband died?"

"I am not absolutely sure, but I have heard him say, 'I have killed to keep the authorities from knowing my business. I shall kill again if necessary. Any man in the business knows what will happen if he says a word. The only murders in this part of Cornwall in recent years have been my husband and the other man I told you about."

There was a pause, then the old crone continued. 'No, Victoria, that is not right. There were two others. Your father and mother."

Victoria looked abashed. "My parents! As a girl I heard questions about their deaths but never a direct accusation."

"I have always known it was murder. Your parents did not just go boating and drown. Your father was too good a sailor. He would never allow a hole to develop in his boat. Both could swim well. They could have made it to the spit. You will have proof in time."

"But who, why?"

"I don't know. But your father knew something was about to happen. He told your mother that. She was worried. After all these years you may have the answer to the who and why of your parents' deaths."

"Perhaps it is better I don't know," Victoria sighed. "Nothing can be done about it if I do learn. If it was murder, those who did it will have their just rewards in some way at some time."

"Better not go searching for answers. You are already in danger and you have done enough sleuthing. It is better for me to do something about your discoveries. Remember, do not do anything until I return."

In her own room, Victoria reviewed all the events of the day. "Surprising, isn't it. I thought traffic in contraband was part of a colorful, romantic past, the subject of exciting tales. But it goes on right now, here, at Kensington House as it did in Castelamer's past. It isn't so colorful or so romantic as the tales would have one believe, not when murder is practiced.

"If Lord Covington is involved, how many other 'honorable' citizens are making illegal purchases. Knowingly. And with the sheriff taking bribes, who among officials can be trusted?

"So Mrs. Tatham thinks I am the one to be careful. It is she who is the object of their wrath. Very well. I shall be careful."

With that Victoria pushed the little table in front of the passage panel. Almost immediately she heard scratching. "I am too tired to play games with him. It is a good time to walk to the abbey." She blew out the candle and left the room.,

Cook was generous with bones and scraps and with these tucked under her arm, she left the house and entered the service area. Ahead of her was Cleeve.

"Why, hello, Victoria. I was just thinking of you. I must ride to Brixton Village and I do not want to go alone. As I passed Socrates, he said to me, 'Tell Victoria to meet me and take me for a jaunt.' You can please two of us if you will say yes."

Before she considered the invitation, a 'yes' popped out. The moment she agreed, she was sorry. "It was his play on Socrates that made me say yes. How can I get out of going?"

Too late. Cleeve had already called the stable master, Socrates was prepared, and there he was now, being walked toward her.

"I would like to go to the abbey on the way," she requested, patting the glistening neck of the horse.

"Have I interrupted a rendezvous?" Cleeve inquired in jest.

"Yes, actually, you have." She spoke as if he were an intruder.

"Well in that case we shall go to the abbey. I want to see who takes your interest." She could not tell if his last comment was said also in jest, for it did seem she detected a tone of concern.

As she rode, she felt a compulsion to inquire about the contraband business and the true owner of Kensington House, but she knew this would be a catastrophe if she did. Instead she opened a conversation by asking, "When do you plan to go to London again?" She was hoping he would refer to his business and tell her more about it.

Instead he beamed, "I am pleased you asked, Victoria, for I was intending to ask you to go with me to investigate the possibility of opening a dress shop. I think we should go."

"Does Mrs. Cleeve fear the plague? Do you think it is safe in London?"

"Elizabeth will not go. She is thinking of going to Oxford with Parliament sitting there."

"Going to London with you, alone!" she exclaimed to herself. The thought of such an act shocked her. In silence she considered the situation. "Such a trip would mean being alone with you in a coach, staying at the same inn, joining you on rounds. How would I escape your advances? You know you are thinking of this trip not to help me." The thoughts angered her, then a new idea surfaced. In silence she thought, "So this is how you plan to take care of the menace to your business, get her to London and no one will ever hear of her again."

Aloud she said, "It is good of you to think about me and to offer help, but I am still Mrs. Cleeve's companion. I need to talk with her."

"You don't need to do that," he commented instantly. "Her need of a companion is only when she is here. She wants to return to London permanently after Oxford."

"How will you manage the property with Mrs. Cleeve absent and you away much of the time?" As soon as she spoke she realized her error. "Forgive me, please. I exceeded my position."

The abbey was in sight and Cleeve did not reply to her question. Instead he asked, "Are we in time for your rendezvous?"

"I am not sure. Let's find out." He dismounted then helped her off Socrates. Cleeve moved apart, curious as to whom she was meeting and felt jealousy mount.

She took her package to the column and placed the contents on the ground. What Cleeve saw made him laugh out loud. "A dog. My competition is a dog!" He relaxed for he fully expected a man to appear, not considering the package. He watched the dog approach the food, wagging its tail and letting Victoria stroke his head. "No, I cannot tell her about my separation from Elizabeth or my termination of this contraband business," he said to himself as he watched. "That time will come. I am still not sure how to get out of this illicit business." He awaited her approach, helped her to mount, and they rode off to Brixton Village.

"Do you often make a rendezvous with that dog?"

"Yes, often."

He noted the enthusiasm of her reply. "I shall change places with that dog," he said in a serious tone.

"Why, you would not eat what I bring him. Cook is generous in giving me scraps and bones."

"I wouldn't eat at all if your would come to see me regularly." He paused then asked, "Why do you turn from me, Victoria." He looked at her, begging an explanation.

"I don't run from you. I cannot, as I told you, accept your advances. You are a married man, and I have too much respect of your wife." There was no question as to her adamant position.

"Would you be of the same mind if I were not married?"

"Indeed I would. I do not consort with men, married or unmarried."

"Oh, that is not what Edward told me." As soon as he made the comment he was sorry.

His statement was a blow. "So Edward talked," she told herself. "So that is what made Cleeve so aggressive. This man thinks I am easy because I fell in love with Edward and consummated that love." Then aloud she stated, "It is Edward who taught me that men are dishonorable."

"Forgive me. I did not mean to say that. It is dishonorable for any man to take advantage of an innocent girl and then talk about it to others. It is equally dishonorable for another man to throw comments to that girl. I apologize. Please accept my apology."

"What has been said cannot be erased." Victoria pulled on the reins, turned Socrates around, and began a trot toward Kensington House, leaving Cleeve staring.

He considered following her but a second thought stopped any move in her direction. As she disappeared around a curve in the road, he turned his horse in the direction of Brixton Village and began a monologue. "Why is it I make such errors when I need that girl. I bumble every effort I make to express my love. She thinks I am going to violate her when in truth I want my arms about her, to kiss her, to love her. I know I appear violent. She does that to me. Those eyes drive me to action. I want my hands on her, my arms crushing her, trying to make her a part of me.

"She keeps reminding me I am married. Damn! I had to marry. I had to have position to get the power I needed, and it was marriage that gave me that position. Elizabeth's family has power at court, power in the financial world and power in the social world. By marrying her

I acquired all I needed to secure my status in the field of trade. I was eminently successful. But I wanted more. I met Wyatt. He made an attractive offer, to be a front man to his illicit business in return for a country estate, an excellent salary and unlimited expenses. I accepted because I could leave my London business in good hands, pile up a small fortune here and gain more status.

"Elizabeth knew my intentions when I courted her, but I was a dashing suitor, and the scar gave her excitement. Our marriage has not been good. At first I tried diligently to make it work, but my absences gave her freedom. She became a female Edward. I brought her to Kensington House hoping that by removing her from the loose social atmosphere of the court, she would care more for me. I hasn't worked. I learned recently that during my absences she has taken on some of the help and particularly a neighbor farmer, Geoffrey Booth.

"Elizabeth and I will be separating as soon as the guests leave. She will work out details in London then I shall be free to marry Victoria. Little Victoria. Because I seek her love, she probably believes I am after every girl I see. There was a time I did. But that was before Elizabeth. Now it is Victoria alone I love. It is Victoria who will one day share my love. No other.

"If I confessed all this to Victoria, she would not believe me let alone listen to me. If I were not so violent in my approach! I must try to be more gentle. She is undoubtedly fearful of me after her experience with Edward." Cleeve was still talking to himself as he entered Brixton Village. "Her eyes will not let me alone!"

Victoria vented her anger after leaving Cleeve, and as she trotted Socrates along the road, she considered her departure from her employer. "Such cheek of that man to throw Edward at me! Edward is a beast to have told Cleeve of our affair. They probably laughed in great guffaws as he described how easily he conquered the little seamstress. It is no wonder Cleeve is so brazen with me. He thinks I am a loose one, and I helped his attitude by letting him kiss me when we were on the beach. Poor Elizabeth to be married to that man. She must know how he cavorts with other women. All women. I hate that man!"

The last words she said aloud, unconscious that she did so, so intent was she in airing her wrath. "No! No! That is not true. I hated him at the moment I left him, but I cannot hate him. He does something to me. I get that strange desire for him, but I don't want him pawing at me. Maybe it is because that first kiss at the inn was so violent that he frightens me and I fear his attack. I do know I do not want him to violate his marriage."

"When are you going to notice me, Victoria."

She was startled when she heard a familiar voice and looked up to find Geoffrey on his horse beside her. "Were you in another world?" he laughed. "I have been your phantom companion for at least a quarter of a mile."

"Oh, Geoffrey, forgive me." She smiled at her unexpected escort. "I guess I was some distance off and did not realize it. Are you enjoying a ride?"

"Not really. I just left Brixton Village and am hurrying home. In fact I saw Christopher in the village. I would much prefer stealing you and taking you home with me." He looked directly at her and added a question begging a positive answer.

"Sorry, Geoffrey."

"Forgive me, but I must hurry. Can you get home alright?"

"Oh, yes. Socrates is a fine guide. Thank you, though."

"My dear, would you attend church services with me on Sunday morning? I shall be honored if you would join me in the Rooth pew. Rooths have been tithed to the church since it was built, and I would like to see you sitting next to me. May I call for you at nine o'clock?"

"Geoffrey, of course."

"Cheerio!" he waved, leaving her to take a path at a right angle to the Plymouth Road.

As he rode on, his thoughts were totally of Victoria. "That girl. She captivates me. Those eyes seem to pierce me, and she has such a charming personality. I want her but she is difficult to reach. I sense she is the gentle type. They take longer to bed. I am in no hurry. She will come around."

A thought of marriage came to mind, and Geoffrey considered it. "Possible, very possible. Victoria has many of the qualities I seek but after being a bachelor a short time, I am not ready to settle down so soon. I can wait, or, who knows. Maybe she will come to me without marriage. Meantime I am enjoying my meetings with _ _ _ _." He caught himself. "I wont say that name even to myself. Why hurry into marriage? That would for all practical purposes put an end to my conquests. Why terminate those pleasures!" A big smile put an exclamation mark on his comments. He followed that with a resounding yell.

Victoria's short meeting with Geoffrey interrupted her thoughts about Cleeve and turned them to Geoffrey. "He is such a handsome man, and that commanding voice. He is so gentle, so considerate, thoughtful. Imagine asking to call for me to take me to church and to sit in the Rooth pew. He doesn't attract me as Cleeve does. He is not so robust, virulent, exciting, but he has lasting qualities. He seems to be the perfect gentleman. He would make a good husband." She adjusted her position on Socrates' back. "Husband?" The thought seemed to develop naturally. "Mmmmmm. That is an idea, a possibility. How would I respond if he should ask? I don't know."

Nagging in the background, serving as a block to a definite decision, was the thought of Chris.

# Chapter Twenty

 rs. Cleeve and Victoria met in the great hall before the masked ball. Staff was completing decorations that would transform the large room into a beautiful setting resembling the Forest of Leigh. Fresh greens had been brought in and arranged to look like trees. Boughs were placed attractively and garlands were strung among the rafters, some hanging to the floor.

"Victoria, you have outdone yourself. Your ideas have made this grand hall a Garden of Eden." Mrs. Cleeve was enthusiastic in her praise, placing her arm around her companion and squeezing to give emphasis. "Is everything ready?"

"Just about. A touch here and there is all that is necessary. The staff has been so helpful. These greens were not cut until early this morning to be fresh, then garlands had to be strung and mounted. Everyone has been working as you can see. Now to talk to cook."

"I shall take care of the food. You get some rest. You must be fresh yourself for tonight."

Victoria accepted the suggestion. She decided a walk in the garden would be fine. The view onto Hythe Haven was particularly lovely with the sun fingering the quiet water to create sparkles. A boat was passing the entrance spreading an array of glitters. From her elevation it looked like a bug skimming on top of the water, an oar on either side chopping into the water to leave momentary foot prints of white. The oarsman tied the boat to a pole and helped his passenger step onto the dock. She could see he was dressed in a cloak, and a hat was pulled over his ears. He appeared to have his face covered. As he moved along the wharf, she could see he dragged one foot and moved slowly.

She expected he would take the path up the hill to Kensington House, but she was surprised when he passed the path entrance and walked along the foot of the cliff at the edge of the water. She followed him with her eyes to the point where he turned the corner of Bodacombe Bluff.

Interested in his movements, she took the garden path bordering the bluff and hurried to the south garden. A quick look over the brink revealed the man walking on the beach. The dragging foot left a broken trail in the sand as he moved along. She watched him for some time, for his progress was slow, and he appeared to be in no hurry.

A commotion behind her took her attention. Instantly fearful, she looked behind the hedge but found nothing. When she returned to the brink, the man was gone. Visually she searched everywhere. She suddenly said aloud, "The cave!

"He drags his foot. He could be the person Mrs. Tatham saw leave the study and walk down the hall. Could he be part of the business? If Mrs. Tatham is correct, that man is head of the business. He would know about the cave. Could it be that he is the person who creates a dragging sound when he uses the passage? Is he the person Mrs. Tatham saw crossing my room? If so, he knows the house well. He may be the owner of the unidentified voice in the study and the storage room. He could be the man who controls Cleeve. If so, he is the man who is after Mrs. Tatham."

Victoria was almost to her room when she stopped suddenly. "If he is the man in the passage, he is the man who uses the peek hole to watch me. He is my tormentor!"

When she entered the room she found that Pall had her bath water ready. She enjoyed the warm water and took time to complete her ablutions. She purposely cut the mysterious man from her thoughts and concentrated on the ball. "Are you ready, Pall?"

"It is going to be a grand party, Miss Victoria. The girls on the staff are as excited as the guests. We may not be in costume with masks, but we will have on the green gowns you made for us. I'll get you a tray of food to hold you over until you eat tonight."

Victoria began arranging her hair, combing, brushing, then braiding, intertwining a green ribbon as she worked. "I must have the classic look of ancient Greece. After all, I am Helen of Troy." The costume she had made for herself was spread across the foot of the bed. She slipped into it easily then stood before her mirror. Her reflection placed her in a simple gown with a square neck, low cut and outlined with a traditional Greek geometric pattern in green to match the ribbon in her hair. The waist was gathered and tied with a ribbon of the same color. Her feet were shod in sandals tied with green ribbons.

The last task was to apply paint to her face, a skill she had learned from Mrs. Cleeve. Colors made her face come alive, highlighting her cheeks and mouth but especially her alluring eyes. A slight patting of powder was all the was required to freshen her skin.

Satisfied with her preparation, she picked up her mask. It could be tied about her head for permanent placement, or it could be held by a short stick that was fastened to the side of the mask to be raised or lowered as desired. Ruffles of lace were used liberally around the eye openings to cover as much of the face as possible.

She went to Mrs. Cleeve's room to assist her with a difficult costume. "Ah, Victoria, my dear, how thoughtful of you to come. I truly do not know how people of Tudor times managed these gowns. I am not sure how to keep from bumping these farthingales into others. You are simply beautiful. You are one of the Greek goddesses."

"That is close. I am supposed to be Helen of Troy. Let me help you with those adjustments. The materials in the gown are truly lovely. You make an excellent Queen Elizabeth. You need a Lord Essex to escort you."

"I tried to convince Christopher to be Lord Essex, but he wanted to be Cupid. He is checking on the musicians and the last minute things. He will be up shortly to dress."

Preferring not to meet him here, Victoria hastened her modifications on Elizabeth's gown. "You look regal in it. Now for jewelry. What shall it be?"

Elizabeth opened a box of diamonds, pearls, rubies and other precious gems. "Use any, my dear. That is what they are for. Some are gifts from my family, and Christopher gave me some. He wants me to wear them."

"Very well. Queen Elizabeth liked jewelry and wore her treasures excessively. So should our Elizabeth. You must have them in your hair, around your neck and on all fingers. I'll place them and you tell me what you think."

Victoria laced strands of pearls through her piled up wig, arranged necklaces around her neck and tried rings on her fingers. After some trial and error, Elizabeth was indeed royal. "Were His Majesty here he would take you as his queen. But you are Mr. Cleeve's queen."

"You are too appreciative. It is you who has created me for this wonderful night. You run along. Christopher and I will make our entrance together."

Many guests had arrived by the time she entered the great hall. Several costumes were unknown to her, those being worn by villagers, neighbors and Mr. Cleeve's business associates.

The color of costumes, movement of people in masks, music coming from the gallery, room decorations, burning candles, all created an enchanting scene. The banquet room was equally lovely. Under beautiful brass chandeliers ablaze with lights, highly polished silver servers had been filled with a variety of foods. Bowls held punch, and ale was available on the sideboard. All was ready for a gala evening.

Mr. and Mrs. Cleeve, Cupid and Queen Elizabeth, entered the hall. She held her mask by the stick before her face, but he chose to wear no mask at all. Victoria had to admit that Cleeve looked manly indeed, for the tights identified his well developed muscular, trim figure. She could hear ladies tittering and voicing words she was thinking. "Look at that chest." "Oh, those handsome legs." "What muscular arms." "Lucky Elizabeth to have a man like that make love to you."

Musicians in the gallery struck up a lively Cornish folk tune, filling the great hall with music. Immediately guests from the countryside formed lines and proceeded to demonstrate a series of intricate patterns as they moved in and out of circles and squares. Laughter was abundant.

Guests from London were honored with music familiar to the court. Dancing was marked by graceful patterns, polite steps, gentlemen making attractive legs and ladies bowing almost to the floor.

This was followed by a mixer, music known to all, and everyone joined in to fill the hall with four lines of dancers. Some were panting noticeably as it ended and many men went to the banquet room to be refreshed with ale.

Victoria was aware of something sharp touching her back. She turned to find Cleeve using an arrow to attract her attention. "I was trying to find your heart, Helen, but as with Victoria, I cannot locate it. Tell me about Victoria. Does she have a heart? I want so much to touch it. I was hoping as Cupid I could pierce her heart with my arrow but my weapon appears to be ineffective. This has never happened before."

Victoria had expected some overture from Cleeve and decided to play the role indicated by her costume. "Oh, but Cupid, you have pierced my heart. And of Paris, too, at the same moment. You made my heart his and his mine. I cannot give it back to Cupid."

"Was I that successful once? Let me try again." With pleading eyes gazing at hers, he gently touched her bosom with the point of his arrow. "Tell me when it is deep enough. When the heart of Victoria is touched, I shall use the arrow on my heart. Then we shall blend our loves forever."

Victoria stood quietly as the arrow remained in place. "You should know, Cupid, that when you created my love for Paris, you created it forever. Your arrow cannot touch my heart again."

"Stay, Helen. I shall return as Paris. And then you cannot deny me. I give you warning, Victoria, as Cupid or as Paris or as Chris, your heart shall be pierced and you shall be mine."

Victoria watched him move away to continue his charade with the bar maid.

Music began again and she was swept up by a ghost who punctuated his dancing with frightening boos.

Later as she sipped a glass of punch the tingle of a bell caught her attention and she watched the approach of a court jester, a person who portrayed his role most effectively by affecting a handicapped leg that dragged as he walked. His baton, topped by a miniature buffoon, was held by a hand whose movement was constricted by an obviously crippled arm. The peaked hat crested a tiny bell that held his mask in place. The handicapped leg provoked a flashback to a view from the brink of a man walking on the beach, and she thought to herself, "He dragged his leg. He went into the cave. He could be the man at the peek hole!" She felt a shiver of fear as she realized she could be facing her tormentor. Her hand went to her throat. She heard him speak to her.

"Oh, Helen. Your beauty dazzles me. It is no wonder Paris stole you. I would steal you, too. Would I were Paris now, I would cause an international scene and defy armies to take you from me."

The voice she could not identify, but she thought she had heard it before. "You are teasing me, Sir Jester, and you are successful in winning a laugh from me," she responded to his flattery trying at the same time to cover her anxiety. "Tell me, whose court do you leave to come here?"

"It is from no court I come. I come only to court you."

Victoria did sincerely laugh at his clever use of words, but the tone of his voice was more serious than the lightness she expected. "Your skill in producing laughs is to be enjoyed. Since you have no court to entertain, perhaps I can recommend you to His Majesty."

"It is only to your court I would go. I would find joy in no other place. My eyes have watched you, and I know your beauty. Your eyes alone move me to action. I am not jesting when I say some day you will be mine."

Victoria had no reply for she was stunned. She again caught the serious tone that accompanied his last comment.

"When may I see you again, sweet Helen?"

"Paris objects to my meetings with strangers," she quipped.

"You jest with me, fair maiden. We are not strangers. We have met. In fact we have met several times. Think on it."

Victoria was perplexed but she tried not to show her reaction. She forced a smile but wondered if he was making silly conversation or if he was serious in stating facts. "Where could I have met him? If I have met him then he is only affecting the foot dragging, for I have never met a handicapped person." To relieve her tension, she said, "It is you who is the jester. Why, I do believer Sir Walter Raleigh approaches." She was glad for the interruption as she saw a man coming toward her. He was dressed in the style of the late Tudor period.

"Forgive me, Helen. I must see to our Queen Elizabeth," the court jester announced as he withdrew.

"I shall watch for our jester when the masks come off. I must know who he is," she promised herself.

"Dear Helen, may I escort you to the dining table?" the person in Raleigh's costume requested. "The music has stopped for a time, but later I would have a dance with you." The voice was unmistakable.

"Indeed you may, Sir Walter."

"May I remove my mask, Victoria."

"How is it you know me without a second guess?"

"How does a bee know a flower" I should know you if I were blind to sight or impervious to touch."

"Oh, Geoffrey, how shall it be if I have no secrets?" she pouted as he removed her mask and then his own.

"These things do get uncomfortable and they are impossible for eating supper. What shall it be?"

At one end of the table was a roasted joint of beef and at the other end a leg of pork. Cheese, green vegetables, roasted potatoes, roasted pheasant, its plumage displayed appropriately, chicken and a variety of fish were placed between. Pates were decorated brightly. A man in livery was in attendance and maids in Victoria's green dresses were assisting.

Once served, small tables for four to six persons were set along one side of the room. Silver service and serviettes were in position at each place.

"The Cleeves do provide for their guests. His Majesty cannot have a better table."

"Mrs. Cleeve has brought London to Kensington House, not only with fine food but with elegance."

Music started again. Not so many party makers were in the great hall, but there were enough for a line dance. Masks were off and it was more pleasing to talk to animate faces. Smiles radiated pleasure and eyes flashed in enjoyment. Light quips were bantered about as dancers moved in and out of patterns. As she danced, Victoria looked about for the jester. He had not been in the banquet room, and she could not find him in the hall. "I want to see his face," but she gave up searching. He was no where to be seen.

"You dance divinely, Victoria. You move rhythmically and with such a light step." Geoffrey was complimentary as a pattern brought them together.

"It is you who leads me gracefully. How is it a farmer dances so well?" she asked quickly before she had to step to the other line.

Geoffrey smiled at her, waiting for her to return. "I practice with a hayfork," he quipped. He bent double as he made an exaggerated leg and she bowed low to end the dance.

"Your costume is perfect for you," he complimented as he led her away from the dance floor. "Helen herself could not have been more beautiful, and I doubt she could have fitted her costume with as much charm. Oh, Victoria, you are love." he stated emphatically, pulling her around to face him. He wanted to take her in his arms and kiss her before the assembled crowd, but he was interrupted.

"The host demands a dance," came a voice over his shoulder. Cleeve was looking directly at Victoria.

Graciously she excused herself to Geoffrey and raised her hand for Cleeve to lead her to a place in line. She endeavored to be formal but friendly, yet she could not help but notice his skill in moving through patterns, the sureness of his step, his sense of rhythm. She responded to his grace and began enjoying his lead. She even smiled at him. but maintained her reserved distance.

"Your eyes, Victoria," he whispered as they took hands to circle. "Your eyes do things to me. Those hazel darts prick my heart."

They released hands and parted to step into a line movement, his eyes following her. His interest was so intent he did not notice a minor commotion developing among the seated guests.

A highwayman, his mask still on his face, was talking to Queen Elizabeth. He was playing his outlaw role, demanding the queen's jewelry. She had given him a strand of pearls, a paste string that was an excellent reproduction. He fingered them, commented on their fine quality and pocketed them. He then raised in his hand her exquisite emerald hanging from a golden chain. He appraised it by whistling through his teeth. She denied him his request saying, "Nay, Highwayman. This is yours only if you carry me off as well."

"My dear lady, that would be a pleasure. But I cannot put you in my pocket. Come, now. Meet my demands or I shall take your jewels by force."

"It will have to be by force then." she laughed.

Her laugh was short lived, for she felt a forceful sudden jerk on the back of her neck, bringing tears to her eyes and prompting a cry of pain.

Quickly the emerald was in the highwayman's hand, and he slipped it instantly into his pocket. He turned to leave the room but got only as far as the door where he was intercepted by Geoffrey, sword drawn, who blocked his exit. "You play the role too well, Highwayman. As the queen's liege I challenge you." His action was not a charade.

By this time the music had stopped, voices quieted to silence, and all eyes were focused on the two men. What had been byplay had turned to serious confrontation.

The highwayman unsheathed his sword and the two men began paring and thrusting, each looking for an opening. Cleeve grabbed two swords from the wall, tossed one to Jonathan, and the two closed in on the intruder. As quickly as it started, the duel was over. Cleeve and Jonathan directed the man to the door and Geoffrey returned to Elizabeth.

To relieve the tension, he bowed to Elizabeth and said loudly, "As your liege I shall defend you before all men and return to you your jewels."

Elizabeth, interpreting the plea on his face, spoke out, "Ah, Sir Walter, would I could knight thee thrice I would do so. But instead I shall grant thee leave to take Spanish galleons with all the loot to be your very own." She offered her hand for Raleigh to kiss, and the guests applauded. Tension was relieved, the music struck up, and dancing was renewed.

Victoria danced with Lord Arlington, Guy and James, then pleaded for a rest. "A bit of sweet?" Geoffrey proposed. She agreed and together they returned to the banquet room. Trifle, blanc mange, a variety of cakes, cheeses, crackers and fruit looked inviting. A selection was made and they sat down to eat.

Their conversation was broken by the arrival of Cleeve. "Thank you, Geoffrey, for intercepting the highwayman. That fellow had a gall and almost got away with Elizabeth's jewelry. Imagine. Just walking in, joining the party, eating, dancing, then accosting her. I owe you my gratitude."

"What did you do to him?"

"He is locked up for the sheriff."

"He provided a bit of diversion for your guests."

"What surprises me, he tried it alone, but he made two critical errors. He wore an authentic highwayman's mask, and he kept it on after supper when all guests had removed theirs. When charades were over, he continued."

"That is what caught my attention. I heard Elizabeth refuse him," Geoffrey explained. "Most untimely for him. Anyhow you had a fine party, Christopher, despite the interruption. And I must be getting home."

The three walked together to the great hall. They found others were preparing to leave.

"Until tomorrow, Victoria," Geoffrey reminded her. "One day I may not have to take leave of you."

Cleeve cringed inside.

# Chapter Twenty-One

S unday morning was overcast and brisk with a cold wind blowing in from the sea. "A Cornish fall day," Victoria thought as she looked out her window. The garden was in motion as wind plucked leaves from trees then waltzed them around vehemently. Branches held on tightly as if fearing to be snatched away, and hedges were rotating as the wind changed cadences.

She took some deep breaths and felt invigorated by slaps of wind on her face. "What is it that gives you such an exhilarating feeling this Sunday morning? Is it the fun you had last night? Perhaps. Knowing that you contributed so much to the success of the party? Maybe. Or is it the anticipation of meeting Geoffrey? You are not a child meeting a young man. Why, Geoffrey must be at least twenty-seven or more. And you?" She stopped before she finished, for another idea had occurred to her. "When was the last time a man called for you at your home? Do you realize that no man, young or old, has ever called on you? And at your age! Tsk. Tsk. Tsk." She smiled at the thought. "Then this is the first, and for church!"

She enlivened her humming with a faster tempo and she tried to whistle, but the effort produced only blasts of air. With no thought at all, she began singing aloud a song she had not thought of in years, a schoolroom round.

All the while she continued dressing, having selected a woolen gown for the weather, something conservative for church, and something with a bit of color for Geoffrey. It was a green dress with lace at the neck and sleeves and embroidery covering the front of the bodice. She placed her mother's locket around her neck, a bonnet went to her head and a cloak was whirled around her shoulders. She considered a muff, then thought it would be a hindrance if he should want to hold her hand. "Fancy that idea. Are you encouraging him? And on your way to church." A glance in the mirror prompted a little more red on the cheeks. She hurried to the window and found him waiting at the entry.

She almost skipped to the door as childlike happiness guided her. With more dignity she went down the stairs, pausing at the entry hall to compose herself.

"Good morning, Victoria." The voice was familiar, but she was completely taken back on hearing it. She twirled to find the expected figure on the stairs looking at her. Cleeve was dressed for riding.

"Good morning to you." She addressed him curtly. The interruption caused a cut in her jovial air.

"I thought you would be sleeping late after the ball." His tone indicated a strong negative inquisitiveness.

The questioning bothered her. She wanted to say, "It is none of your business," but she replied, "Geoffrey Rooth is calling for me."

"Rooth," he considered to himself, "is seeing too much of her." He stood for a moment then spoke dryly. "Have a good time." The lack of feeling conveyed his thoughts. He watched her open the door, then he returned up the stairs. "I must do something or I will lose that girl.

Victoria went out the front door upset by the brief confrontation but as casually as she could, she presented herself with a bright, "Good morning, Geoffrey."

On hearing the door open, he alighted his rig. A broad smile revealed the pleasure her presence gave him, and he bowed in jest saying, "My Helen of Troy has vanished, blown away in the Cornish night leaving me with Victoria, a sprite of beauty, the modern Helen."

The deep voice was even more thrilling to hear on this occasion. "You speak like a poet," she said as he took her hand. She felt his warmth in the clasp that gave her hand an added welcoming squeeze.

"You inspire me with words poetic," he responded, helping her step up and into the simple rig pulled by a single horse. He took his place in the driver's seat. As he lifted the reins, he took her hand and slipped it through the crook of his arm warning, "Hold tightly, my dear. This Roman charioteer is wild! Inflamed! Ged up, Trojan." The horse responded instantly and the rig was in motion, slowly at first, then Trojan broke into a trot. Wind increased with the speed, and she snuggled closer to his warmth. He put a free hand on hers.

Chatting about the masked ball shortened the distance to Brixton Village. Victoria paused in their conversation to listen to the melodic peel of bells from the old church as their clash and clang floated over the countryside. For as long as she could remember and for generations before, Cornish families had been called to church and then welcomed in their approach by these clarions. Bell ringers standing within the base of the tower pulled ropes in designated rhythm to activate the bells. Clappers tumbled against metal to create euphonic tones that together produced the peel.

Geoffrey reflected his feeling for Victoria as they came to a stop near the church. "All too soon the joy of your nearness is gone. We must be proper as we leave our chariot." He put his hand at her elbow to assist her over rough ground outside the churchyard. Other church goers were drawing near, friendly greetings were exchanged with Geoffrey, and he introduced her to several of his acquaintances.

The grey stone church was old, the square tower and rounded Norman arches identifying its origins as being in the thirteenth century. Geoffrey and Victoria passed through the entrance porch and half way down the nave to where he guided her to his family pew.

She felt at home in the familiar church. Every Sunday for years she had joined members of the Castelamer household staff to worship here. She caught herself analyzing the intricate geometric designs decorating the great Norman chancel arch as she had done as a child.

Brixton Village church was unique among Cornish churches, indeed among all village churches in Britain, for on its south wall were primitive murals, simple but expressive paintings, interpreting scenes from both the Old and New Testaments. Paints had been applied to the wall by traveling religious students in the fourteenth century, and early vicars had used these paintings to illustrate lessons to children of their parish.

After the service of matins, Geoffrey escorted her back to his rig then spoke. "It would please me very much if you would join me at my home for your noon meal. It is not far, and I shall get you back to Kensington House in good time."

"I would be delighted to see your home, but I must not stay much after."

The lane Trojan took bordered a copse giving the countryside an appearance of wildness, then it rose to a hilly elevation that allowed a view of the west country. The wind had calmed, but Geoffrey kept her hands covered with one of his. "This part of Cornwall is so lovely," she beamed. "I thrill to the pleasure of just looking at it. One can see for miles from this spot. It is so beautiful with its rolling hills, stretches of cultivated land, forested areas, meadows, a wooded dale. I do believe I could live in no other place and be completely happy."

"You are on my land," he explained, pleased with her appreciative comments. "I inherited some with my house, but I recently bought an additional section. It is productive soil if cared for. The cattle and sheep are mine."

"You like being a farmer, don't you?"

"It is the only life for me."

Trojan stopped on a rise. Below lay a small wooded glen washed by a stream. Beyond, on a low hilltop, was a manor house of grey granite. "What a dramatic setting, Geoffrey. It looks like a fortified house with those battlements. It is no wonder you love this place."

"I have the same feeling of satisfaction whenever I arrive on this spot. The house was built at the same time as Castelamer by a member of that family. It has been modernized by successive generations, and it is quite livable. Come. I shall show you."

The exterior design of the entry was much like Kensington House, but it opened directly onto a very large room with an inglenook fireplace at one end. Swords and shields decorated either wall. Furniture was heavy oak, hand made. "This is our great hall. Let me give you a tour of the house." The kitchen was a miniature of the one at Kensington House. Delicious aromas permeated the house as cook prepared the noon meal. Freshly baked bread was cooling on the work table.

Upstairs were bedrooms. The master bedroom she was shown was a smaller version of her own.

The noon meal was served in a small dining room, a heavy refectory table in the center surrounded by large oak chairs. Brass candlesticks lighted the center. Thick soup in pewter bowls was served first with chunks of fresh bread. Mutton and vegetables followed. "Oh, Geoffrey.

Strawberries with clotted cream. You remembered my weakness. What a thoughtful way to finish the delicious meal."

"Pleasing you has given me new purpose to my life," he replied, looking directly at her.

"I am not sure I want to leave this room. It is so comfortable. Do you think this table came from the abbey?"

"Such is the story, but I do not know for sure." Her interest pleased him.

"Come. Let us sit near the fire in the great hall." He led her into the big stone room. As they sat side by side on a comfortable sofa before the fire, Geoffrey took her hand and kissed the open palm. "I brought you here, Victoria, to see some of my estate and to show you my home. All of it is incomplete without a mistress. I want you to be that mistress. Will you marry me?"

She was taken back by his proposal. It was not entirely a surprise, for many overtures had been made. She sat still, pondering, making no visual effort to reply.

"I know this is a sudden and serious question. I do not want an answer now. You need time to consider. I want you to know what you will have when you come here. I believe you have many offers from other gentlemen, such a lovely creature as you."

Geoffrey had just considered asking his question. He had learned only the past week that the married woman with whom he had been enjoying escapades was leaving Cornwall, and this development led him to believe that he might do just fine married to Victoria. He had already concluded that he could not have her without marriage.

"I must tell you that I have been married. I lost my wife in childbirth last spring." Still no word did Victoria speak, her eyes fixed on the fireplace. She was about to express herself when he spoke again. "Come, Victoria, I shall return you to Kensington House."

He rose and went toward the entry. She put on her bonnet while he retrieved her cloak. With her back to him, he placed her wrap on her shoulders then let his arms slip around her waist. She turned to look up at him. He bent over her and let his eyes dart about her face. "Your eyes are beautiful. Every time you look at me my heart thumps, then skips, and I want to take you in my arms and do this." He kissed her gently. She returned his kiss with ardor.

When they parted she looked at him, eyes glassy with the beginning of tears. "Do not speak, my love," he whispered. "Think on it. I want you, your love, all, completely. Let your heart give the answer."

The way home was quiet, she thinking, he holding both her hands, drawing her close to him. Victoria felt a wonderful glow inside, the radiance that comes from being loved.

Unexpectedly a picture of Chris flashed. "Why thoughts of him? He can't possibly marry me. What can he give me? I want marriage but he cannot ask for my hand. What is it that brings him to mind?" She fought the realization then admitted, "He does have meaning for me. Could a thought of him be an omen I must heed? Wait, Victoria. Hold your answer to Geoffrey. Be sure."

Finally she spoke. "You are love itself, Geoffrey. But I cannot give you an answer now. I am seeking answers to some questions, and when I have those you shall have your answer."

"I have patience. I shall wait, for your love is worth the wait." He looked at her longingly, then thought to himself, "Perhaps it is better this way. I would feel guilty being avowed to Victoria then seek the bed of someone else."

They parted at the entry to Kensington House. He wanted to take her in his arms but thought better of it. She thanked him graciously for a lovely day.

On Monday morning early, Jonathan picked her up in a wagon, its bed loaded, the contents covered from view. "I have two purposes for this trip. One is business and the other is pleasure." Looking at her face when she saw the wagon, he added smiling, "I trust you will be comfortable. I have tried to care for bumps by adding cushions." He helped her mount the front seat and headed the horses toward Plymouth.

"You have not told me, Jonathan, why you arrived at my bedroom door with a stable boy."

"I have not asked your forgiveness for such an inconsiderate act. A woman was seen in the stable area. She acted with suspicion, but my associate could identify her only by her clothes and her hair. We searched the garden where she ran but were unsuccessful in locating her. I had orders to search until she was found. We think we looked at all the ladies in the house, even the guests. We think whoever was there changed clothes and got away. Isn't that what you would do, Victoria?"

"It all depends. If I found out what I wanted to know and was being chased for that reason, I might have gone down the palisades and hid myself among the rocks."

"We did not think of looking there. Is that where you went, Victoria?" He looked at her feeling assured he knew the culprit.

"How could I when you found me in my room. Why do you ask?"

"The description the stable boy gave of the woman he saw fits you perfectly except for the clothes and hair. We cannot figure out how you got from the garden to your room and changed clothes and your hair arrangement so quickly. Somebody would have seen you entering the house or passing through the hall."

"Then it was not I the boy saw."

"Possibly. Do you know another lady at Kensington House who could be mistaken for you?"

"Perhaps not. Tell me, why is it so important to find this lady?"

Feeling himself being pushed too far, he hesitated, then said, "I don't know that it is so important. We just have orders to report suspicious people, and the young man was doing his job."

"I would like to know, too, the right reason why you came to the cave to check on me."

"For the same reason. Suspicion. Mr. Cleeve has a standing rule. All strangers or suspicious people must be identified and reported. Furthermore, you could have been hurt crawling around those rocks and no one would have been around to help you."

"It seems somebody was around to help me. Who was the man with the grey hair who was looking down onto the beach from the brink along he south garden?"

"It could have been one of the help. I was asked by Mr. Cleeve to get to you immediately."

"Interesting," Victoria reasoned to herself. "I am surprised Cleeve did not come to the cave himself. He would have trapped me. He is so intent on compromising me. Perhaps the occasion did not suit his fancy. Then aloud she asked, "Did he direct you to intercept me or protect me?"

"I do not recall his exact words, but he did say, 'Don't let anything happen to that girl.'"

The tandem team of horses was moving along at a fast gait for wagon horses. The sun was bright but the air was cool. Victoria pulled around her a blanket Jonathan had provided and watched the countryside skip along beside her. The rhythm of the wagon's movement on the dirt road must have lulled her to sleep, for she became aware of a tugging. "Have we arrived? That was a short trip."

"Its length is always related to the amount of time you sleep. I am going to stop at the inn first. Please get something warm to drink. Wait for me. I'll not be long with the business."

When he returned, he motioned for her to follow him. At the top of the stairs he stopped at a room and knocked. Greeting them was the lady whom Victoria thought could be a cousin. A table in the center of the room was set for lunch. Victoria held out her hand and spoke. "I shared your room not too long ago. I regretted your absence after you left for I wanted so much to talk with you."

"Of course, dear. I remember. It was as I told you. I was busy."

"Diana," Jonathan joined in, "you surprise me. I told Victoria I had a friend I wanted her to meet and you already know each other."

"It was a short meeting unfortunately. Are we ready to eat?"

All agreed and she left the room briefly. When she returned a man followed with a tray of food. The three talked as they ate, Victoria telling them how Mrs. Cleeve called attention to the similarity between Diana and herself.

The meal over, Jonathan said, "May I ask both of you to stand with your backs to the mirror. Diana, where is the hand mirror I asked for? Good. Now. Will you help each other bare your left shoulders. Look in the hand mirror as I hold it. Tell me what you see."

"A birthmark," Diana replied instantly. "That is no secret. I have had mine for years, ever since I looked at myself in a mirror. Friends often remark about it." She laughed.

"I did not discover mine until a short time ago," Victoria confessed.

"Fine. Now look." Jonathan removed his jacket, unbuttoned his shirt and pushed it across his shoulder.

"I see a birthmark," Diana smiled.

"All our birthmarks are the same, and they are in the same position. Same size, same shape, same color. Let's all look in the mirror. Smile. What do you notice about our teeth?"

"Why, we all have a protruding tooth, and it is the same for each of us," Diana declared.

"Diana, what was your childhood name?" Jonathan continued questioning.

"Why, Penelope."

"And yours, Victoria."

"It was Patience." Her eyes reflected dismay then she exclaimed, "Penny! Penny! You can't be Penny. I saw you in bed, dead! You had just given birth to a child. You can't be my twin sister."

"I am Penny, Patty."

The girls embraced. Instantly questions rang out, both talking at once.

"Quiet!" Jonathan yelled, slamming his hand on the table. "One at a time. We all want to ask and answer, and I want to hear it all."

"If we are sisters, you could be the brother we have not seen in years," shouted Diana.

"I am! But let's take us one at a time. Victoria, you go first."

Before we sit down to talk, let's go to my home," Diana proposed. "It is not far and we might as well be comfortable. We could make more than an afternoon out of this reunion."

She led the way to a quiet street of fine brick houses. She used a highly polished knocker and shortly a maid opened the door. "Come in," Diana invited. "Molly will bring some ale. Get comfortable. Victoria, you start us off."

Victoria selected highlights of her life since leaving Castelamer, omitting all but the most appropriate details. "It is not a very exciting story. I left the day Penny died. I settled in Exeter where I found a position as a seamstress. Mrs. Cleeve found me there, asked me to make some gowns for her, then she asked me to serve as her companion at Kensington House. Now I am back at our home."

"That is a strange circumstance, almost as if it were planned by someone. Now to my story," Diana volunteered. "I'll start the same day Patty used for her beginning. It was true. I was taken for dead. Mrs. Battey told the staff I had died in childbirth, and she assigned two women to prepare my body for burial. When they began washing me, one noticed I was breathing, ever so lightly. Mrs. Battey finally found a doctor who worked on me. Then Mrs. Battey nursed me back to health.

"It is also true I gave birth to Mr. Wyatt's child but unfortunately it did not live. That man was a devil who fascinated me, and I must admit I liked him. He did wonderful things to me even before I left our room, Victoria. It was always in the study when the Framsdens were gone. He wanted me to meet him, then he would undress and fondle me, whisper beautiful words, then he would take me, often.

"When I became pregnant, he threatened me with death if I should tell. Then he left me. I never saw him again. What he taught me I could not change. I wanted men. When my health was restored, I came to Plymouth in search of a man who would take Mr. Wyatt's place.

"My life is interesting to me. I wouldn't change it for any other. I earn good money, dress well, and I have an established clientele. I bought this home and I maintain a room at the fashionable inn."

Victoria volunteered her experience with Mr. Wyatt that day on the brink. "Wasn't his disappearance ever discussed at Castelamer?"

"Mr. Wyatt was not well known by the staff," Diana explained. "He talked only to Mr. Framsden. He came occasionally to the socials although he was in the study frequently. He only became sociable with me."

"Was his body ever found?"

"If it was I never heard."

"What was said about me?"

"Every bit of news about you was withheld from me until I regained my strength. When I asked about you, everyone said you had gone away for a time. I thought that was strange, but your absence was pushed to the background when the Framsdens left. That announcement made all other events minor. Because I had regained my strength, I decided it was time for me to leave. I cut off all contact with Castelamer."

After more questions, Jonathan began his story. "You already know that when our parents died, I was sent to relatives in the north of Cornwall. They were wonderful to me. With that as a background, I'll start my story when I was seventeen. The father of the family who raised me called me to him and said, 'Son, I have a paper for you. It was found among your father's things. It has your name on it. I have kept it for you until you grew up.' He handed me the paper. I noticed it had a seal on it, and the seal was unbroken. Then he said, 'You read it, and if you want to talk about it, we'll talk.'" From his pocket Jonathan pulled out a paper. He read:

My dear boy,

On a day when you are old enough to understand, you will be given this letter. It carries with it the greatest love of your father and mother.

I am writing this because we believe there is expected danger for our family.

Quite by accident I learned an illicit contraband business is being conducted at Castelamer. A Mr. Dudley Wyatt has somehow manipulated our uncle to permit Mr. Wyatt the use of Castelamer for this business.

I have learned also that Mr. Wyatt controls our cousins, Cecil and Anne Framsden, for his own ends.

Because Mr. Wyatt knows I have information about his business, 1 fear for the lives of your mother as well as my own. He is an unscrupulous man and will do anything to protect his interests.

It is for this reason I am writing this letter. If anything should happen to me and your mother, know it is not been an accident. It has been murder.

Should your mother and I die, you, Penelope and Patience are to be heirs to Castelamer. You uncle provided that I inherit and my children after me.

I am fearful, however, that Mr. Wyatt, because he has acquired so much power, will manipulate the will as he manipulated our uncle.

This sealed letter is being placed in the hands of Mr. Evston with the instruction that it be opened only by you when he thinks you are old enough to understand.

If indeed you and your sisters are not the recognized heirs to Castelamer, you will know what to do.

We give our blessings and ask for His protection on you.

Lovingly,

Your devoted Mother and Father

"I read and reread the letter, thought at length about it and made plans. I knew the two of you were placed at Castelamer. I thought if I could get to Brixton Village and find work, I could learn about conditions at the house. Then I could decide what to do. I discussed this plan with Mr. Evston and he agreed.

"I arrived in the village using the name of Jonathan Kemper. I got a job as a farm worker. Of course I found out that the Framsdens owned the house. It was easy to get information. Everybody talked about Castelamer. Some discussed our parent's deaths as murder even though their deaths occurred years ago. They also talked about the missing Patience, many charging murder as well. They knew about Penny's illness and some said it was attempted murder. When she went to Plymouth, they thought she had been forced out of the house.

"It was said the Framsdens went to France.

"I wanted more information and decided I had to get to the house for it. I asked the stable master for a job and he gave me one. I kept listening for the name of Wyatt, but not one person spoke of him. The men in the stable did not discuss much of anything.

"Then the Cleeves arrived. He talked of himself as the owner and word went around that he had purchased Castelamer. He certainly acted like the owner. He dismissed all the house staff and hired new help. He changed the house's name and started redecorating some of the rooms. I asked for an inside job and got one. That is when I first entered the house.

"Mrs. Cleeve wanted socials. She gave parties, had house guests and the house livened up considerably. He went riding often. Once he asked me to accompany him and we became friendly after that. One day he called me to his office. 'Jonathan, we have need of a capable, dependable young man,' he began. 'I am in charge of a very important business, and I need a lieutenant to assist me. You show promise. The person I hire, however, must be willing to pledge that he will speak to no one a single word of what he learns about the business on pain of death.'

"His voice gave no doubt as to the seriousness of the statement. He spoke the words 'on pain of death' with emphasis.

"I thought immediately of our parents. What father had learned he paid for with their lives. But for me it was an opportunity to get into the business to learn what was going on and to avenge our parents if indeed they were murdered.

"I took the job and learned. Mr. Cleeve imports without paying taxes, he sells without paying taxes, and he involves the best names in Cornwall, Devon and the shires beyond. I call on clients, make deliveries and for that I earn an excellent salary.

"All this time I thought Cleeve was in charge. But one day I was called to the study. Cleeve was at his desk. A folding screen was standing beyond him. A man was behind the screen. I was not introduced and I did not see him. Even now I cannot tell you his name or can I describe him.

"This man is the owner, the power. He makes decisions. He owns Kensington House. It could be he is responsible for our parents' deaths and for taking Castelamer. I only think this. I cannot prove it.

"Now I must speak frankly. Victoria, you are in danger, grave danger. Your name is never mentioned, no name is ever mentioned except Cleeve's name, but it is obvious you are the girl 'that man' wants to use for revenge. Cleeve and that man know you have been in the cave. They think you are the woman seen in the stable. You know too much. They are only waiting for him to have a go at you, then Cleeve will kill you.

"Go to London. Start your business. Perhaps if you get away you will save yourself. I'll help you with money. Please go!

"One final word. Nothing of what I said cannot be repeated. I shall face death if word gets back to Kensington House that I have spoken one word."

Victoria considered her brother's advice. "I can't go now. I have found a man who loves me and I love him. I would lose all if I left. And Mrs. Cleeve has great need of me."

"But you must, Victoria, for our sakes. We have just found each other and we can be a family again."

"I cannot go now, but being forewarned is being forearmed, as the saying goes I am prepared. I shall be alert to both Cleeve and that man."

"You said you found a man who loves you, and if you left you could lose him. Is he a farmer? Does he visit Kensington House?" Diana questioned.

"He is a farmer. He comes to socials at Kensington House, but I don't know how much he visits the Cleeves other than the socials."

"Is his name Geoffrey Rooth?" Diana interrupted.

Victoria was stunned. "Why, yes it is. Why do you ask?" She suspected he had been seeing her.

"I met Elizabeth Cleeve at the inn where I have my room. She spoke to me about knowing someone who looks like me. We struck up an acquaintance and since she suspected my work, she asked if I could help her with a private party. I offered her my home and she accepted. The party was small, she and a man. I could not help overhearing their discussion about Kensington House. They talked about Victoria. She is fond of you, Victoria, and he would like to know you better. He said he was even considering marrying 'Victoria so he could know her better.'"

Diana continued to watch her sister as she spoke, and she could see how overwhelming the story was to her.

"Elizabeth here, with Geoffrey. Elizabeth!"

"Yes, dear. They have come often. In fact she has a party as she calls it for next week. We have an understanding, though, that a cancellation may be required."

Victoria stood up, walked a bit, then sat down. "Forgive me for being so upset. I never dreamed that what you have told me could be true. I need some time to think."

"I am so sorry I am the bearer of this news. But your safety is more important than Geoffrey Rooth. If he loves you, he can wait. He can call for you wherever you go, even to London. Think on it."

The discussion continued through the rest of the day, over supper, and into the night. Questions were asked and answered, more details were explained, and by the time they separated they had established their family identification with one another.

Next morning when Jonathan picked her up, he had the wagon partially filled with supplies for Kensington House. Both talked about the threat to Victoria and possible courses of action for her, and Jonathan cautioned her about over friendliness toward him when they met.

By the time she arrived in her room, she was ready to sit down and think through all that had developed. To have found her brother and sister was exhilarating and the pleasure of their company had given her new spirit. "I must not let anything come between us now. I need to build our relationship, strengthen it and make sure we see each other often."

Feeling more secure for having family members near and knowing they were readily available and willing to help her, she moved to the next consideration. "Geoffrey is a surprise to me. I did not expect he would be acting like one of his farm's roosters. He just does not seem to be the kind of man to do that. It may be that Elizabeth sees no problem in meeting other men. It is the way of London's social life, and she may have brought his part of London with her as she did the entertainment. I wonder if Cleeve knows. If he does, he may consider he also can take freedoms, and that is why he makes advances to me."

Jonathan's warning came under consideration. "So Mrs. Tatham was right when she said someone is interested in me. My tormentor is head of the business and he knows I have found out too much about what he is doing. Well, get him before he gets you, Victoria. Set a trap. Be in control. Get him in your web."

The expression on her face was somber. After some time a sneer appeared on her lips. "Now I know what to do."

The next day Victoria took her scissors to the blacksmith for sharpening. The shop was in the service area next to the stable. She stayed to watch the smithy shoe a horse and chatted with him for a time. "I wont have these scissors ready until this afternoon. Can you call for them then?"

"That is fine. I think I will go to the abbey and read. I'll return by early afternoon." When she turned to leave, she almost bumped into Cleeve. On guard instantly, she wondered how long he had been there and if he had heard her comments. She tried to cover her obvious negative reaction by saying, "Good morning."

"And a good morning to you, Victoria. I should like to ask you to go riding with me. Would you like to go? It might be more interesting than going to the abbey. I would enjoy your company."

"No, thank you,. There is work to be done before I go to the abbey. But perhaps you will ask me some other time."

"I shall do that and soon." With that she watched him ride off.

Victoria went first to the kitchen to ask cook for a pasty and some bones for the dog. She puttered around her room for a time then stopped to see Mrs. Cleeve to offer to do anything for her, and the two talked for a time.

"Some of our guests are returning to London after tomorrow. There are reports that the worst of the plague is over, and authorities believe it is under control although deaths are still occurring. Kensington House will be quiet again when they leave. I do wish Christopher would plan a business trip to London. I, too, would like to return for a while. There are times when I wish we could go there to live for good. Lady

Arlington has asked me to go to Oxford, and if Christopher agrees to it, I may."

"Perhaps we should plan a series of small parties when the guests leave," Victoria suggested. "The neighbors so enjoy coming here, and you entertain with such a flair. Small gatherings are often more pleasurable than large ones."

The proposal brought a smile to Elizabeth's face. "You are a dear, and you helped so much with the guests. Perhaps we should entertain. Let's put our ideas together and then we will do something."

Victoria picked up her pasty and a large collection of bones with a warning to the cook, "What you are feeding that dog will make him too fat for his own hunting. You have made him a beautiful animal. His ribs have disappeared and his coat is sleek. We both thank you for the meat and bones, and I thank you for the pasties."

The dog more and more was making the abbey his domain. Sometimes he came to meet her, or at other times he made an appearance during her visit. She always placed his food at the base of the column where they met. Frequently he sat by her as she read, and when she walked about, he sauntered nearby. It was obvious a friendship had developed, for the two enjoyed each other, even seeking the companionship of one another.

On this day, overcast and cool, Victoria chose to walk to the abbey. Her purpose was to consider in more detail how to force the issue with her tormentor. "The scissors will be under my pillow. The light will be bright enough so he will have no trouble seeing me. When I hear the scratching, I shall undress slowly, in full view, my back to him. I shall take time, enticing him. Once in the room, I shall see who this person is." Thoughtfully and deliberately she rehearsed mentally the flow of action in a setting she would create.

She was not aware of a person watching her from behind the south transept arch, so involved was her concentration. As she entered the chancel area, he took long, silent strides until he placed himself in back of her, and copying her cadence, joined her slow but regular walking rhythm, step by step. At the altar, she turned and bumped head long into him. Startled, she cried out, extending her arms in a quick reflex action to protect herself. Anticipating her movement, he opened his arms and she fell into them. Like a trap, he enfolded her. Instantly she recognized her captor, the feel of him, the smell of him. She had only to raise her head to confirm her identification, and she looked directly into Cleeve's eyes.

"Ah, Victoria. Since you wouldn't come riding with me, I accepted your invitation to see you among the ruins. You did tell me you were coming here."

"Not so, sir. You overheard my comments to the smithy." Her tone was defiant.

"Now, Victoria. Please don't be so formal. My name is Chris. Use it. Please."

She remained silent, her eyes fighting his. She felt his strength building gradually in the arms that locked her, the pressure of their crunch increasing about her chest, a hurt beginning and building.

"Say it."

Capitulating, she snarled, "Chris," adding, "What is in a name?"

"No matter how you say it, you said it. Chris. Get used to it, for you will be saying 'Chris" as you beg for me."

"Beg for you. Why, such insolence." The snap in her voice was filled with anger.

"You don't know me yet. You shall know joys you never have experienced. Your passion shall mount upon wings. You shall soar with eagles. Come, let me show you."

"No!" Her refusal was adamant, strong, filled with hate.

Equally determined he spoke, "You shall."

He backed a step, freeing her arms. She struck a blow that found his cheek. A moment of anger covered his face, and he acknowledged the slash of pain with, "I like a struggle. The reward is so much more gratifying."

Suddenly he moved, and she felt a pull on her arm. Something struck her foot.

She was aware she was falling, the ground seemed to rise up, she was on her back, he was over her, looking down, directly into her face. "One learns to reject refusals. I use a technique born out of need, but never twice with the same girl. You will never give me reason to use it. Make yourself comfortable as I prepare myself."

As she watched, his jerkin came off. Under it he wore a white linen shirt with full length sleeves. He released a few top buttons, partially exposing his chest. Her thoughts went back to Edward. She saw him again, above her, strong, muscular. Somewhere he heard, "Victoria, touch me. Let your fingers touch me." It was Edward speaking, so gently, so softly, compelling.

"Edward, I want to touch you. You are beautiful. There. I feel you. Strong. Edward!"

"Release the other buttons, Victoria."

With her right hand she jerked the shirt from his body and tossed it away. His naked torso rose in full view above her. In the distance she heard, "Touch me," Her finger tips roamed randomly about his chest making freeform geometric designs, pinching at his nipples, getting lost in a light matting of hair.

The action was driving him to ecstasy. He was about to lose control when he mumbled, "Bring me to you, Victoria. Pull me down on you." The voice was anxious, hurried, loud.

Her arms went around his chest to his back. She directed her hands to press into the muscular flesh, and slowly she pulled him down to her, he moving down willingly.

A bark disturbed the unfolding scene. It acted as a negative interruption. She blinked several times, rapidly. "No. You are not Edward. No. No. It is you. Where was I. Where are we. You! Let me up!"

Her senses returned. It was Cleeve over her. Cleeve! Quickly she pulled back her arms, sickened by what she saw.

"That was lovely, Victoria. Help me with these trousers."

"No!"

"Come now. You are no stranger to love. Remember?"

She saw a smile develop slowly on his lips, satisfaction gleaming in his eyes. He saw contempt form on her face. He spoke a warning to himself. "That was wrong. You are losing her. Damn! Can't you learn! You say the wrong words. Be gentle" As he looked down on her, he saw her face involved in a series of emotions, surprise changing into aghast, shame.

"You are mine, Victoria. Here. With me and no Pall this time to interrupt. Look at me, Victoria. I want to see those flaming eyes." He leaned over her and slowly lowered his face, kissing her lightly, gently on her mouth, then with soft pecks on each eye, her nose, again on her lips, her chin. A feeling of fascination returned to her. She felt a compulsion to give in. The meekness of his actions was creating a fantasy.

As his lips moved down her neck, she felt him pulling on the draw strings of her bodice. His action jolted her and brought her back to reality. "The gall of him to do that," she shrieked to herself. Her arms now loosened were free for swinging, and she struck him again and again, driving clenched fists at his chest, face and arms. Wherever they landed they pummeled him.

At first he gave her full freedom to flail her arms, then his hands became manacles to drive her into submission. "Victoria, listen to me! Hear me! Her panting quieted, but her eyes glared at him. "Victoria, I love you!" His tone was mellow, sincere. "I love you, Victoria. Believe me. I want to be gentle. I am trying, but you fight me. You say I am married. I am. Not happily. Elizabeth is leaving Kensington House. She is leaving me. She is giving me my freedom. Then I want to marry you, to be your true love, to give you my devotion. Let me share my love."

She became aware that he had stopped his aggression. She controlled her attack long enough to see his eyes staring in fear at something past her head. She pushed herself free to turn and look. Glaring at Cleeve with hate in his eyes, his body tense, fangs bared, was the dog, ready to attack. Fear mounted for Cleeve, not knowing what the dog would do.

A deep throated growl rumbled. It gathered force then exploded in a loud bark. The dog moved to its right as if selecting a better place from which to attack, its snarling and barking becoming more vociferous, more threatening, his flesh quivering, causing his fur to glisten in the sun. He reared, preparing to lunge. Cleeve moved as the dog leaped, avoiding the attack. Cleeve stood and retreated, the dog forcing him away from Victoria.

It became clear that he was not after a kill but was keeping up his aggression to protect her.

A horseman appeared, surveyed the scene, then directed his mount between the dog and man. "Get up!" he directed. Cleeve leaped onto the horse's back, glad for the intrusion, but eyeing the dog as it moved close to Victoria, panting loudly, alert, his eyes on the two men.

"Oh, Geoffrey! I am so glad you are here!"

The horse pranced about nervously, keeping his eyes on the dog. What Geoffrey saw disturbed him. Victoria looked disheveled, her clothes in disarray, her hair mussed. "Christopher, dismount." Cleeve slid off the horse and stood, his eyes on the dog. Geoffrey leaped down and faced Cleeve. "Christopher, explain yourself."

Cleeve remained silent for a moment. "Explain to him!" he snarled to himself. "Darned insolence! This man who lays with my wife. This man who would take Victoria from me." Looking directly at Geoffrey, he said aloud, "No explanation is necessary."

"That dog was attacking you. He had reason to attack. What gave him that reason?" Geoffrey pursued the question. Inwardly he hoped to impress Victoria.

Cleeve could feel pressure building inside, a red color to his skin. He fought for control. "It is not your business." The words were spit out in anger.

Geoffrey stepped forward. The two glared at each other. "Victoria's cries brought me here. They were not the sounds of Sunday's games." He raised his right arm. Victoria expected a blow to be struck, but instead he grabbed Cleeve's forearm. "Tomorrow I shall call for Victoria. You may tell Elizabeth anything you wish since she could not accept the truth."

Cleeve broke the grip with a slash of his free arm. He started to speak but backed off, grabbed his clothes, and mounted his own horse, trotting off, down the nave in the direction of Kensington House.

The two watched him go then Geoffrey turned and approached Victoria. The dog stood solidly, keeping eyes on the man coming toward them, then loosened a growl, low and meaningful. She patted his head and in reassuring words said, "It is all over. Geoffrey is our friend." The growl stopped but his eyes and body remained alert.

Geoffrey reached out for Victoria's hand and instantly felt iciness. "It is over for you, too, my love." He pulled her to him, embracing her warmly, looked into those eyes, then bent to kiss her. She returned his kiss and felt a warming glow extend from his body to hers. "Stay, my darling," he whispered. "Never again will you fear the abuses of another man."

The two remained, arms enfolding one another, he providing protection, she receiving. The dog looked at the two, not budging. His eyes reflected his bewildered thoughts, not understanding that one man she fears and this one she receives.

"Come, dear heart. I shall take you to Kensington House. Tonight get your things together. Tomorrow I shall call for you to take you home." He helped her onto his horse then he mounted. Slowly he guided his mount, making their togetherness last as long as possible, her arms around his waist, one of his hands closed over hers. They arrived in the service area where they dismounted. He kissed her affectionately then reminded her to be ready tomorrow.

The next day he came for her but not to take her away.

# Chapter Twenty-Three

ictoria called first for her scissors. When the blacksmith handed them to her, he warned, "They are sharp, Miss, sharp enough to cut leather. I have put a point on each blade as you asked."

Thanking him graciously, she tested the edges and the points and agreed they had been honed expertly. "They are sharp! I shall be careful."

She took them to her room and immediately placed them under her pillow. She then prepared for Geoffrey on the morrow. From under her bed came her portmanteau and traveling bag, carefully filling each one. Her gowns she left in the armoire for morning.

As she worked, events at the abbey poured down on her. "So Elizabeth is leaving him. Is it because she lost her love for him? It was Geoffrey who took my love today. Tomorrow I shall go with him. But first my tormentor. See to it!"

Victoria found Pall and ordered bath water. After soaking in the hip tub, she bathed, sprinkled her body with scent, then dressed. She brushed her hair, letting it trail over her shoulders and down her back. Her tresses never looked more beautiful.

Pall brought a tray of light food, but very little was eaten. Victoria bolted the door and tested it to make sure it was in place. She went to the window, breathing in the fresh air. It was refreshing. Night had closed in and the clear, sharp sky was covered with flickering stars. She could make out Ursa Major and smiled to know that she could recognize one constellation. A quarter moon shed light on the landscape.

A stroll took her to the front of the bed where she stood opposite the wall mirror, and glancing at the peek hole to visualize herself in the scope of its view, she observed, "He will have no trouble seeing me here."

She waited patiently. As minutes passed, she became tired of standing. The longer she waited the more she wondered if he would come. Giving up, she sat on the edge of the bed and started to undress.

Scratching!

She took a deep breath, trying to calm a nervousness that suddenly appeared and remained seated. Slowly she rose. Like an actress who knows her craft well, Victoria walked to the designated spot at the foot of the bed. She was nonchalant as she began disrobing, her back to the peek hole. Her undergarments were loosened and dropped to the floor. She was brazen to entice her viewer. Naked now, she ran her hands slowly along the sides of her breasts and down her hips establishing a half front view of her nakedness in the wall mirror. She reached for her nightgown and raising it above her head, she let it slide over her shoulders and fall slowly into place.

The scratching continued, strengthening confidence in her purpose and reassuring herself that whomever it was, he was still watching. "Keep in control." Slowly she blew out one candle, leaving one burning on the table next to the priest's hole. That light, she thought, would illuminate him and place her on the fringe of its light and in a little shadow.

She got into bed noisily for she now was out of view of the peek hole, and she wanted her tormentor to know where she was. She placed herself on the window side of the double bed, for, she reasoned, this would give him the left portion making it possible for her stronger right arm to commit an awful deed. She felt for her scissors, making practice strokes by stretching her right arm under her pillow and reaching for them. Quietly she waited. "Stay in control."

The scratching stopped. Time passed. Nothing. "He left?" She held her breath, intent on listening. "No! He is not coming. He is only antagonizing me again." She lay quietly regretting the whole business, wondering about tomorrow and thinking what she should do about Geoffrey.

A noise! She became alert to its identification. The priest's hole panel was sliding. She continued to lay prone as she was, fear engulfing her. Her body was beginning to tense. "Maybe I should have left the door unbolted. No one can come in to help me." She closed her eyes and pleaded prayerfully for help.

A new noise! She identified it as his effort to crawl through the opening. As planned, she raised her head and shoulders to rest on one elbow and watched for her tormentor to rise from the floor.

Slowly the figure of a man took shape. As he straightened beyond the perimeter of light he appeared to be above average height with broad shoulders and a square frame. The unidentified person moved forward with a dragging step, his left arm crooked and his right arm hidden behind his back. He moved into the light. A medallion swinging slowly like a pendulum at the end of a chain was reflected in the light.

It was his face that caught her attention. It was scarred extensively with one eye closed permanently. His hair was grey and disheveled. "Who is he?" Victoria challenged her memory. "I have never seen him!" As he moved toward the bed, his face took on more of the light. His appearance was loathsome to her. She shuddered in fear. All confidence left her. She wanted to scream but her mouth was too dry and her throat closed.

"Good evening, Patience." His voice was calm. "You await me, Patience. Ready for me. In bed. You fill me with joy. You have done so often. Tonight you revealed to me in your nakedness the lovely lines of a matured woman. In days gone by you were more of a child, just showing promise. But tonight you thrilled me. You aroused my passion. I can await your joys no longer." He gazed at her and as he did so, a smile emerged, breaking the tissue like appearance of scarred skin. He caught the quizzical look on her face.

"You don't know me? Come now, guess. I just gave you a clue to my identity. I called you Patience."

Victoria stared, apprehension filling her face. She was losing control. It was a critical part of her perilous plan to manipulate her tormentor as a puppet, keeping him at bay and unbalanced, then guiding him into position for the kill. First the ghastly face unnerved her and then his cavalier attitude, coupled with his knowledge about her identity, placed her in a negative position. She realized that it was he who was in total control.

"No. You don't know me." The smile slowly left his face and was replaced by a contemptible glower. "I shouldn't expect you to know me. Let me give you more clues. You spied me looking over the brink while you were on the beach. On the evening of the play you saw me watching from the gallery. You talked to a court jester at the masked ball. Remember?"

Victoria looked puzzled. She recalled the events but could not identify the man.

"No. You still do not know me. Let me add another clue." He obviously was enjoying the guessing game. "The most notable moment of recollection occurred in the garden. You lay on the brink gazing at the heavens. How attractive you were! I explored your welcoming position from behind the hedge until I could stand it no longer. I offered to make you a woman that day, but you rejected my advances."

Victoria gasped in disbelief as he offered the clue, for instantly her mind went back to the time of which he spoke. "Yes! The brink! That day! Mr. Wyatt!" She spoke half aloud. A shudder of shock passed through her body. The revelation shattered her confidence entirely. "I thought you were dead!" Her mumbled comment just slipped out without any expression whatsoever.

"No. Almost. You wanted me dead. You pushed me over the brink." His statement was delivered in staccato fashion through his teeth. The charges were thrown at her like slaps on the face.

The accusations not only angered her, but the ire that began building replaced the initial shock of his identity. A feeling of self reliance returned as she challenged his cowardly indictments. "It was not I who met you. It was you who met me, nay forced yourself on me. You fought my resistance. You. An adult, a strong muscular male, fought a child. In your shameful craving you maneuvered yourself to the brink. I did not push you. You grabbed for me and loosened the ground under you. It gave way. At that moment I did not want you dead. I grabbed for you. I tried to save you! You are despicable in your accusations of me. You cannot face the fact that a mere girl beat you at your own vile scheming!" Her delivery of the facts spurred her conviction and she felt herself gaining control. "I saw the edge give way. I reached for you. The brink collapsed. I tried to grab you. It was not possible."

His face flushed. The scars changed to a livid color. Hatred reflected in his intense eyes. The right arm appeared from behind his back. It held a sword. The left arm moved awkwardly to hold the scabbard as the right arm unsheathed the blade.

"Look at me, Patience! Look at me! Look at this face. This is what you did to me. This is how you killed me. Look at my hair, grey before my years. Look at how you disfigured me." His anger intensified as he resumed his attack, reciting new charges. "Look. You created this. Look at these scars. You carved these as if you used a blade. This eye that cannot see. You blinded me. What woman would want me now! No woman has looked at me without revulsion!" The allegations were made in hateful snarls.

He ceased his tirade to give her an opportunity to observe his mangled face. He threw the scabbard on the floor. The sword he slammed on the table where it bounced before it came to a rest. Painfully he maneuvered his arms to remove his coat and shirt, dropping them to the floor. He spread his naked chest before her to reveal more scars, one of which was wide, cruel looking, revolting. In abhorrence she viewed the disfigurements he displayed. The sight nauseated her.

"Look at me! Look at this chest! These scars! You did this to me! My arm is crooked." He moved his arm, expressing pain as he did so. "No strength is left to me. I can no longer clasp any object and lift it."

Victoria heard his shoes come off. He reached down and removed his stockings. As she watched, he unbuckled his belt and dropped his trousers, kicking them aside. Only a single under garment remained.

"Look, Patience! Look at these legs!"

She looked. Both were scarred like his face and chest.

"Look at this leg! This left leg. It wont bend! It drags. It is completely useless to me. You did all this to me!"

Victoria heard and saw so much by the time he had almost totally disrobed that a callousness was developing. At first she agonized over his vandalized appearance, but his constant badgering, the repetition of his charges, the placing of total blame on her for his mutilations renewed her spirit to fight back. "No, Mr. Wyatt." The tone was calm, more confident. "I did not do this to you. You did all this to yourself. Your depravity, your utter animal appetite led you into difficulties. You were so intent on ravaging my body that you ravaged yourself. You misplace the blame. Had you left me alone, there would have been no fall."

"Be honest, Patience. You caused my fall. Then you left me crushed on the rocks. You did not seek help for me. I lay on the rocks suffering excruciating pain for two days.

"When I was found it was too late to set my leg and arm properly. For lack of attention, the wounds healed very slowly. Look at me, Patience. Look at me! I repel anyone who sees me. A full, complete life is impossible for me. You ruined me. Though I live, I am dead. The pleasures of life are denied me. I know that death means nothing to you, but it will! Listen! Listen to me. I am going to use your body. You are going to know a man fully, completely, erotically. Then you are going to know death. Yes. Death!"

Victoria listened as the tone became violent. She watched the scars on his face move as his lips made a mocking smile. He snatched the sword and held it over her.

"I am going to kill you, Patience. My sword is marked, a tally for each of those who has menaced my purposes. See these slashes, here, near the handle. The first is for your father's uncle, the old man of Castelamer. I just hurried his death so I could take the estate. Then there was Tatham. He couldn't keep his mouth shut, so I thought. After I killed him, I found out I murdered the wrong man. The third tally is for the right man who interfered.

"The fourth and fifth tallies are for your father and mother. Yes, your father found out about our illicit business. I was just getting well established when he blundered onto my activities. He told your mother. They had to go, both of them, but my associate made a mess of things. That boat should never have been found. Framsden, I soon learned, botched it. I forced him to take you and Penelope to raise and to send your brother away. I wanted girls raised for me. I was willing to wait. Penny I seduced early and easily. She kept me busy but happy.

"Framsden knew what I was doing. He laughed about it and wanted some side attractions of his own, but his wife was too maternal about you two girls. Then Framsden started making too many errors including talking about the business. Two tallies were added to the sword when they got on the ship for France. They never saw France.

"You, too, Patience, know more than you should. You became too curious about the signal lights, and then you found the cave. You searched out the storage room. The next tally on the sword is for you. Would you like to know the pain of a living death in the time you have left? Make a record of your own death on this obituary blade. Come. Patience. Mark!

"And that Tatham woman will be a tally when she joins her husband. That fool Cleeve let the inquisitive old lady have lodging. She fussed about until she learned too much. Anyone who uncovers one iota of fact about my business is a menace to me.

"My loathing for you grows as you look at me. You are mine to ravage and then kill. I shall do the killing!" A snarl distorted his angry scars as malice flushed his countenance. He pushed the sword in front of her face. "Look at this. Feel the edge. Sharp! Newly honed by the blacksmith. The point is like your needle."

The point of the sword was thrust at her. "You have looked at my scars. Now I'll create some marks on you, carving as I would a joint of beef, then I shall gaze with pleasure at my handiwork. Fearfully Victoria saw the point of the sword coming toward her, slowly and steadily. The candlelight made it glimmer as the blade trembled in the hand of the madman. It touched the bodice of her nightgown and entered the material. A sudden upward thrust, expertly maneuvered, cut a straight line through the garment from the waist to the neck.

Quickly dropping the sword on the bed, he grabbed the left side of the bodice and tore it open, exposing one breast and part of her torso.

Seeing the sword on the bed, she grabbed for it, but his hand reached it first. "Ah, Patience. You would try to take my weapon. I cannot make you look like me unless I have it. Now, remove the other half of your bodice." The voice carried authority, direction and thrust, but she hesitated to act, flouting him.

"Come, Patience. Do it!"

She remained as she was, defiant.

Taking up the sword again, he pointed it at her. "Do it!" His shout was uncompromising.

She challenged him with a hateful stare.

The sword continued coming toward her. The point touched her left breast, was flicked, and then withdrawn. A spot of red appeared. It grew as blood bulged upward then spilled to create a trickle.

"Remove the other half!" The demand was deafening.

The sword again came toward her. She watched the approaching ride of the point directed at her neck. A voice told her to act. She raised her right hand and pulled the remaining half of her bodice free from her body leaving her torso completely exposed to the waist.

"Lovely! This is what I have been waiting for. I watched you often. I became completely enamored of you. I became aware that you were warned of my presence in the passage by the scratching of my medallion on the wall. You did not know it was I looking at you, but you knew someone was.

"I thought you enjoyed being watched for you did not once try to cover the peek hole or destroy it. I deliberately made the medallion scratch the wall to please you."

A crooked smile again took form on his lips. "Why, Patience? Why did you not cover the hole?" He spoke in a mechanical manner, emphasizing each word. "You wanted to be seen," he challenged. "You wanted to entice the watcher to enter your room, to share your bed. That is right! Tonight you enticed me in. You want me. Tell me you want me."

He waited a moment, his eyes crawling over her. "You like to be tormented. It is a fetish with you. Why didn't you report these noises to Cleeve? No. You wanted these playful acts to continue. I opened your closed door. I took your scissors and put them in Mrs. Tatham's room. It was excitement for you, wasn't it?

"You discovered the secret passage. Clever of you to do that. It was I who found you in the passage. You fainted or hit your head, but you were on the floor of the passage when I reached you. What a perfect setting for me. You were stretched out. Darkness was hiding you. I had your clothes pushed up when I heard noises. It was silly of me to panic, but I did. I did not even stop to learn the source of the noises.

"Why didn't you cover the priest's hole, Patience? You could have put an end to this cloak and dagger business, but it fascinated you. Didn't it, Patience? You liked the mystery of the games we played. You didn't want to close out the unknown man you knew would one day use the passage and the hole to come to you. I am here, Patience. You have waited long enough for me. You planned this meeting. Let us begin our frolic."

He lowered his head, kissed her on the abdomen, then raised his head again. "Many times I saw you. You have a beautiful body. It was made for me. Often I have watched you standing naked before your mirror. Why didn't I come in? I wanted to see more, to torment you more, to wait for the right time. I enjoyed the game, too. It pleased me to delay our confrontation. The right time is now."

His scars seemed to consume him as his face moved toward her. Her arms came up to defend herself. His right hand pushed them aside as if they were toothpicks. He towered over her. His eyes were like glass. "For three years I have waited for this moment. Three years! Since the day you returned I have watched you undress and prepare for bed. But tonight you were glorious. You must be mine. Totally mine. Completely mine. MINE!"

With great pain, he manipulated his body onto the bed. His eyes dwelt on hers. Then they began roaming about her body, here and there, stopping long enough to enjoy each portion of her nakedness and savoring enticing sights. Suddenly, without warning, his face fell on hers, crushing her mouth in a violent kiss, his one good hand making light swirls on her stomach as he gave vent to his emotions. "You are lovely. I like the view of your body, the kiss of your mouth, the feel of your skin, so smooth, alluring. You drive me to madness."

His one sound hand, rough to the touch, continued to roam over her body. She twinged waiting for an opportunity to reach for the scissors. Quickly his head lowered over her and rested on her breasts. She felt a nip. His tongue began probing the spot clipped by the sword.

Slowly her right arm curved above her head and moved toward the pillow. Her fingers found the edge and crawled under it toward the scissors. They touched the cold metal and gently pulled them from their hiding place. With as little movement as possible her fingers formed around the handles. She squirmed her body to hold his interest and placed her left arm on his head, pressing his face deeper into her breast to camouflage her action. She raised her right arm high above his back to provide as much force as possible to the downward plunge of the scissors into his body.

As she prepared to plummet the sharpened points into him, he felt her muscles tighten and instantly the warning triggered a reflex action. He twisted sideways. The scissors flew downward, clipped his shoulder, opened the flesh and caromed off to land between them. He cringed at the sudden pain and looked at the weapon. He felt blood dribble down his side. His eyes sought hers. "What you could not do three years ago, you are trying to do now. You tried to kill me again! You vixen! You slut!"

Victoria saw fury in his eyes. She rose with the intention of pounding on the wall, but she remembered Mrs. Tatham was gone.

Wyatt's right arm pushed her back. He executed a painful turn to place his body over hers. His hand grabbed the skirt of her nightgown and began ripping it. She pounded him with both fists, driving blows to his face and chest, but they had no effect.

So intent was his anticipation that he did not hear the slight noise of a person crawling through the priest's hole. He did not see a hand seize the sword. Victoria caught the flash of light on the blade as the sword was raised, and she recognized Mrs. Tatham as the old lady stepped into the light. "Mr. Wyatt is it!" she boomed with as big a voice as possible.

He froze, recognizing an unexpected voice which was angry in quality and threatening. Quickly he tried to rise to his knees. Excruciating pain in his right leg reflected in his face. His balance shifted to his right knee and he turned to face the intruder. Identifying the old lady, he relaxed. "So you have come to taunt me," he addressed her. "How easy you make it for me. Two new tallies waiting to be scratched on my blade."

"You speak too soon." Mrs. Tatham's aged voice was firm. Her hand held the sword steady, the point aimed at his chest. "I could never find proof that you killed my husband or that you ended the lives of Patience's parents. I knew you were the murderer, but I had to have evidence. You have just given me the proof I needed, your own confession. I, too, learned about the secret passage. You left the panel open so it was easy to listen to your confessions. You condemn yourself, Mr. Wyatt. Your bragging was too much and in the wrong place. You violated all your own orders to others. You became a blusterer, proud of your murders, speaking where you thought you wouldn't be heard. It is an eye for an eye and tooth for a tooth. The next scratch will be your own."

A shot rang out! The blast split the quiet night. Instantly two more shots further fragmented the silence. Mr. Wyatt guessed the meaning of the salvos and tried to get up. He came toward the edge of the bed with the intention of going as quickly as possible to the scene of the shooting. As he rose from the bed, Victoria tripped his leg. He extended his chest to gain balance and raised his good hand to break his fall to the floor.

Mrs. Tatham was not bothered by the shots. She held her position with the sword still aimed at Wyatt's chest, the point adjusting to his movement as if lured by a magnet. The point took his chest as Mrs. Tatham released the sword. The falling weight pushed on the blade, passing it through the body to exit below the rib cage.

Each woman looked at the other aghast. Revenge was theirs but the act was sickening to them. Automatically Victoria got up, removed the portion of the night dress still clinging to her, and donned her robe. She turned to Mrs. Tatham and said, "Come, dear, let me help you to your room." As she spoke she heard hoofs beating rhythmically on the road below.

"No. I shall stay. The constable will want an explanation of this. The shots must have been his."

The shots! Quickly Victoria donned shoes and cloak, unbolted the door, and ran though the hall, down the back stairs and out the rear entrance. There was a mingling of people in the service area and a few in the stables. When she passed the horses in their stalls, she saw two bodies lying on the ground near the wagons, each covered with a blanket.

# Chapter Twenty-Four

Mrs. Cleeve was standing near one body enfolded by the arms of Lord Arlington, her head on his shoulder. Smothered sobs were coming from her covered face. Lady Arlington was next to her husband patting Elizabeth's back and saying quiet, comforting words. As Victoria approached, Lady Arlington recognized her and stepped away to speak with her.

"There has been a dreadful shooting. The royal constable and his men were here to conduct an investigation. They heard an argument in that room. They saw Jonathan come out with Christopher behind him, gun in hand. A gun was fired. Jonathan fell dead. There was another shooting and Christopher was shot. He is dead, too, his face completely ripped away. Elizabeth made the identification because of the clothes he was wearing." Victoria fainted at Lady Arlington's feet.

In the morning, a wagon drove up to the front of Kensington House. Geoffrey was met at the main entry by Osborne, the butler, who told him Victoria would see no one.

"I just learned about the events of last night. I know she needs me. I must see her!" He pushed by Osborne but realized he did not where to look for her.

"Sit here, Mr. Rooth. I'll find out if Miss Victoria will see you."

He returned shortly to say, "Follow me. She will see you."

Geoffrey tried to hurry Osborne along as they climbed flights of stairs to Mrs. Tatham's room. Inside he paused to look at Victoria resting in bed. She saw him and raised her arms in greeting. He rushed to fall into them and the two embraced. He covered her face with kisses, murmuring endearments. "I heard the news when I passed through the village. I would have been here earlier had I known. Are you alright?"

"Of course, dear. I had a shock, but I am fine."

"Good. I came for you. The wagon is ready. I can take you away from thus place."

"Dear Geoffrey. The events of last night have changed our plans of yesterday. I cannot leave Mrs. Cleeve just yet. There will be a time, and soon."

"Of course. I was thinking only of myself and how much I need you. How may I help you?"

"Be my comfort. Stay with me. I shall get up and we will walk in the garden. The sun will be refreshing."

The two walked slowly along the geometric paths, his arm around her shoulders holding her close to him. She felt comforted having his protection. He asked no questions about the night before. Instead he talked about the future, hoping to restore her confidence and confirm his place in her life. "All my animals know you are coming and just the anticipation has improved their nature. Cows are giving richer milk already. I talked to the house and the walls are chattering happily to one another. With all that joyfulness around the house, you know how exuberant I am."

"What did you say about the animals?" Victoria laughed out loud. It was the first laugh she had experienced for some time and it gave her a good feeling.

Geoffrey kept the banter light and punctuated it with kisses. She was beginning to have a glow. Such was the setting when Pall interrupted. "Mrs. Cleeve needs you in the study," she announced.

Waiting for her were Elizabeth, Lord Arlington and his wife, Mrs. Tatham and the royal constable. The official made his apologies for calling a meeting so soon after the tragedy. "It is regrettable," he said, "however, I have been informed that Lord and Lady Arlington are preparing for the Oxford meeting of Parliament and will take Mrs. Cleeve with them. There is information all of you must know, for each of you will be affected in one way or another, directly or indirectly.

"First, you should know about the business being conducted at Kensington House. The crown has known for some time that an illegal activity was underway in this part of Cornwall, but the authorities could not identify the participants, so secretly was the business being conducted. A few days ago we had reports providing the information we needed to take action. Briefly, Mr. Dudley Wyatt, the organizer and conductor of the business, was extremely competent in operating the foreign importation of goods. Items from France were shipped to Kensington House, buyers were found in this country, and deliveries made to them. He hired a minimum number of people whom he swore to secrecy.

"Second, it was difficult to analyze the operation since it was widely accepted that Mr. Cleeve was the owner of Kensington House as well as the owner of a perfectly legal foreign trade business in London. Mr. Wyatt stayed completely in the background, gave no evidence whatever of being identified with the business here, and was known by few people hereabouts. He used Mr. Cleeve as a front man who in turn conducted his legal business at Kensington House as well as the illicit business.

"Third, there was a clever organizational structure. Only four or five men were involved. Goods arrived on the shore below Bodacombe

Bluff at irregular times and always at night. They were transferred from a boat to a cave which was kept a secret. The entrance to the cave was small and well camouflaged.

"Fourth, not one person ever discussed the business. All involved had been sworn to silence, the penalty for talking being death. Since death was the reward for talking, I shall disclose point five.

"We have testimony that Mr. Wyatt had identified those whom he thought were about to inform on him.

"Now we have complete records of those who purchased his goods and avoided crown taxes."

Lord Arlington blanched at this statement but said nothing.

The constable continued, ignoring the fact that he was aware of Lord Arlington's reaction. "The community has long believed that first Mr. Framsden and then Mr. Cleeve owned Kensington House. There is written evidence, however, to show that Mr. Wyatt was the legal owner."

"Just a moment, Constable. Are we, Mrs. Cleeve that is, to understand that she is not to inherit Kensington House?"

"The rightful owner undoubtedly will be determined by the court. A paper was found among Mr. Wyatt's things in the storage room to indicate that he acquired ownership of Castelamer when Mr. Framsden's uncle died. If the paper is ruled to be legal then the property goes to his heirs.

"A search of the records is continuing at this moment. We have one agreement between Mr. Wyatt and Mr. Cleeve. It involves free rent to Mr. Cleeve for the house in return for services rendered. It stipulates also a salary. The search may reveal other agreements."

"See here, Constable. Hadn't we better get Mr. Wyatt in here. Let him clarify the questions that are being raised," Lord Arlington insisted. He was visibly agitated.

The constable cleared his throat as if to indicate that disturbing news was imminent. "Mr. Wyatt is dead. He was killed by his own sword as he attacked Mrs. Tatham." The constable glanced at Victoria, assuring her that he would not reveal all the sordid details.

Victoria asked, "Have you had an opportunity to determine why the deaths of Mr. Cleeve and Jonathan occurred?"

"A man in the storage room at the time of the shooting is still reluctant to talk. It is believed, however, that Mr. Cleeve accused Jonathan of planning to talk to authorities. Jonathan denied the charge and left the room. As he passed through the door, he was shot. It is not clear at this moment who did the shooting. Mr. Cleeve picked up another gun and passed through the door. He apparently saw me, raised the gun, and then one of my men shot him."

"Thank you, Constable," Lord Arlington interjected. "I shall have Mrs. Cleeve's solicitor contact you. I am sure he will want access to all records. Meantime I must hurry to Oxford. Mrs. Cleeve will be coming with us. If you have need to contact her, please notify me."

"Very well, Lord Arlington. Is there someone whom you would designate as Mrs. Cleeve's representative until either she returns or the court makes a decision regarding the the legal owner."

"Victoria, dear. Do you feel equal to this task?" The question was spoken dolefully by Elizabeth. "I have such high regard for you and so does the staff."

"If you wish, Mrs. Cleeve. I am sure your solicitor will guide me when he comes." Her reply lacked her usual enthusiasm. She did not feel comfortable about accepting the responsibility, but she could not deny assisting when she had been treated so well. Her decision would not be at all pleasing to Geoffrey, and she cringed at the thought of his reaction.

"My appreciation to you all," the constable smiled. "If there are no more questions, I shall renew my work with the investigators."

Victoria turned immediately to Mrs. Cleeve and the two women embraced, speaking endearingly to one another and walking arm in arm to Mrs. Cleeve's room.

As soon as the study cleared, Mrs. Tatham interrupted the constable. "Please, sir, I need to talk to you." The two sat and faced each other. "I should tell you, sir, that I have known Victoria since she was born. Her mother told me before her death that the original will to Castelamer, prepared by Victoria's great uncle, was hidden in this house's secret passage. It was hidden by the uncle because he knew Mr. Wyatt was trying to acquire the house and property by illegal means.

"I found the secret passage and, at the end of a long search, I found the will. No one else knows about this will, not even Victoria. What shall I do with it?"

She handed the paper to the constable who unfolded it and read it. "This looks to be valid in every way. It is witnessed by the man who was vicar at Brixton Village church at that time and by someone else I do not know. It has the official seal of Cornwall. I shall take it, Mrs. Tatham, and present it to the court with other papers. Thank you."

As Victoria expected, Geoffrey was not pleased when she saw him after the meeting and told him of her decision to stay at Kensington House. His reply was, "I understand, but it is to be for only a short time. It would be better anyhow to arrive at my manor as Mrs. Rooth, not as Miss Victoria."

As Geoffrey listened, Victoria reviewed the main points of the constable's presentation. His first reaction concerned Elizabeth. "Her leaving is timely. I do not know how I could have broken our liaison without a major confrontation and certainly without Victoria learning about us. There would have been difficulty in continuing to see Elizabeth after my marriage to Victoria." He broke his silence by saying, "This has been a trying time for you, dear. I know you had no use for Christopher, so his departure is no loss to you. Elizabeth's leaving will be felt for I realize how much you like her and she you. But all this should be settled soon. When it is over, you will be in my protection. Goodbye, my sweet, for this moment."

The two embraced then she saw him to the door. He turned on the step and kissed her again.

Victoria hurried to Mrs. Cleeve's room. She noticed that tears had stopped, inflamed eyes had almost cleared, and puffiness on the cheeks had disappeared. She even detected that she was evidencing some pleasure in the leaving. "I cannot take everything, just enough for Oxford," she said to Victoria. "I am not sure I want to take anything. I doubt if I shall ever come back. Please, dear, use whatever you can and what you can't use, give to the staff." She paused to place some under things in a trunk. "I never felt at home here." She sat down and stared at the floor. "Whatever possessed Christopher to get involved with that awful Wyatt. He had enough money, and his London business was doing well. Neither he nor I wanted for anything. What a loss."

A maid appeared to announce that the Arlingtons were ready, and the trunk was removed. Elizabeth embraced Victoria saying, "I do wish I could take you with me, my dear, but you are helping so much by staying. Now do come to London when this is settled. We shall get that dress shop of yours opened, and you shall dress the social ladies in your fashions. Do come. I shall expect you!"

The quiet of the house descended on her like a tumultuous crash as soon as she closed the door and stepped into the entry. She went to her room, took a heavy wrap from the armoire and twirled it around her shoulders. "I must escape this house until I get myself under control," she muttered to herself. She stopped by the kitchen, picked up some bones and scraps for the dog, and began a rapid walk to the abbey. After depositing the food for the dog, she began a quiet walk though the ruins. Calmness returned slowly as she let the quieting atmosphere work its charm. She gave thought to her future. "I must give a reply to Geoffrey's proposal of marriage. Strange isn't it. I felt more sure of my decision when he asked me than I do now. It is Chris' going that has made me uncertain. When did I know I loved you, Chris? It was not at our first meeting. You frightened me then. Was it on the beach? I think it was on the beach. I was so terrified by the falling boulder, and then you held and kissed me. You were gentle that day."

She watched the dog approach the food, sniff and then slowly walk toward her. She knelt on the turf to greet him. He sent out a long tongue to touch her extended hand and sat next to her. "Were you to come to me now, Chris, this dog would be gentle to you. Not like the last time. I was fearful then and the dog knew it. Today he knows I am overcome with sorrow, and he has come to me to fill a void. You would have done that for me, too, Chris. After Elizabeth freed you, you would come to me. Together we would have let love be the victor."

# Chapter Twenty-Five

Jonathan, Wyatt and Cleeve were buried in Brixton Village churchyard. Mr. Cleeve's body was placed there temporarily until his wife could make a decision as to his permanent burial site. It had not been decided whether his remains should be interred in the London plot of Elizabeth's family or returned to the village of his birth.

Mr. Wyatt left no will and no person came forward to claim his effects. Neither was there any evidence of his permanent place of residence. A portion of the storage room was used as his abode while at Kensington House. It was strange that he chose to live that way, for he could have been more comfortable within the house, or the wealth he had accumulated could have purchased any property in Cornwall. He had placed a money box in a well concealed hole under the flooring of the storage room. A record book was stored with the money itemizing weekly the sum he had placed there and the sources from which it came. The court would have to consider a letter he placed with the cash. The letter was addressed to Penny and Patty and briefly provided that each sister should receive an adequate sum to compensate for the loss of their parents.

Mrs. Cleeve's solicitor visited Kensington House. Since he could find no record of Kensington House finances, it was concluded that

Wyatt gave Cleeve enough money to run the house, pay hired help, and keep up the social amenities required of landed gentry. It was possible, however, that Cleeve could have placed his money elsewhere and deliberately avoided record keeping because of its illegal source. All bills had been paid and no monetary demands were made on the estate.

Jonathan's estate went to Diana. It was surprising how much money he had accumulated considering the short time he had worked for Wyatt. His savings were found in his living quarters with a short note dated only two days before his death. Victoria deduced that he must have anticipated trouble when he decided to terminate his association with Wyatt.

After a full investigation, the constable was able to reconstruct the steps leading to the shooting. "When Jonathan announced his decision to quit, Cleeve objected. Heated words were exchanged. Jonathan started for the door, Cleeve following. It was first believed that Cleeve shot Jonathan, but after study it was determined that Cleeve shot passed Jonathan, probably to frighten him, and that the constable's men, thinking the shot was meant for them, fired at both Jonathan and Cleeve, killing both.

Victoria took charge of Kensington House. As she explained to all employees, her role was temporary until the court determined legal ownership of the estate. Her first act was to invite Mrs. Tatham to stay on. She was moved to a guest bedroom, and orders were given that she was to be treated in that capacity.

More and more the house endeared itself to Victoria. Although everyone referred to the old mansion as Kensington House, she began to think of it as Castelamer. In rummaging about in the north tower, she found all her childhood effects and these she returned to her room.

Each time she met with Mr. Evans, overseer of the estate, Victoria realized more and more that Kensington House was a business. She learned that hundreds of cattle and sheep roamed the lands, and that they produced income. Crops were raised as well. He pointed out problems which had to be met and made suggestions. At times, Mrs. Cleeve's solicitor participated in these meetings and checked record books. Fortunately there was enough money to pay all help and keep the estate going until the court made its rulings.

Geoffrey was a constant support to Victoria. He came to the house frequently to offer his services and advice, but he did not take part in business meetings. He had a man come from Plymouth to survey structural problems of the house, and it became evident that work was required to support the foundation. A plan was prepared to restore structural strength, and the solicitor approved funds only for the most critical portions.

During one of these discussions regarding the house, Victoria spoke abruptly to Geoffrey. "I must talk with you about a matter of concern." She had wanted to talk about her future with him, but each time she approached the topic, it seemed expedient not do so.

"Yes, dear, what is it?"

"I am considering going to London to investigate the feasibility of opening a dress shop." No sooner had the statement been made when he shouted, "You are what?" The sharpness in his voice was emphasized by its customary deep quality. The usual gentleness was absent. "What brings on this thought?" he demanded.

"I must make a living, Geoffrey."

Again he broke in, giving her no opportunity to explain her thoughts and that angered her. "Making a living!" He was shocked and again his voice conveyed his consternation. "How can you consider such a thing? I am perfectly capable of providing for you. Your only concern is to manage my home!"

There was no question about his definiteness. It was evident to her that he assumed she was to be his wife.

"Forget that notion about London. I wont hear of it." The statement was made with finality. This was a new side of Geoffrey, a side she did not know existed. He had terminated any chance of discussing the topic that was of great importance to her. She had wanted to talk about the dress shop objectively and to get his considered opinion. She decided to drop further mention of it.

He recognized she was perturbed and he tried to soothe her. They talked of other topics and his voice returned to gentleness. Soon he took his leave. "I am looking forward to our ride tomorrow, Victoria, but if the day is damp, we'll wait for a sunny one."

Two days later the sun was shining and she waited for his arrival. He did not show. She assumed he could not get away from farm duties so she walked to the abbey. It was no longer necessary for her ask cook for bones and scraps to take to the dog. Recently he had felt secure enough first to follow her to the service area and then later to stay near the stables. Cook fed him daily and the men took a liking to him. Someone began calling him "Wolf" and the name stuck.

Wolf usually met Victoria when she left the house and today was no different. As soon as she passed through the door, he came running to meet her, tail wagging energetically, his body twisting and turning in leaps much as an acrobat at Brixton Village Fair. She had taught him to chase sticks, and as they walked he hunted for a broken branch for her to toss. Once in the abbey grounds, however, he became quiet, and for the most part stayed on the perimeter of the ruins, keeping an eye on her.

The assizes court would be meeting in Plymouth in two months to consider the legal status of Kensington House. "I shall have to leave and the options open to me require reflection." Actually Victoria did not have many options. "I can get married and be cared for. That will end consideration for anything else. But I am not sure of Geoffrey. That is why I have not yet given him an answer to his proposal. His actions and attitudes toward me make it plain he considers me his wife. I am beginning to see a dominant side to his character, an attitude that bothers me. My years of self support have given me a feeling of independence, something I enjoy, and I do not want to lose it completely. I understand well that my role as a wife in this modern world of 1666 is one of subservience, but I do hope for a marriage that will respect me as a human being. I want a husband who will discuss problems with me and see to it that we make decisions together."

Victoria heard Wolf bark. She looked up to see a horseman whose figure grew larger as he neared. Geoffrey. "There's my love," he called. He took Victoria in his arms, caressed her gently, and spoke tenderly. "My heart's desire. I missed you so. Tell me you love me."

"I do love you, Geoffrey." She returned his kiss and reveled in his smothering embrace.

"Victoria, it is so good to be near you. I knew you would be here. I cannot stay apart from you. I must be with you." His voice was eloquent in its urgency. She could feel his body tense. His arms tightened around her. She was not prepared for these intense expressions of endearment.

He lifted his mouth a fraction, his lips still on hers, and mumbled, "Victoria, love me. Victoria, I want you. Kiss me." Again his lips fell full on hers, pressing hard. His mouth opened and she felt his teeth tearing at her lips. His tongue began probing, trying to enter her mouth. She thought of Chris, his violence, his urgency, his manner of conveying his feelings.

Now it was Geoffrey.

Suddenly he stopped the crushing. He raised his head and looked into her eyes. "Victoria, forgive me. I forgot myself. My longing for you has made me wild. I am not this way." He relaxed the power in his arms, but he did not release her. "I love you. How else can I show how much I love you? Let me embrace you gently." He kissed her eyes, her nose, her lips. Lovingly he placed a kiss on her forehead and then on her neck. She could feel a reaction to his tenderness building in her body. Looking into her eyes he murmured, "Marry me, Victoria."

"Yes."

Instantly his lips were on hers again. "I shall make you happy." The words slurred through his lips, still covering hers. "I have such need of you, my dear. Let me make you mine. Now. Here. I want you so much. Please!"

"But we are not married. Wait, Geoffrey. Wait until we are married."

"We are married, Victoria." He stated the words mechanically as if the act were done. "We need only the vicar to bless our union. We have already pledged our love to one another. We are man and wife. Please, Victoria." He pulled her to him, bending her back as his body curled over hers and pressed hard. "Life is so short," she heard him say. "We must not wait another moment. Please. Here in the abbey. You love this place. Let our love bind our pledge here. Now!"

"No, Geoffrey. It is the vicar who will bind our pledge." The statement was firm and direct. The look on his face was one of deep disappointment.

"Then I shall ask for the banns to be read at once. I will go to the vicar." He kissed her lovingly then released his hold. She watched him mount and ride off.

That afternoon he called on her. "It is arranged. On Wednesday following the third reading of the banns the vicar will bless our union and I shall make you mine. That is a long time to wait, Victoria. Life is so short." Later she would consider his words to be prophetic.

She began instantly preparing for the wedding by fashioning a gown with a tight bodice and a full skirt almost touching the floor while quantities of Flemish lace flowed from the neck and sleeves. Geoffrey came every day, even if just to say hello. They talked about a move to his home, the plans he had for them, and what he wanted to do to the house to modernize it. He suggested buying more land so their children would have enough acreage to inherit. One day he said he wanted to buy Socrates for her.

On the appointed day for the trip to Plymouth and the court hearing, the coach appeared at the house entry. Victoria had accepted Geoffrey's offer to accompany her, and Mrs. Tatham had been asked by the constable to be in court. Diana had invited all three to stay with her in her home. He was visibly shocked when the coach stopped in front of Diana's home. His consternation increased when Diana appeared at the door and called him by name.

The next day all four went to court. There they met Mrs. Cleeve's solicitor and the constable. Victoria was fascinated by court procedure. A judge wearing an impressive wig sat behind a large desk at the front of the room. A man announced the case and a solicitor for the crown spoke about questions to be resolved. These included the dispensation of Mr. Wyatt's funds, a decision as to the rightful heirs of Kensington House, and the crown's claim on an illegal business.

Several documents were submitted to the judge for review and each was explained.

The constable was called to the witness chair placed next to the judge, and he told of finding some of the documents during his investigations. Mrs. Tatham followed with her testimony. She told of finding the will and why she knew it existed. A discussion among the solicitors and the judge followed then a recess was called.

When the court reconvened, the judge reviewed the questions submitted to him and gave his verdicts. He ruled that a fair portion of Wyatt's money be given to Diana and Victoria. The rest of the money would be taken by the crown for taxes. In the disposition of Jonathan's will, the judge gave Diana all of his estate. He then reviewed the total aspect of the Kensington House estate. His decision was to disallow any claim by Wyatt's heirs, should there be any. He stated that the evidence proved Mr. Wyatt acquired Castelamer by illegal means, including the duping of an old man who intended that the property go to his blood line. He ruled the rightful owners were Diana and Victoria.

Mrs. Cleeve's solicitor had learned of the will, but he was hoping a legal maneuver would gain consideration for Mrs. Cleeve. He then offered to place the estate in Victoria's name since Diana declared instantly that she would renounce all her rights. She said that her attachments had terminated long ago and that her interests were in Plymouth. The money left to her by Wyatt and Jonathan would care adequately for her.

The court's decision granting the estate property to the sisters was a complete shock and even more so to Victoria with Diana relinquishing her share. Geoffrey was stunned. He had planned on Victoria being mistress in his house. They agreed to resolve the question of house occupation after the wedding. While the property was in Victoria's name now, it would become Geoffrey's when they married.

Victoria laughingly stated that it wouldn't be necessary for him to buy Socrates, but he replied unhappily, "I wanted to give that horse to you as a wedding gift."

On her return to Kensington House, Victoria immediately called the staff together to explain the court's decision. They accepted her completely thinking that nothing had changed for them.

News of the court's decision swept through Brixton Village and the surrounding countryside. There was a mingling of shock, scorn, delight and anger as the story was told and retold. It was a topic of conversation in the pub, shops, at church and as people met on the street. Harsh words were used by some who chastised Victoria for running away and causing terror for those who kept up the search for her. She was blamed unmercifully for not informing the Framsdens of her whereabouts. It was suggested that it was her disappearance the provoked problems for her foster parents and was the cause of their deaths.

It was her audacity to live among them incognito and play the sham that caused so much criticism. "The idea of that girl fooling us. She has a nerve. Cheeky thing. She needs a willow stick on that behind," one lady was heard to say.

Victoria knew the reaction of the community and rather than answer the charges, she thought it best to let the talk run its course. In time it would end. She did not go into the village unless it was necessary, and she attended early morning communion at church rather than the more popular matins service.

It was not Victoria's nature to cause conflict or create animosity, and the situation was exceedingly upsetting to her. Only time would take care of the gossip and heal wounds.

Victoria wrote to Elizabeth immediately for she wanted to explain her identity and to apologize for the need to use an assumed name. She did not tell all the details, such as Edward, but she was specific about Mr. Wyatt, and she told about her forthcoming marriage to Geoffrey.

The most trying time came during a meeting with Mrs. Battey, the former Castelamer housekeeper. Mrs. Battey asked to see Victoria and a time was set. The two met over coffee. Mrs. Battey was hostile and resentful, primarily because she was removed from her position by Mr. Cleeve, for she was convinced she would still be housekeeper if Victoria had not run away. She blamed Victoria for three years of deep concern.

Victoria listened, nodded, and agreed it was most unpleasant. After Mrs. Battey was talked out, another pot of hot coffee was served. Victoria explained her fear of being tried as a murderer, that is childish to have run away, and the other circumstances influenced her action when she returned. She also assured Mrs. Battey that should an opening occur in the household staff, she would be considered above all others for the position. Although she arrived filled with malevolence, she departed more friendly and reassured. Victoria thanked her profusely for all the help she provided to the Framsdens, to Penny particularly, and of course to her. "I think the possibility of a job in the future and hot coffee helped," Victoria smiled when the ordeal was over.

As owner she looked at the old house with new meaning. "I am no longer a sojourner abiding time. I am mistress. In my blood is the blood of the founder to be passed on to my children's children. I am the flesh of Castelamer, a part of Cornwall, a part of England." She felt a cascade of loyalty overcome her. "This is my heritage. Never again will Castelamer leave the family."

She walked through the rooms letting this feeling of appreciation deepen and adding resolve to her aim to protect and retain this mansion and its properties. "I must," she promised herself, "bring Geoffrey here to share this experience with me, to accept this house as his and create our lives within its fabric."

# Chapter
# Twenty-Six

Victoria was greeted on her wedding day by a sun blazing a bright ray of light across her bed. She lay quietly to luxuriate in anticipation of the many joys that would be hers. Pall readied a bath and admonished, "Soak, Miss. Let the cares of the past roll off and drown in the water. You are to be off to a new life." When she had dried herself, she sprinkled scented water on her body and stepped into her under clothing. A little paint was applied to her face and Pall brushed her hair vigorously to put a sheen on it, letting it fall in tresses about her shoulders. She then raised the wedding gown high above Victoria's head and it fell across her shoulders to the floor. "You do make a beautiful bride, Miss."

All the staff was assembled in a line of carts and wagons in front of the house. They applauded when Victoria appeared in the entry and was helped into the lead rig. She sat next to Mr. Evans who was to give her away. Someone started to sing. Soon it became a musical parade that reminded her of the happy group that went to Brixton Fair. "It was on that day I met Geoffrey," she smiled to herself. The procession passed the stone column at the entrance to the estate drive. The old marker was in place. CASTELAMER.

Bells in the village church came into hearing. Someone recognized the hymn being toned and began singing the words and others joined in. They were moving in 2 - 4 time when a rider came into view, an arm waving wildly. Mr. Evans read the signal and he gave a commanding yell to halt the horses. The carriage was completely at rest when the horseman drew along side, his mount showing evidence of hard riding. Singing had stopped. All eyes were on the horseman. Between breaths he said fitfully, "Miss Victoria, there has been an accident. It's Geoffrey. He is at his home. Come quickly!" His excited voice was loud enough for all in the wedding procession to hear.

"Oh!" gasped Victoria. "Is it serious?"

"I'm afraid it is."

Without hesitating further, Victoria quickly clipped orders. "Mrs. Tubby, please continue to the church and tell the vicar what has happened. Mr. Evans, please come with me." To the horseman she said excitedly. "Please lead the way. We shall follow." Immediately the rider turned and Mr. Evans shouted for his horse to move out.

Victoria found Geoffrey prone on his back, his clothes disheveled, eyes closed and his face very pale. She dropped to her knees next to the sofa on which he lay and placed one hand on his. It felt cold. She looked up at a man staring at him. "I am Dr. Peers. Are you Miss Victoria?"

"Yes, I am. I am Geoffrey's avowed. We are due to be married this very moment. What is the problem?" Her voice was anxious, alarm expressed in her plea.

"Mr. Rooth was found this morning in the field north of his house. His horse came home alone. It appears Geoffrey was thrown from his mount, but we do not why or how. He has a broken back and is paralyzed. I am waiting for signs to determine what can be done."

Victoria's reserve which she had tried so hard to maintain, broke and she gave way to tears. "When will you know?"

"I am not sure. Nerves and vertebrae are involved. It is a critical situation. If we move him and the nerve is severed, we will lose him. To be honest, I am surprised he survived the move from the field. I am afraid to transport him. I would like to get him to the hospital in Plymouth, but at this moment I don't know how without jeopardizing his life."

The gravity of the situation took time for Victoria to comprehend, but when it did come, her alarm was expressed in deeply moving sobs and pitiful cries of "Geoffrey." She kissed him again and again believing her demonstration of love would help restore his health. She stayed on her knees as tears rolled down her cheeks. She left her hand on his and watched his face.

Sometime during the night he died.

The church received Geoffrey's body and committed his soul to heaven. He was placed next to his wife and baby in the church cemetery. "In a few weeks I have lost all the men in my life." The thought came to Victoria as she looked across at the unhealed scars in the cemetery earth. "What does all this portend for me?"

The clear sky that had cheered the mourners at the start of the service was being screened gradually by threatening clouds from the channel. By the final blessing, a smokey grey overcast added to the depression Victoria was experiencing. No word was spoken to her after she made final statements to Geoffrey's mother and father. Mr. Evans drove her home, sympathetically leaving her to her thoughts.

The rig went to the service area where Victoria was greeted by Wolf. She knelt down to pet and caress the big dog who licked her hand. Once inside the house, she started for her room but decided against it. She wanted to be alone, but she did not want to be alone. She went to the kitchen where cook was preparing the evening meal. "Come, sit down, Love," came the welcome. "By the fire. We've turned cold all of a sudden. Let me fix you something hot, a coffee. As the suggestion was made, cook began grinding coffee beans, placed small bits in a little pot, poured boiling water on them, then placed the pot next to Victoria. The first sip was bitter, but the heat was healing. She continued to sip and stare into the fire.

After a time of silence, she spoke. "The vicar conducted a fine service and gave a lovely talk about Mr. Rooth. Geoffrey was fine man. I had known him only a short time, but I knew enough of him to love him. Did you know him?"

Cook of course knew Geoffrey Rooth, not intimately, but as most of the villagers knew him from being raised in his early years on the family farm, participating in community activities, attending church and conducting business in the village shops. She knew his reputation. As a young man before his marriage, he was a gay blade. It was said he had to marry, and the birth of his baby so soon after marriage was cited as proof. It was said that even during the pregnancy of his wife, he was away from the marriage bed more than he was in it.

"He had gone to the home of a friend for a bachelor's party," Victoria continued without waiting for an answer to her question. "All the men drank too much, but Geoffrey was well in control of himself. About midnight Geoffrey mounted his horse and rode home." She stopped her recitation as if she could not bear to go on. Soon she continued. "How he landed on the ground is a mystery. There was no hedgerow nearby to indicate he tried to jump. No holes were found that his horse could have stepped in. There were no bruises on the horse's legs to lead one to suspect he tripped and threw Geoffrey. It is odd that the field in which he was found was not in a direct route from the house where the bachelor party was held. Strange that."

It was well known to cook that from talk being bantered about the village following Geoffrey's death that the accident was not totally an accident. The question was bound to be raised as to why he was in a field north of his house when the party was to the west. The answer according to prattlers was that after the party broke up, Geoffrey made a call at a neighbor's, was caught in the act by an outraged husband, was struck across the back by a heavy object, the body slung over the saddle of his horse, and it slipped off before the steed could get him home.

How much of it was true, cook wasn't sure. It was fact, she knew, that Geoffrey had been told previously by the offended husband to stay off his property since the man suspected Geoffrey of clandestine visits during absences from home. It was also fact that the aggrieved husband had been in Plymouth on business and had come home sooner than expected. Any facts beyond that would mean the husband would be charged with murder, and he had not even admitted to seeing Geoffrey.

Cook went about her work quietly wondering how long it would be before a comment would be dropped by someone and Victoria would know the whole story.

"Then he lay for such a long time with that broken back before he was found." Victoria sniffled, took a sip of coffee, and went on. "A youth who helps Geoffrey found him."

Cook stepped out of the kitchen and called Mrs. Tubby. "Come, Miss Victoria. It is time to rest." With an arm around her, the housekeeper guided the grieving girl up the back stairs. Pall helped Victoria prepare for bed while Mrs. Tubby poured a brandy. Victoria accepted the liquor mechanically, letting her face express a firm dislike for it. Once in bed, Pall arranged the covers over her, drew the drapes, and left the room.

Victoria slept the clock around. Mrs. Tubby and Pall had been in to check on her from time to time, for the long sleep concerned them. Pall opened the drapes so that, should Victoria bestir herself, it would not be a dark room. When she did awaken she lay quietly. Her mind became active, and she let it wander anywhere it chose to go, sometimes into crevices it had not been for ages. It slipped over the cleft that sheltered the memory of Geoffrey, for that, she decided, was a story with a lovely beginning but a tragic ending. "No, it is time to put that past behind me. Let me learn from what has been to guide me to what shall be. My chief purpose is to protect Castelamer for here is my life.

"The house and the estate must be secure at all costs. It is my duty to see to it that in so far as it is possible, the estate pays for itself. I know I must go to work to protect it. Now, first things first."

Mr. Evans was sent for. They met in the study, and she asked for a part of each day during the next four weeks to ride about the entire estate, to learn in detail the estate as an economic venture, to review the books and to explain income and expenses.

That being over, Victoria went to the storeroom used by Mr. Wyatt. She entered through the sliding door before which the shooting of Jonathan and Chris had taken place. It was the first time she had been in the storeroom. It was in great disarray. Boxes were open, goods were scattered about, furniture was turned over, books were tossed here and there, and holes were dug in the floor. Bales were open and either the contents were pulled out completely or they were left intact after a cursory inspection. All fabrics were the same as the excellent selections she had made into gowns for the plague refugees. "These I can send to London for my shop if I go to London." She worked steadily to repack, taking considerable time to shake, smooth and fold carefully.

An inventory was recorded as she worked and when the task was completed, she realized she had ample material to make several prime quality gowns. "I suppose all this is mine. The court took enough money to satisfy taxes and the constable did not say I could not have it. If the crown wanted it, the constable would have been back before now."

Other bales contained spirits, mainly wine and brandies. "My, there is enough wine here to last the rest of my life even though I live to be an ancient crone," she joked.

The top of one bale was covered with a thick matting of straw the same as she found on the others, but as she pulled the straw out she noted that the bottles were not placed in the same position and that there were not so many as in other bales. She removed the bottles and pulled out more straw. She found boxes, small boxes, each tied with string. Victoria picked up one box, untied the knot and lifted the lid. Instantly her eyes widened in disbelief. Pound notes! A stack of notes!! She looked inside other boxes. Pound notes!!

"How could the constable and his men have overlooked these boxes? They looked so carefully, or so I was told. They must have thought all the spirit bales contained wines and brandies." She looked at the codes on the exterior. Yes, all the markings were identical. The lettering on the bale containing the money had no variations. "They must have given up finding anything other than the bottles before they got this far."

She considered the money. "It is very likely the money belonged to Chris since Jonathan identified his, and the constable found Mr. Wyatt's. If this money belonged to Chris, it is now Elizabeth's."

Not only did Victoria wonder how to keep the money a secret for safety purposes, she did not know where to hide it until it could be delivered to Mrs. Cleeve. After much cogitation, she placed the four boxes in a large square of material and tied together the four corners. Taking the bundle with her, she found Mrs. Tubby and requested that she have the spirits moved to the wine cellar then meet with her in the study. "And have Osborne come to the study after our meeting."

Victoria went to the classroom and hid the boxes in a compartment she and Penny once used as a secret hiding place. In the study she awaited Mrs. Tubby. "Please sit down. It is possible I shall have to go to London on business. I so want to make sure Castelamer is well secure in your good hands. Also, until finances are adequate to maintain the estate, we shall have to be as economical as possible. May I ask you to determine the minimum needs of the house, considering both services and goods, to maintain it for a period of six months. I shall appreciate meeting with you next week to discuss your report."

"I must tell you now, Miss Victoria, that even with the London guests here, we kept an economical staff. Do you anticipate entertaining?"

"No."

"Very well. I shall have a report for you on Monday."

A knock was heard on the door and Osborne entered. "We are making a concerted effort to economize, Osborne. I may go to London shortly, but I do not want to close the house during my absence. I need to have your thinking about our absolute basic needs for staff."

"Why, that is easy Miss Victoria. I can manage everything. We can release support staff at once. That will save money.,"

"Fine. Next, I want to continue our program of restoration on the house. Please be in charge to see that all moves forward as we have money available."

After Osborne left, Victoria gave thought to her name. "I have had so many," she chuckled to herself. "Out of respect to my parents, I shall return to my family name, Tatham. That is a firm decision. Patience is not a favorite. I have used Victoria for so long, and people know me by that name. I have grown accustomed to it. I like it. That is my name. Victoria Tatham, Mistress of Castelamer."

# Chapter
## Twenty-Seven

or the next four weeks, Victoria kept every one at Castelamer busy. Having made up her mind to go to London, she decided she could not leave until she assured herself all was secure both within and without the mansion. Mrs. Tubby brought to her a plan for the care of the house, proposing that only Pall and cook be retained after all the main rooms downstairs and rooms in the south wing were cleaned and placed in order. Furnishings were to be covered with sheeting as cleaning progressed. "Pall and I can keep the house together during your absence."

Victoria and Mr. Evans met to discuss the estate as an active farm. The two studied maps of the land, he identifying crops raised and she asking questions, offering suggestions and proposing some changes. Many of these he evaluated and pointed out as being impractical. Others he agreed to try. After a discussion they usually rode to the sites discussed so she could see first hand what had been planned. Record books were reviewed in depth, he explaining the system used, identifying the best crops and specifying the profit in raising sheep and cattle. "Of course you realize that adverse weather, animal and plant disease, lack of adequate help and other conditions influence the profit of our operation." He also justified the number of employees retained for service. "I took the liberty of releasing from employment three of the five men hired by Mr. Cleeve."

At the end of the learning sessions, Victoria was well schooled on farm economy and knew well the operation of Castelamer.

Mr. Osborne secured the help of a builder from Plymouth, and a priority list of restoration jobs was developed with a price set on each one. He reported enough cash on hand to do the foundation work. "Please start as soon as possible," she directed.

"Now to prepare for the trip to London," she considered. "No, I wont take the coach. I wont have a use for it there. Better to take a wagon and a driver. I can haul all I need in the wagon, use the driver to help in the shop for a time, and either send the wagon home or sell it there.

"Money is a problem. How can I carry my money and Mrs. Cleeve's money in the wagon and not lose it to highwaymen? She gave considerable thought to the question then wrote some notes. "Make a padding for the front seat, sew some money inside. Ask the stable master about hiding some money in the horses' harnesses. Scatter money in the boxes of materials. Carry in my bodice enough money for trip expenses. Ask about a false bottom to the flat bed."

At their next meeting, Victoria asked, "What man, Mr. Evans, would be best qualified to drive a wagon to London, provide protection for me and help with the preparation of a shop should I decide to open one?"

"I do believe William Tyler is a good man. He is an experienced driver and he has driven to London before. He handles a gun well. I recommend him."

"Fine. I respect your judgment. Please schedule time with Mr. Tyler so he can instruct me on handling horses and shooting. I have never shot a gun or driven a team. Is it possible to use a false bottom or even harnesses for hiding money?"

"I can arrange something. I think that whatever we decide to do, we must keep to a minimum those who know. I am sure you are aware of what money can do to the most dependable men. At our next meeting I shall have ideas for you. As for Tyler teaching you to shoot and drive horses, that can be done quickly. Is tomorrow morning alright?"

"Fine. I shall be in the service area tomorrow morning after breakfast. I do thank you for all your help."

In her own room she continued sewing. The more she worked, the more she felt assured that the idea of ready-to-wear gowns, while novel, would help her get started in business. "I can make alterations on a ready made dress to fit the buyer. I can have dresses to show the first day the shop is open."

The next morning Tyler had a wagon ready with a team of two horses. Standing on the flat bed was Wolf, proud and pleased, acting as if he were in full command. Victoria greeted him warmly, and he licked her hand while his tail whipped the air vigorously. "He is master of the service area," Tyler laughed. An idea occurred to Victoria, and she held it abeyance.

Tyler demonstrated the principles of wagon driving, giving her cautions and encouraging her to use verbal commands as he held the reins. After a time he inquired, "Ready to try?"

The two changed seats and Victoria took the reins. At first she kept the horses at a slow walk to practice starting and stopping. Later she felt secure enough to direct them in a fast trot. At the end of the session she returned the wagon to the service area.

"Are you ready for guns?" Tyler produced a gun, made sure it was unloaded, then started instruction, pointing out the sight at the end of the barrel, the trigger and the loading chamber. Without a bullet, he demonstrated how to aim, squeeze the trigger and load the chamber. She followed the procedure under his direction, then he said, "Take the gun with you, practice aiming and squeezing the trigger. There is no bullet in it. Get used to the feel and weight of it. Tomorrow we'll try shooting bullets after you drive us into the country."

For several sessions, Victoria drove the wagon and shot the gun. More and more she gained confidence in handling both the horses and the weapon, even adjusting to the kick produced by the firing. Tyler complimented her, but never once did he ask why she wanted to learn. Pleasing to Victoria was Wolf. He was not bothered by the shooting, and he obviously enjoyed being in the wagon. She made a note of this.

The following week as promised, Mr. Evans reported to her his efforts to provide for secreting her money. "First, there is a false bottom to part of the wagon bed. Second, a few pockets have been put on the inside of the harnesses, and one wheel spoke will be hollow."

"Why, that sounds excellent. How many men know about this?"

As far as I know, only our harness man and the carpenter. They made the chambers. They do not know why they did so, but it is very possible they can guess the reason."

"Thank you, Mr. Evans. I can use these concealed places very nicely."

Once alone Victoria considered the money. "I shall take Wolf with me. Above all he is loyal, and he will defend me against anyone. I must be realistic. A wagon full of something, with a cover over something, becomes a target for a highwayman. He may not expect jewels, but be certainly would expect money to be carried.

"It is very likely the word is out about a false bottom, hollow spoke and a fancy harness. I can place a little money in those places and use other places known only to me. I can put some in the padding I made for the wagon seat. I can make a soft collar for Wolf and pad it with pounds. A collar wont take much money but it will help. Now for other places."

By the end of the month Victoria was ready. She had made five mostly completed gowns and packed those. The materials in the storeroom were condensed to three bales. She gave Mr. Evans some pound notes to place in the chambers provided. Wolf was supporting a cloth collar with a red tag that read, WOLF CASTELAMER CORNWALL. Traveling cases and the old portmanteau were packed.

The next day the wagon was loaded with a large area in back of the seat reserved for Wolf. Everything was covered for protection from rain. Tyler had his case ready and his gun was conveniently next to him. A second gun was given to Victoria with some light jests that brought smiles to her face. She found a place under the cushions to hide it.

Before sunrise the next morning, Victoria was ready. Cook handed up a basket of food including something extra for Wolf, then the wagon rolled around the house, down the lane and onto the Plymouth road.

"Since the load on the back is not heavy, the going should not be difficult," Tyler anticipated. "It should take us five to six days allowing rest stops for the horses and overnight stays providing we leave early each morning."

"Tell me the best way to get to the center of London."

"Since I always made deliveries to Mr. Cleeve's warehouse, I entered along the river."

The two chatted amiably and the morning passed rapidly. They entered Plymouth where the horses were rested and watered. A little after noon they stopped near a stream and ate from the basket cook had prepared. By late afternoon they came to the outskirts of Exeter, but since it was still light, they decided to continue to a small inn Tyler had used on previous trips.

Apprehension began building as Victoria faced the reality of leaving the wagon and its contents alone for the night in a strange place. She could not, she believed, ask Tyler to sleep in the wagon and she was fearful of robbery. Wolf calmed her fears for immediately on arrival, he stayed near the wagon, taking command and growling when anyone came near. Just the size of him was enough to cause any intruder concern. After supper Victoria fed him and talked to him about his duty. She hugged him affectionately. The innkeeper, aware of her misgivings, assured her that the gates to the courtyard would be locked for the night. Victoria looked on the horses and found that the innkeeper's son had cared for them. She went to bed tired but assured.

The next morning Tyler jovially asked, "Would my pupil like to take the reins." She did. The horses responded to her handling as she took them through the courtyard and out the gate. She laughed out loud as the pleasure of driving stimulated her. "I don't know how I would be maneuvering around other wagons, but on the open road driving is delightful!" More confidence developed as she drove, but by midmorning she tired and was glad enough to return the reins to Tyler.

"Did you enjoy working for Mr. Cleeve?"

"Yes, I did. I found him to be fair, and he was never demanding. I am truly sorry about the shooting,"

"Did he have a sizeable warehouse in London?"

"It was a large building, and it was well stocked when I made the last delivery. I never saw him there. An assistant always had the wagon unloaded. I got the impression that Mr. Cleeve had a substantial business."

A thought came to Victoria. "I wonder if a supply of materials is still in the warehouse. If so, Mrs. Cleeve may not have disposed of it, and she may sell to me." Aloud she queried," Do you remember how to get to his warehouse?"

"Oh, yes. I went there several times. It is along a section of the Thames they call the Pool, below the part of London they call the City. I don't recall the street name, but I can go to it. I remember a sign in front that says, 'GOODS AND SPIRITS - WHOLESALE.'"

Further discussion was interrupted when Tyler saw three horsemen approaching in the distance. "Now, Miss Victoria. Can't be too careful. Get your gun and put it under your cloak. I have mine ready. Pay no attention as we pass. Never know when highwaymen show up."

Victoria did as she was directed. A rise of dust was thicker as the men came nearer. She could see they wore no masks, and their coats indicated they were men of means. Tyler nodded and spoke a greeting as they passed. There was no incident.

"In all my runs up to London, I was never bothered. Highwaymen don't go for wagons as a rule. They prefer coaches. But you may get a desperate wag, and he'll try anything to get a farthing. It's best to let them have what they want. I don't want to get hurt."

The advice was strange, Victoria thought, for Tyler had advised her to have her gun ready when the three men approached. "What good are the guns for them?" she asked.

"Just in case," he responded. Without explanation he went on. "What is the use of getting hurt or killed. Offer no trouble. Cooperate. Let 'em take what they seek. Of course, with all the money you have here." He broke off the sentence before it was finished and caught himself from going on. "Anyhow my suggestion is to give in," he added in a flat tone and looked straight ahead.

In the afternoon Victoria took the reins. She concentrated on her chore, but in silence she thought about Tyler's remarks. "So he knows there is money aboard. If he knows, so do others. There must have been talk about the secret locations. Be alert," she warned herself. "All may not be well."

The next day was miserable. Drizzle started in the morning and kept up, changing at times to rain. Both Victoria and Tyler stayed under a cover of blankets, but Wolf did not mind. He barked at passing horsemen and wagons, although they were few. She was glad to get to the inn at Salisbury.

Sunday was brighter although clouds remained from yesterday's storm. Bells from the tall cathedral spire sent their message over the landscape, and village churches replied in meeker voices. The wagon was not far out of the city when Tyler notified Victoria, "I feel a strangeness in a wheel on the left side. We may have a problem." He stopped the wagon off the road, got out, then returned in a moment. "I can fix it but it may take a few minutes. You and Wolf go for a walk. Stretch your legs a bit."

He helped Victoria down, and she called Wolf who instantly was at her feet. She did not notice movement behind a clump of trees a short distance off as she and Wolf started across a field. She found a stick to throw. She noticed as she glanced back at the wagon that Tyler was talking to a man while he worked at the wheel. "Strange. He reported a wheel on the left side and now he's working on the right side." Pretending to lean over to look for a stick, but keeping eyes on the wagon, she saw the stranger walk to the horses and put a hand on the harness. "That is not strange," she warned herself thinking of the money, "That is robbery!"

Instantly she ran toward the wagon. The stranger heard her approach. He turned, pulled a gun, directed her to stand before him, then grabbed her by the arm. At the same moment he yelled, "Tyler!" Tyler left the wheel and started for Victoria. She tried to pull away from the man, screaming loudly. Wolf was angered by her cries. He gave a stupendous lunge at the man, throwing his powerful body at his back. As the huge animal crashed into the stranger, the gun exploded. The unexpected blow threw the man smashing into Victoria, knocking her down. He crumbled at her side.

All three were on the ground with Wolf pawing furiously at Victoria. She opened her eyes to see the massive animal panting in her face. The pummeling to the ground had knocked her out. She lay quietly trying to retrieve her senses. Looking up, she saw not a foot away, the intruder, face down on the ground, his gun clutched tightly in his hand. Next to the wagon was Tyler, stretched out, his face to the heavens. She pulled at both men but neither responded.

A wagon was coming down the road. Victoria stopped it and asked for help. The driver looked at the situation and offered to get assistance. While waiting, Victoria scrutinized the wheel Tyler was manipulating. She found he had loosened the spoke and was about to remove it when either his name was called or he heard Victoria's scuffle with the stranger. As she tightened it, she noticed a groove had been cut into it, apparently a mark to show which one had the money. She also reviewed the harness on the horse near the fallen stranger. "Evidence," Victoria said to herself, "that the man knew what he was doing." She pushed the notes back and turned up the right side of the harness. She heard Wolf growl and turned to see a few people collecting. One man called out, "Can I be of help, lady. Heard a gun on a Sunday and that's unusual hereabouts."

"No, thanks. Help is coming from the city."

The curious milled about discussing the situation among themselves until two horsemen and a wagon approached from Salisbury. They identified themselves as sheriffs men. Victoria explained what happened. "Both Tyler and the stranger are dead," one of the men announced after inspecting the two. "The stranger's money fold has an address in

Plymouth. It looks to me as if these two men were about to steal the wagon or something in it, and the dog spoiled the try. What's in the wagon, lady.?"

"Why, have a look. I carry goods to London." She started to untie the cover, but the sheriffs men finished the job. They saw bales, opened one, and briefly inspected the material.

"Maybe it was just a highwayman who bungled it. He could have wanted a wagon and horses. I am no doctor, but I would bet a farthing that the dog's blow to the back snapped that one's neck, and the blow caused the finger to discharge a bullet that hit Tyler. If they were acting together, it's a strange quirk of fate."

Victoria gave the men all the information they required, and they told her to go to London. Taking the reins, she drove off. "So Tyler had it planned. He knew the location of Mr. Evans' secrets. But how did he get the stranger to help? Maybe it was planned in Brixton Village. He knew what he was doing regardless."

Victoria did not have the strength to maintain a steady pace, but she felt no distress about her safety. Wolf was her protector, and he appeared more alert since the shooting. Traveling alone added a day to the exhausting trip. She chose an inn on the outskirts of London even though it was midday when she arrived. She knew the horses would welcome a rest and she certainly would. After a bath, she slept until early morning. She arose at once, ate breakfast, and was told the way into the city.

As congestion developed and as streets became more numerous, she had to ask for directions. A lad heard her and offered to go with her for a price and she agreed. The young fellow guided her a ways then took the reins himself. Victoria constantly had to reassure Wolf that all was well. The boy obviously knew what he was doing, for after what to her was a struggle, the wagon pulled into the courtyard of a small inn near Blackfriers, close to the heart of the City.

After paying the agreed upon fee, she asked him to return in the morning. It was a request that would have influence on her the rest of her life.

# Chapter
# Twenty-Eight

When Victoria arrived in the courtyard the following morning, Wolf was atop the wagon in full command. The lad she had told to return was trying to coax the dog to be friendly, but the animal sensed that his assignment did not include making acquaintances unless he was directed to do so by Victoria. "It is alright, Wolf, she called. "We have a friend."

The new friend turned to face her. He appeared older than the boy of yesterday, perhaps because he was cleaner and his hair was combed. "Eighteen, possibly nineteen, I judge," she commented to herself. "Younger than I." He is over six feet but thin, very thin. It could be he doesn't eat. Aloud she added, "Please have breakfast with me before we work."

He followed her into the inn. She encouraged him to order a full breakfast, as the innkeeper called it, and she asked for coffee and a scone. When a plate was placed before him, he looked down on three eggs, four sausages and a large slice of bread. A bowl contained porridge. As he ate ravenously she studied him. She was taken first by his blond hair of which he had ample. "It could be he has not had a cut in months," she decided. His coloring was light, too, with some rosiness in the pale cheeks. He looked at her with deep blue eyes, reminding her of the

English Channel in summer, clear and warm. The brows and lashes were blond, too. "You are enjoying your breakfast. I am pleased."

He smiled. "It is all delicious!" A grin broke into a smile, revealing a fine set of white teeth.

"You haven't told me your name. I should know it since we shall be working together. My name is Victoria Tatham. I live in Cornwall."

"My name is Sebastian Lowe."

His speech was different from any she had heard in the west country. "It is not like that used by the Cleeves or the refugees," she discerned. "I have to listen carefully or I do not understand him. He talks like the innkeeper here."

When he finished eating everything that had been placed before him, he looked at her and with a broad grin said, "Thank you. I was hungry. You asked me to work for you today. What do I do and how much do I get?"

"His smile is a winner," she noted to herself. "I am pleased you ate well. I want to open a dress shop. I need a place in the shopping area, one that has living quarters and a place to stable the horses and store the wagon. Do you know London well enough to help me?"

"Of course, Miss. I know London. I was born in the City and grew up in it. I know just where to go. We can look for a shop. I am not sure about a shop that includes a stable for your horses, however. You did not talk about money."

"Shall we find a place first and then talk about a salary?" Victoria stopped a moment to talk to the innkeeper then returned to the courtyard to give Wolf directions. She put an arm around his neck, petted his head and spoke endearing words, cautioning him to be a good watch dog.

The two young people walked into the City. The streets were dirty with refuse, horse droppings, debris of all kinds, puddles of murky water, and at this time of day, crowded with people, horses, wagons, coaches and push carts. Men and women were hawking wares and some shop keepers had samples of their goods hanging before store entrances. It was all Victoria could do to keep up with Sebastian and avoid the impediments.

Suddenly he stopped. "This is Ludgate Hill. Up there is Saint Paul's Cathedral. All about you is the heart of the City. Now to look for the kind of shop you need." He made inquiries and was directed to a few places. Choices were not many and what Victoria saw was grossly inadequate. After spending the entire morning searching, they stopped to rest.

"Pardon me, Miss. I could not help but overhear. There is a shop to let on Watling Street." The man who spoke had been standing nearby. Thanking him, they entered Watling Street, a thoroughfare that led away from Saint Paul's toward Cheapside, and it had its share of traffic. The empty shop was found and Sebastian located the owner. The business location was just right and living quarters were adequate. "But there is no stable," the owner cautioned. "Most of us use the commercial stable at the bottom of Watling. It is good enough and not too dear. You can get the wagon in this yard, though."

She and the man discussed a rental price and he agreed to a six month lease. "It is working. After that I will need help in running the business."

"I don't know a thing about dresses, but I can help with other work. I accept." It was not the work that appealed to Sebastian. It was the guarantee of a place to sleep and steady meals that prompted his reply.

"Agreed. First, let's see about making a decent living area. What do we need to do to move in tomorrow?" A paper came out of a pocket and she made notes as the two walked about. "A good cleaning is absolutely necessary. Sebastian, find two girls to start washing walls and woodwork. Buy coal, soap and rags." She gave him money and off he went.

A rickety table and two chairs graced the center of the kitchen. In the cupboard were odds and ends of battered pewter. Some pots and an old kettle were above the stove. Water, she had been told, had to be carried from a pump on Watling Street. The two front rooms were bare. Upstairs were two bedrooms, one facing the street, the other overlooking the back yard. Each had a bed frame nailed to the wall and floor. A window served to light and ventilate each room.

"Well, it is a beginning," Victoria told herself. "I shall make it livable and I can soon know if I can make a living." The first pangs of disappointment were settling in, all motivated by the amount of work that had to be done, the high expectations she had set for herself, and the second thought she had about the location. "Well, I made the decision to try. Just sitting wont make the dream come true."

Sebastian returned with two girls. All began an active afternoon that launched a new business she called "Victoria's Gowns."

Sebastian's knowledge of shops put new mattresses on the beds, a good used table and two chairs in each bedroom, new pewter in the cupboards, a new kettle, some pots near the fireplace and some flatware in a kitchen drawer.

Early next morning, Sebastian drove the wagon up Ludgate Hill, around St. Pauls and into Watling Street. Wolf barked most of the time, warning those who came too close to beware. A friend met Sebastian and the two moved the contents of the wagon into the shop. Bales were piled in the front rooms, both beds were made with linens and blankets Victoria had packed, towels were arranged, the wagon stored in the yard and the horses were placed in the public stables. Sebastian brought back the harnesses.

Victoria shopped. She purchased furnishings for the two front rooms, materials to make drapes, and by noon she returned with bread, cheese and ale. Her confession that she knew nothing about cooking led to the hiring of Mollie, one of the cleaning girls, who agreed to come each afternoon to clean and cook, and Sebastian reported he had secured the services of a sign painter.

Watling Street was lined on either side by small shops, each operated by a family. All buildings were of wood construction, and all but the corner stores had common walls. The house Victoria rented was unique since an entry to one side allowed vehicle passage to the rear yard.

Sebastian proved to be a handyman and was not afraid to work. He partitioned one front room to create a small reception area and a larger work area to take advantage of the front window. Fittings would take place in the second room. A mirror was installed.

By the third day Victoria was prepared for customers. A sign reading OPEN FOR BUSINESS was placed on the door and a ready made dress was hung in the window. Materials were neatly arranged on a table. Victoria began sewing so that when passersby looked in the window they could see her.

The entry bell tinkled. In her most charming manner, Victoria greeted her first customer. Chris' fabrics were shown, but the lady thought they were too elegant for her social station and departed. After four such encounters, she came to a conclusion, "The clientele in this community need cheaper fabrics. I was afraid of that. Well, tomorrow I close and Sebastian and I will search for something less expensive."

The two spent the day along the river front visiting wholesale houses. She found exactly what she wanted and paid cash for everything.

On Saturday morning the shop opened for a second time. Sebastian was on the street walking up and down in front of the shop carrying a sign DRESSMAKING and Victoria hung one of her ready made gowns outside the shop entrance. "That is the way we do it, Victoria," he had insisted. "You have to get people's attention, at least at first." Several women came in during the morning to "get acquainted with the new shop and to meet the new seamstress," but not to buy.

Both Victoria and Sebastian were discouraged when they sat down for the noon meal, but he cheered her by saying, "You have only just opened. Some women came in. Londoners are careful buyers. They look about for the best bargains. You'll be fine."

The first lady to enter the shop in the afternoon was beautifully groomed. "I saw the hanging dress in the window, and it is beautiful. I want to try it on." Victoria showed her to the fitting room and fashioned the dress to her by making tucks here and there. "I like it. What is the price?" There was an exchange ending with agreement on a fair price to both.

"I'll have it ready Monday," Victoria assured her.

"I like your work. What other fabrics do you have?" She was shown both Chris' materials and the newly purchased cheaper ones. "These are exquisite," she purred, running her hands over the goods from Castelamer. "Do you have other ready made dresses?" She examined the remaining gowns Victoria had brought with her and exclaimed, "You are a master with your needle, young lady. If you will give those to me at the same price, I shall take all. I shall return on Saturday and I shall bring some friends with me."

Victoria showed the lady to the door and watched as a coach stopped. A footman helped the lady inside. "Sebastian!" Victoria called, full of excitement. "We sold all the ready made dresses to that lady! We are a success!"

"She's quality. You are a success!" He hugged her in his joy for her. His action was so natural, he was not even aware he did so, but she reacted to him. It was pleasant having a man's arms about her.

"Let's celebrate," she proposed. She gave him some money and told him to buy whatever food he wanted. "Let's go to the country tomorrow. We'll take the wagon, have a picnic, and give Wolf a run."

Sunday was beautiful with a clear sky and a warm sun. She attended church and when she returned, Sebastian had the horses hitched, a basket of food ready and Wolf was in the wagon. Traffic was surprisingly heavy with people getting out of the City, but Sebastian guided the horses expertly all the way to Hampstead Heath where fields were green, trees covered hills and a stream cut through a dale. They found a spot by the water and in the shade of a tree spread a blanket for themselves and the basket. They romped with Wolf until his tongue hung out and he panted loudly. "How's for a walk," Sebastian proposed.

"Even the weather is celebrating with us," she laughed gaily. "Do you know, Sebastian, you have lived in the shop almost two weeks, and we have yet to get acquainted. Tell me about yourself."

"I have a short story. I was raised by a woman who found me on the street near Saint Paul's when I was a baby. She died when I was ten, and I've been on my own since."

"How did you manage to live?"

"I stole when I had to, worked at odd jobs when I could get them, just like all the other boys I know."

"The other boys?" His statement shocked her.

"Yes. There are thousands of homeless brats running around London. All of us do what we have to do to live. We manage."

"How old are you, Sebastian?"

"I think nineteen. Mrs. Lowe wasn't sure how old I was when she found me. She thought a year."

"Have you been in school?"

"I was in school off and on when I was little. A lady came to the church to teach. Oh, I can read a little and write some. Even figure a bit. But I was educated in the streets. I don't have an education like you, Victoria."

She noticed he did not call her Miss Victoria. "Would you like to learn?"

"I would like to read and write and have good manners. "Like you," he added after a pause.

"Very well, we begin tonight. You must promise to spend a part of each day studying."

During the following week, Victoria completed the order for the ready made dresses and was given orders for three more gowns. She sewed constantly to keep up, even at night. On Saturday morning a coach stopped in front of the shop and three ladies alighted. Sebastian was alert to the arrival, for he intended to find out about the ladies. "Good morning," Victoria greeted them warmly. "Please be seated and enjoy some coffee."

From the kitchen where everything was held in readiness, Victoria brought mugs of steaming coffee, scones and serviettes. All chatted, mostly Victoria answering questions and she could tell the ladies were impressed. "Your dresses are ready. Do you mind trying them on." Her spoken English was on a par with theirs and they were generous in their compliments as the dresses were fitted and her handiwork scrutinized.

"Do I understand these gowns are from your own creative ideas?" one lady queried. Assured by Victoria that they were, the lady added, "I do want to see the same fine materials." By the end of the session, Victoria had been given orders for four more dresses and she was paid in new pound notes for those being carried out.

As soon as the coach drove off, Sebastian came bouncing in. "That, Victoria, was Mrs. Houghton Miers. She bathes in money! We have arrived!"

Both laughed merrily and Victoria felt greatly encouraged, for she saw success developing. But luck was not to be. Orders did not multiply and although there was sufficient cash coming in to provide for an adequate living, there was not the business to provide for Castelamer.

Sebastian's initiative added to her income somewhat. During the day he worked for business men in the City. Victoria permitted him to use the horses and wagon with the understanding that the horses be well cared for and that the wagon be kept in constant repair. He did so with a portion of his earnings. The rest he shared with Victoria. Wolf went with him to provide watch dog services and the two became firm friends.

When he was home, Wolf had easy access to the house. Victoria had tied a plaited cloth to the outer knob of the back door. With the door unlocked, Wolf learned quickly that he could reach Victoria when she called by pulling on the cloth and scooting inside before the door closed.

As summer moved along, Victoria saw her life developing into a pattern, sewing during the day, studying with Sebastian during late evenings, and weather permitting, Sunday afternoon excursions. "This is not the way I planned it to be," she decided one night as she lay in bed. "It is routine that is giving me no promise. True, I am making a living. True, the house and shop are well organized, but after expenses, there is little left to protect Castelamer. And I have yet to meet a potential husband."

It was to the future that her thoughts turned, for the present had not developed as she had hoped. "Learn what you can from it," she admonished herself, "and start over." It was almost dawn when she came to a decision.

The next evening when Sebastian sat down with her in the kitchen, Victoria said gently, "Instead of a lesson, I need to talk with you. I am not happy. I am returning to Cornwall."

The comment stunned him. His eyes shot back at her in disbelief. His lips moved, but no words came out. His hand automatically went to hers, fingers touching fingers, palm closing over palm. He gave her hand a squeeze. His touch communicated what he could not say.

Seeing his alarm and recognizing his inability to express himself, she added, "It is the best thing I can do."

"Are you unhappy with me?"

"Sebastian, you have been my strength. I could not have done one thing without your help." Her hand squeezed his to emphasize her statement.

"Victoria, I love you!" His feeling was conveyed not so much in words but in the sincerity of their presentation. She caught the pathos in his voice.

It was her turn to be stunned. She had not looked at Sebastian as a potential husband. To her he was a boy who had guided her into the city, helped her to establish a business, then assisted her in maintaining it. True, they were about the same age, but to Victoria he seemed a boy, immature and lacking in refinements. She respected his determination to improve himself and his resourcefulness in earning money, but beyond that she gave him no consideration.

Her lack of response to his confession hurt him. He fully expected Victoria to acknowledge immediately her love for him. He looked at her with pleading eyes, but did not release her hand. Recognizing the barrier of silence, he dropped his head and spoke softly. "Forgive me. I should not have said that. I forgot my place. You are above me in a class with background and position. I am from the streets."

"You are a fine young man, Sebastian, hard working, intelligent, and you have goals that are worthy of any gentleman. It is just that I have not thought of love, Sebastian."

"I have thought of love, Victoria. Often. The first time I sat next to you in your wagon, the day you entered London, and you were lost. You looked at me with those beautiful eyes. I felt so proud. I knew you were my girl. It was the first time I even felt that way. Since then I looked forward each day to being near you, helping you, wanting you to succeed. I am trying hard, Victoria. I want to speak and act like you. I want to be a gentleman you could love in return."

"You will be that gentleman, Sebastian, and you will be successful. I want to help you be both." She watched her words, for she could not return the feeling he had for her, and she did not want him to think she could.

"But you are leaving. I wont see you again." He sounded as if the bottom had fallen out of his world.

"I wont be leaving for a while," she reassured him, "and I may be back. I haven't decided yet. Let's take advantage of our time and do our lessons." She had to act to redirect his interest.

For the next several days, Victoria pondered her decision to return to Castelamer. She was more aware of Sebastian and warned herself, "He is no longer a boy. He is a man."

# Chapter
# Twenty-Nine

Sebastian entered the kitchen breathing hard, obvious agitation showing on a face besmirched with soot. "I hope I am not too late for dinner, Victoria. I ran most of the way. I've been helping on the fire lines."

"So that is what is causing the smoke. I noticed a black pall over the east when I returned from church. It must be a big one."

"It has already burned many homes and shops and several warehouses along the river front. It was pretty well under control when flames reached a shed filled with tar and pitch and oil. The explosion spread the flames again. Men and women are passing buckets from one to another, but those wooden buildings are old and dry and the flames eat them like cake. The Lord Mayor was having a look around just before I left."

After eating, Sebastian asked, "Would you like to see the fire with me? I've seen a lot of fires in the City, but this is the largest."

"No, you go. I am going to take a walk and then go to the cathedral for evensong." When she stepped outside, she caught instantly a strong odor of burning wood and noticed fine ashes on the street. They fluttered down like snow and caught on her shawl. She touched one only to have it disintegrate to nothingness between her finger tips.

She walked to Canon Street where she saw crowds of people standing around piles of household goods and heard parts of discussions about escapes. All looked dejected. Other people were carrying bundles of goods in their arms and on their backs. Two men were moving a bed with a sick person stretched out on it. Dogs and cats were running wildly about. A caged parrot was jabbering noisily.

A man ran by her, his face white with fear, chased by three men yelling, "Kill the Frenchman." Blame for the fire had to be placed, and it was being charged to the French and to the Dutch who were currently at war with England. Even Catholics were being denounced for causing the disaster.

When she entered the cathedral, she joined a large congregation for worship. Prayers were offered for the City's deliverance and the welfare of the people.

Sebastian returned to the fire area where crowds gathered to watch and to help on one of the fire lines formed by volunteers. Leather buckets were filled with river water then passed from hand to hand to be tossed on the fire. Quickly they were returned along another line to the river's edge. Pumps under London Bridge were providing water to other fire fighters.

As heat intensified, fighters were forced back. Vicious winds created by heat escalation encouraged flames to greater effort and to move faster in what ever direction capricious gusts directed. The stench of burning wood and burning flesh of rodents mingled with thick swirling smoke made it necessary for Sebastian to copy others. He dipped a rag in the river and tied it about his nose and mouth. His eyes smarted until tears ran. He saw Tom who called to him to help a family remove their belongings from a house, and Sebastian joined the effort. Once on the street, the goods stayed, interfering with the efforts of others to pass. A man was hollering for a wagon, begging for assistance and waving pound notes he would pay for the service. He was ignored. Refugees from the fire passed him intent on their own problems of escape. Every member of one family from a small child to an ancient grandmother carried bundles. A few tied a chair or other small furniture to their backs before escaping the flames.

Some refugees from homes along the river were using London Bridge to cross the Thames to Southwark on the opposite side. Because of shops and houses on the bridge and the narrowness of the passage way, two way traffic was slowed to push and shove forcing some men with ready cash to hire boats to carry their families across the river to safety.

Dogs and cats dashed about the streets overcome completely with fear, their homes gone, separated from their families, not knowing what to do. One dog stood at the door of a burning home barking angrily at those who would throw water on it.

Sebastian paused, thought about the man calling for a wagon, and saw an opportunity. He grabbed Tom's shoulder and called, "Come on!" Together they ran up the hill to the stables. Entering they found the place in turmoil. The owner and his aide held guns to ward off the efforts of pillagers to seize the horses. Owners were trying to get their steeds, but smoke and general excitement made them nervous and they were balking. Sebastian worked to calm Victoria's two horses. He and Tom managed to place harnesses on their heads and lead them out of the stables. With difficulty the boys got them to the shop, having at one time to strike a man who attempted to seize a lead.

Victoria was not home. Only Wolf was there to welcome him. Quickly Sebastian wrote a note, found some pieces of wood he and Tom could use as clubs, hitched the wagon to the horses and returned to the fire area. The going was difficult getting through the morass of people leaving the affected region. The flow of traffic was against him as refugees made for Moor Field outside the walls.

Sebastian and Tom kept themselves alerted for hooligans who would overwhelm them and steal the wagon. What he had was at a premium, and he intended to protect it.

An offer came near the perimeter of the fire. A well dressed gentleman bid an outlandish price for the wagon, and Sebastian accepted instantly. He piled bundles and furniture on the wagon as Tom kept guard. The family climbed on top of the accumulated mass.

At the first open space beyond the walls, the goods were deposited.

His return was laborious, for the exit surge had thickened. He decided to go around Saint Paul's and attempt an approach from the west. He was making good progress when three young men attacked. One went for the horses while the other two jumped on the wagon, the first one coming at Sebastian while the other assaulted Tom. Sebastian caught his adversary on the head with a swing of his club sending him crumbling to the street. He turned to help Tom, unaware that the attacker who had stopped the horses had climbed aboard and from the back grabbed him by the shoulder. As Sebastian turned he received a blow to the face. Stunned, he dropped his club and reeled, falling to the bed of the wagon. Recovering from the momentary shock, he took a knife from his boot and rising to his knees, he drove it into his assailant's abdomen as his own club, now wielded by his opponent, struck him on the shoulder. The pain was excruciating. He floundered on the wagon bed but recuperated sufficiently to grab the last aggressor's leg and bring him down. Tom finished him off with a crushing blow.

Left unattended, the horses, becoming more frightened by the passing crowd and the rumpus on the wagon, had moved forward. Someone passing by, angered at facing a hazard in his hurry to flee, gave one of the horses a strike on the rump. The horse responded with a leap which excited the other. Both started running. People scattered, dropping bundles which were struck by the wagon. Sebastian struggled forward to the driver's seat and grabbed for the reins. Pulling with both hands despite the pain in his shoulder and yelling words of command, he brought the team under control. While Tom held the reins, Sebastian went to the horses, talked softly to them and patted them gently. The run, however, had brought them close to the perimeter of the fire, and mere patting and talking could not calm them completely.

Fearing another attack and concerned that he was undermanned, Sebastian returned to the wagon seat where he stood to seek out another friend. His scanning of the passing crowd was rewarded. He called loudly, "Henry!" A young man responded. Sebastian quickly explained his predicament, and for a fee, asked him to walk the horses and to shout their availability. A man came shouting from his store, gesticulating wildly. "Here! Here!" He waited impatiently for the wagon to arrive then haggled with Sebastian over the price. Once settled, the flat bed was filled with goods and the family mounted the wagon, all but the father who stayed behind to protect what he could not send away.

Sebastian sat, his two friends next to him. "Three are better than two if we are attacked again," he cautioned. "Keep an eye on the crowd. These ruffians know the value of a horse and wagon as well as we do."

The next run was easier, but night had squeezed out the last trailing of dusk by the time the final family and goods were deposited. Sebastian drove the horses to the stables where the owner refused to accept them. "It is too dangerous," he explained. "The horses are nervous to begin with, and if we are attacked by ruffians during the night, I can't protect them. We are in no immediate danger, but the fire could strike us, and if it does, we could not possibly protect the animals. Put some hay in the wagon and take the horses with you."

The boys filled the wagon with hay then drove it to the shop where they managed to get wagon and horses in the back yard. Wolf welcomed them with his deep throated bark. While his friends saw to feeding and watering the animals, Sebastian went inside to speak to Victoria.

"Sebastian, you had me worried! I read your note. You look a sight. Soot all over you. At church I heard so many stories. Those poor people. I am proud of you for wanting help. Did you have trouble?"

"Yes, but we managed. Two friends helped me. But because the stable owner would not take the horses, we had to bring them home. Can we feed my friends? We plan to sleep in the wagon tonight to make sure the horses are not stolen. Here is the money I earned." He placed a pile of pound notes on the table.

"Why, Sebastian," Victoria said in shock. "So much money. I had no idea you would charge people. At a time like this we have to help without a service charge. But now that you have earned it, the money is yours."

"Those wealthy men wont miss their money. We plan to return tomorrow if the fire is still burning and if you don't mind."

"Of course. We must help, but be fair with your charges. Pay the boys for their help."

"I did already."

"We have cold mutton, bread, cheese, and there is ale. Send the boys in."

"One at a time. We need to watch the horses."

"We can take some refugees here if we are asked to. I don't plan to open the shop tomorrow. I doubt if any woman would be interested in dresses at a time like this."

Before going to bed, Victoria went to the back of the house to check on the boys. The sky was a mass of orange red. Thoughts of her own safety swept across her mind. As she prepared for bed, she considered what she would do if she had to leave. "I doubt if that will be necessary. They surely will have the fire under control tonight."

The next morning, Sebastian was out early leaving his two friends as guards. He went immediately to the fire zone which he discovered had expanded. The perimeter was closer to Watling Street and burning ferociously. He circled the flames to the river side where before him was an unbelievable spectacle. London Bridge was on fire! "There goes our last hope of saving the City," one man predicted when they saw a section of the bridge near the shore collapse. "Our water pumps were at that spot."

Sebastian hurried home, depressed by what he had seen and knowing what was about to happen. Rats scurried in his path. He heard screaming and ran to provide assistance. A woman was in the street before her burning home crying, "Help! Help! My baby!" He started into the house, but a rumbling sound followed by a crash of the roof blocked his entry. The woman fell to her knees and sobbed bitterly. Two houses away a woman bent out her second story window laughing and waving at the passing crowds as the roof burned over her. Pigeons continued to roost under eaves, oblivious to the fire, or like some people, reluctant to leave. Looters were everywhere, entering abandoned shops, taking what they wished, and walking off with filled sacks knowing they would not be apprehended.

"Victoria!" Sebastian yelled when he entered the house. She came from her sewing room, needle in hand. "Victoria, get ready to leave. The fire wont be brought under control. We are not safe. Looters are in every shop. Bolt the doors and keep them bolted. Let no one in. Stay in the kitchen with Wolf. Load the two guns and shoot anyone who comes in. They will be after money. The fire will not be to Watling Street for a time. My friends and I are going to make some runs with the wagons. We have a chance to make some good money."

Victoria followed Sebastian's instructions instantly. All doors were bolted, and she pushed the backs of straight chairs below the bolts for extra safety. Wolf seemed to sense the danger and stayed with her while she prepared bundles. She spread sheets on the floor and put Sebastian's clothes in one and her clothes in another. The portmanteau was pulled from under the bed. Money was taken from the mattress and from under the floor and placed in it.

She went to the fitting room and piled fabrics in empty bales with finished and unfinished dresses placed on top. "These I shouldn't take but I need material for a new beginning."

Believing she had done everything that could be done for the time being, she returned to the kitchen where she continued to sew. A rumble was heard followed by an explosion. It jarred the house, and instantly she grabbed the edge of the table thinking someone was trying to break in the front of the house. A second explosion followed. "Ah," she surmised. "It must be they decided to blow up houses to stop the fire."

She continued to work as other explosions jolted the house. A rattling noise took her attention. She paused and stared at the kitchen door leading to the front of the house. Wolf, stretched out near her feet, raised his head and listened. The noise was repeated. He growled. A crash made the dog jump up and trot to the door where he barked viciously. Victoria went to the door and listened, her ear to the panel. Someone was in the front room. "Looks like a lot of material for dresses," a man's voice said. "None of this is any good. Just look for money."

Victoria backed to the table where she had placed the two loaded guns. She snapped her fingers to get Wolf next to her.

"Let's go to the back of the house," Victoria heard a man say. She put one gun in her hand. Foot steps approached the door. The handle was tried. The door was pushed. It held. The door was kicked. It flew open. Two men stared at her. Wolf attacked the first man who entered the kitchen. Victoria fired. The bullet hit the man and he slumped. The second man grabbed his partner as Wolf tore into him. Quickly the second man shoved his injured friend at Wolf and reached for the second gun on the table. He raised it and shot at Wolf. The dog cried pitifully then crumbled.

"You are just what I want. Money be damned. You are a looker." The looter glared directly at Victoria, his eyes glazed. He reached out a hand to grab her as he spoke.

She recognized the eyes. She knew what they portended. Stepping back instantly, she avoided the long reach and sudden snatch of the hairy hand. She feinted a stride to the kitchen door. He anticipated her move and shifted his balance to block her. Ready for his action, she turned swiftly to reach the open door. Her stride was not long enough. Her foot caught the open coat of the man on the floor and she fell, striking the floor with a crash to the head that momentarily knocked her senseless. Recovering, she rolled herself over to look directly into the hairy face of the despoiler who was on his knees grinning at her.

"You planned it perfectly for me, lady," he laughed out loud. "There is only one thing better than money. Get your skirts up."

Victoria tried to raise her leg to kick him, but he clenched her ankle and twisted it. She let out a scream partly in pain, but with the hope that Sebastian was returning to the yard. She screamed again and again as he dropped his trousers, pulled up her skirts and fell on her.

At that instant a black blur crossed the ravager's back, and he felt sharp teeth pierce his neck. A spurt of blood gushed out, striking Victoria, covering her face. His eyes opened widely in disbelief. He released a muffled sound and collapsed on her.

She lay in shock, stifled by the man's weight and smothered by the beard in her face. She had thought Wolf dead.

When she had pulled herself free from the attacker, she crawled on her knees to Wolf whose mouth was riveted to the man's neck. She patted the black head and spoke reassuring words. The dog's eyes moved slightly then released his grip. Quickly she looked about his body for the bullet wound and found it in the hip. "No wonder he could not lunge," she realized. "He can't use his hind quarters. He must have used his last bit of energy to raise himself, pull his body across the floor, then throw himself at the man's neck."

She exerted great strength to move the dog off the man and into a position so she could wash the wounds. There were two. She heated water and used a wet cloth carefully to clean both areas. Very little blood oozed from the openings. "Is the bullet inside?" She probed with her lingers and Wolf flinched. He raised his head and looked at her in question then lay back. "I can't tell. I must wait for Sebastian."

The day was long in coming to an end. Smoke became thicker as the fire advanced. After cleaning herself, she sat next to Wolf, petting his head and stroking his prostrate body. He made no move. His nose was warm and dry.

After dark the boys returned, covered with soot, exhausted and hungry. The horses were cared for while Victoria explained to Sebastian what happened. With Henry on guard, Sebastian and Tom examined Wolf under candlelight and decided the bullet must have struck him in the hip at an angle, grazed the bone, and caromed off to leave the body at the second opening. "If so the bullet is out," Sebastian commented encouragingly, "but the bone probably is damaged. It will take some time before he is well. It must hurt him, but he is not complaining. Best to let him rest."

"What to do with these two?" asked Victoria gesturing to the two looters.

"We'll dump them in the wagon then throw them on a burning house tomorrow." Sebastian's disgust was evident in the comment.

The three moved the bodies and Victoria cleared the remaining mess, mostly blood that left a stain on the floor.

The boys continued to take turns guarding the horses and wagon. Sebastian reloaded both guns and told everyone to shoot to kill if a looter attempted to steal anything. "So many people are going crazy."

Each boy washed and ate then spelled each other to come inside to escape the polluted air.

"The king and the Duke of York came to the fire area today. We watched as they looked around and made a gesture of helping," Sebastian reported. "You must have heard houses being blown up. Too late. The Lord Mayor too late accepted the advise of experts to blow up some houses in the fire's path to create an open area the fire could not jump. But the fire is still out of control. Houses and shops are going street by street. We'll get the flames tomorrow. Are you ready to leave, Victoria.?"

"Yes, Sebastian. Anytime you say." She had reconciled herself to the inevitable. "Where shall we go?"

"I am not sure. I'll do some checking. Moor Fields is crowded and there is no control. I just hope the plague doesn't break out again with the filth all about. By the by, here is what we collected today. The boys have been paid."

On the table was spread a quantity of pound notes. "Why, Sebastian! You are a business man!" Her compliment was sincere and said with enthusiasm.

"Only because of your horses and wagon," he responded dryly.

"And your know how!"

"I just hope we get out of all this without losing it to looters. They are everywhere. The boys are happy, though. They have never earned so much."

At daybreak Sebastian set out on foot to do some exploring. He was back as his friends were getting up and Victoria was preparing breakfast. Wolf lay still in the same place. All four ate together and discussed plans for the day. "The fire has swallowed two more streets, but we can last the day here. Now, Victoria, will you be safe if we leave? If so, we can work. By dusk we can be back to move us out. Some warehouses are still standing. We can get into one of those."

They decided to leave the shop door open with drapes pulled back from the windows, and they placed boxes and furniture in disarray to indicate that the premises had been entered and ransacked. The door to the kitchen was reset, but they had no way to hammer it shut. The two loaded guns were given to Victoria for protection with the admonition that Wolf would not be able to help if looters entered.

When the boys left, Victoria bolted the back door and took up her sewing. At times during the day, she knelt by Wolf to pat and brush him, saying quiet endearing words. She looked at the wounds and noticed they were festering. "Water wont help much. Perhaps salt water will." She washed the wounds several times. "What else can I use?" she considered. "Whiskey!" She hurried to the front door, waved a pound note and hailed a boy. "Get me some whiskey, and you will have one of these for yourself." The boy was back in no time. "We had some at home. Mum said to sell. Where's the quid?" She smelled as the bottle was handed to her. It was almost full. The boy took the note and ran off.

Wolf flinched when the whiskey was applied. He had not moved and Victoria's concern grew. "If I thought that by giving those looters all our money and Wolf could be freed from all this, I would have. But their interest was in me. No money would have stopped their lust."

By dusk the boys returned tired and dirty. "It is best to leave now," Sebastian directed. "Most people in the City have given up saving their homes. They realize there is no hope, and they are getting out."

They loaded the wagon with everything Victoria decided was worth saving. Wolf was placed on the broken kitchen door and carried to the wagon after it was loaded. The air was dense with smoke, and ashes fell like rain. As they drove to the river, she could not believe the devastation. Street after street had been burned completely with only a few chimneys standing where houses had been. Parts of churches could be seen in the ravaged landscape.

When they rolled around Saint Paul's, she looked away, knowing that the old cathedral could not be saved. She could not bear to think of its loss. Even at this late hour other refugees were leaving the City, most on foot and all carrying what goods they could manage.

Sebastian drove the wagon along the river and reined to a stop before a warehouse whose entrance sign read GOODS AND SPIRITS - WHOLESALE. Victoria blanched. "Is this part of the Thames called The Pool?" She recalled Tyler's description.

"Yes," Sebastian replied. He tried the door. It opened. Surprised that under the circumstances a warehouse door would be unlocked, he entered and looked about. No one was in sight. He motioned for Victoria to come.

Inside she looked immediately for bales or stored materials. At the far end of the building was a collection of bales and boxes. Her heart leaped up.

The boys opened the main entry door and brought the wagon inside. They were careful with Wolf as they lifted the kitchen door and placed it on the floor. After the horses were cared for, they unloaded the wagon and prepared for bed.

The next morning, all four debated the question of returning to assist the refugees, then agreed to work as long as the wagon was needed. After the boys left the warehouse, Victoria bolted the door and hid the large collection of notes in various places. Her attention was then given to Wolf. His wounds did not appear to be festering.

To satisfy a burning curiosity, she went to the collection of bales and boxes at the end of the warehouse. Number codes were marked on each one, but they were different from the ones in Wyatt's storage room. Not one was open. She was concentrating on a practical way to open one bale when she became aware of someone watching her. She turned quickly to find a man. Below the matting falling from the forehead was a scar next to the left eye.

Victoria's right hand went to her neck as she grabbed a bale to support herself. She mustered all the strength possible to overcome a sweep of emotion that dashed her composure. A feeling of lightheadedness made her dizzy, but she bottled the sensation. An arm went around her waist, and she felt herself being pulled to the man in front of her.

She was senseless for a moment, for she fought doggedly to master her passion. A hand pressed under her chin to lift her face, and she looked up to a countenance dominated by piercing eyes, hair that flowed from a moustache to a trailing beard. His eyes burned with passion, demanding. Slowly they became larger as his face neared hers, the glow of infatuation burning brighter until her eyes closed and she received his lips on hers, gently, softly. She responded to his tenderness, returning his kiss, and raising her hand to the back of his head to press his lips more vigorously on hers, to feel more a part of him.

He released his arms from her waist and quickly reformed them to lift her up, his lips still on hers, she completely relaxed in the strength of his loving. He carried her some distance, she not noticing where, not caring, lost in the rapture of his loving. She felt herself being lowered gradually, he not releasing his lips from hers, she keeping one hand at the back of his head, not wanting to release him. She felt herself on a bed.

Together they felt ecstasy, the crowning achievement of devotion, the paradise that made them one, a rhapsody of love.

After, they lay together, not wanting their desire for each other to end. He thought of the times he tried for her. She thought of the doubts she had for him. They were no more, dispersed forever. At last the man she had searched for was in her arms. She smiled as she knew at last that love provided the one true answer.

They continued to lay together, he with his arms around her, she resting snugly next to him, her head on his shoulder. To this moment neither one had spoken one word. There was no need. Conversation was complete but silent, meanings being communicated by articulate eyes, a stimulating touch, an expressive glance. Neither one wanted to break the spell by uttering a sound.

But the question had to be asked. It was done by a statement. "I thought you dead." It was spoken meekly, almost reverently, with no challenge.

"I was. Not being able to see you was like being dead." He paused. "There was a heated exchange between Jonathan and me. He threatened to go to the constable. I pleaded. He started for the door. A driver working in the storage room grabbed a gun, followed him out the door, and shot. Other guns exploded. I left the room by going out an escape hatch. I jumped on my horse and flew to Plymouth. With all haste I made for this place."

They continued to lay as they were. Neither looked at the other. She waited for him to continue, but wanting him next to her, close, touching.

"I escaped because I could not face the authorities for the illicit business I was in. I don't know why I let myself get so involved with Wyatt. He promised the world, a mansion, money, position. I wanted to match Elizabeth's wealth. The reality of it all hit me later when it was too late to get out.

"My true love is you, Victoria. At first you were infatuation, but more and more I recognized you as the woman of my life. You came to mean everything to me. Always your eyes. The more you refused me the more I had to have you, but it was love that drove me. If I had not been married to Elizabeth, you would have been my wife.

"Lord Arlington is about to clear my record of Wyatt's business. Participants in the business, all the purchasers of Wyatt's goods, are buying their way out. It is costly business but worth it."

"Have you no money, Chris?" The first words she spoke were of her concern for him.

"Yes, I have adequate funds. I have been told not to conduct business until Arlington has the king's permission. Meantime, I am staying here, making no appearances. Keeping out of the way seems to be best for the moment."

"Elizabeth named you as one of the dead men."

"I learned she identified one as being me, but she was hysterical at the time and the bullets that struck him tore his face away. There was little to identify, and since the constable thought I had done the first shooting, she assumed the constables' men shot me.

"Tell me about Victoria. You are mistress of Castelamer."

She skimmed over events since the shooting, but was more detailed in her efforts to start a business. "Now I have need for all your material."

"My dear, all those bales are yours. You will want for nothing."

"Chris, I went to the storage room. In one bale was a quantity of money. I brought it all with me."

"Mmmmm. It must have been Wyatt's money. It is certainly not mine. Keep it. You can use it."

"I want to start afresh in London and make enough money to sustain Castelamer. Then I will return to Cornwall."

Feeling a wave of satisfaction and reassurance, she pulled at him. He responded instantly, not wanting to lose the treasure he just found. Answering her silent plea, he moved, remembering to be gentle. She hardly knew he was making her part of him. Embers were reignited, the fire of desire rekindled, blazing to wondrous fulfillment the fits of passion.

She knew that for her, she had let love be the victor.